LIFE STORIES

CHARLES H. TUTTLE

1879—1971

LIFE STORIES

OF A CELEBRATED LAWYER
IN NEW YORK AND LAKE GEORGE

The Memoirs of Charles H. Tuttle, Esq.

by

Charles H. Tuttle

Edited by

CHARLOTTE TUTTLE LLOYD WALKUP

COLLEGE AVENUE PRESS
Clinton Corners, New York

LIFE STORIES

Copyright © 2002 by The Charles H. Tuttle Literary Trust

Unless otherwise indicated, photographs and illustrations are from the Tuttle family archives. Aerial photographs on the front cover: Empire State Building/New York City by Highwing Aerial Photography; The Narrows/Lake George by Dean Color Photography.

COLLEGE AVENUE PRESS

is an imprint of
THE ATTIC STUDIO Publishing House
P.O. Box 75 • Clinton Corners, NY 12514
Phone: 845-266-8100 • Fax: 845-266-5515
E-mail: CollegeAvePress@aol.com

PRINTED IN THE UNITED STATES OF AMERICA

10 9 8 7 6 5 4 3 2 1 FIRST EDITION

Library of Congress Cataloging-in-Publication Data

Tuttle, Charles H. (Charles Henry), 1879-1971.
    Life stories of a celebrated lawyer in New York and Lake George : The memoirs of Charles H. Tuttle, Esq. / by Charles H. Tuttle; edited by Charlotte Tuttle Lloyd Walkup.
        p. cm.
    Includes index.
    ISBN 1-883551-71-4 (alk. paper)
    1. Tuttle, Charles H. (Charles Henry), 1879–1971. 2. Public prosecutors—New York (State)—Biography. 3. Lawyers—New York (State)—Biography. I. Walkup, Charlotte Tuttle Lloyd, 1910– II. Title.
KF373.T89 A3 2002
340'.092—dc21

                                                                2002006664

FOR MY FAMILY

Past, Present and Future

CONTENTS

TABLE OF CONTENTS   vii

LIST OF ILLUSTRATIONS   xv

FOREWORD   xvii

PREFACE   1

Chapter One

FOREBEARS AND FORMATIVE YEARS   3

Section

1. The Rev. Isaac Henry Tuttle, D.D., Founder, Builder, and Grandfather.   3
2. Father and Mother.   6
3. Winter 1881–82 at Lake George. Effort to Arrest Tuberculosis.   10
4. Life as a Child in Oak Ridge, New Jersey, 1883-8. One Room on a Farm.   12
5. Early Life at 218 West 46th Street, New York City, Old St. Luke's.   14
6. Later Life at 218 West 46th Street. Trinity School. A Decision.   16
7. Life in Columbia College. A New Iliad. Red Flag of Anarchy.   18

Chapter Two

A CAREER, A HOME, and A WIFE   21

Section

1. Life in Columbia Law School. Admission to the Bar.   21
2. The First Three Cases.   25
3. A Great Man Heeds a Long-Dead Friend's Call. Life in "the Dog Hole" at Davies, Stone & Auerbach.   29

4. A Home and a Fiancée. 34
5. Summer and a Gun in Philadelphia in 1905. 41
6. Admission to the Bar of the United States Supreme Court in 1906. 45

Chapter Three

TWENTY-TWO YEARS AS A PARTNER IN DAVIES, STONE & AUERBACH 47

Section

1. The Case which Exorcised "The Ghost of Wall Street,"
   Clarence H. Venner. 48
2. The Racetrack Cases and the Dead Salmon. 50
3. The Titans of the Bar Battle over $25. 52
4. Three Men on a Horse. 53
5. The Case of "My Nose" and the Boss of Baseball. 54
6. The Beautiful Countess and the Marriage at Sea. 56
7. "The Bird of Paradise" and the Fire Goddess Pele. 59
8. The Case of *The New York Times'* Drama Critic
   Alexander Woollcott. 61
9. The Hotel Woodward and "Mutt, Jeff and Sir Sidney." 63
10. The Forger and "The Merry Maidens." 65
11. "Exhibit Q," the Poor Russian, and the "Saving Hunch." 67
12. The Too-Quickly-Sold Stock and a Woman's Courage. 70
13. Reading and "World-Blindness." 72
14. The Thomas W. Evans Museum and
    Institute Society: A Judicial Reform. 73
15. On My Life's Wall: Some Portraits from Davies, Stone & Auerbach. 75

Chapter Four

LIFELONG SERVICE with the CITY'S BOARD of HIGHER EDUCATION BEGINS 79

Section

1. A 1913 Libel Suit Marks the Beginning. 79
2. The 1926 College Merger. Encounter with Tammany's Boss. 82
3. The Case of Lord Bertrand Russell and
   the Chair of Philosophy at City College. 84
4. State Control of Salaries of the
   the College of the City of New York. 90

Chapter Five

LIFE in POLITICS BEGINS 93

Section

1. Seth Low ... Edward M. Shepard ... Fiorello La Guardia ...
   Judge Seabury. 93
2. Service as a Member of the State Reorganization
   Commission. 97

Chapter Six

ADVENTURES as UNITED STATES ATTORNEY
for the SOUTHERN DISTRICT OF NEW YORK 99

Section

1. April 7, 1927: My Adventure as U.S. Attorney Begins. 99
2. The Book, "The President's Daughter." The Vice Society. 105
3. The Sinking of the *Vestris*. International Reforms for
   Safety at Sea. 106
4. Murder on the High Seas. The Double Standard. 109
5. The Conduct of Federal Judge Winslow and its Tragedies. 111
6. County Judge W. Bernard Vause—
   "The Hanging Judge"—Hanged. 118
7. Supreme Court Justice Joseph F. Crater Vanishes. 120
8. The Alien Property Custodian and the $50,000 Bribe. 121
9. The Snaring of Daniel P. O'Connell, "the Boss of Albany." 123
10. The Bishop's Warehouse and the Double "O." 126
11. The "Doctor for the Elimination of Business Ills"
    Who Loses His License. 129
12. The Tong Wars in Chinatown. "Peace or Pack Up." 133
13. The Theatre Tickets Tax Frauds. 134
14. The End of Bail Bond Gouging. 137
15. The Founding of the Grand Jury Association and
    the "Run-Away" Grand Jury. 138
16. A *New Yorker* "Profile." 141

Chapter Seven

NOMINATION FOR GOVERNOR.
THE ENSUING CAMPAIGN. MY DEFEAT.   145

Section

1. Gubernatorial Nomination on September 25, 1930.
   Stand for Repeal of the Prohibition Amendment.   145
2. Declaration of All-Out War by the Anti-Saloon League
   and the Women's Christian Temperance Union.   154
3. Campaign for Governor. The Fun.
   The Insurmountable Obstacles.   156
4. The Three Days After the Election in 1930.
   Up from the Bottom of the Well.   167
5. A Cup of Tea with Governor and Mrs. Roosevelt. Its Sequels. 171
6. The Tuttle Boys' Association. Lifelong Friendships.   174

Chapter Eight

SOME CASES OF PUBLIC NOTE
AND HUMAN INTEREST AFTER 1930   183

Section

1. The Remarkable Case of Richard Whitney,
   President of the New York Stock Exchange.   184
2. The Seizure of the Steel Mills in 1952 by the President
   of the United States.   193
3. Indictment of James J. Davis, U.S. Senator and
   Secretary of Labor. The Drunken Juror.   197
4. Spyridon Catapodis Sues Aristotle Onassis.
   A Contract with the King of Saudi Arabia.   200
5. Gene McCann Sues Wall Street for Millions.   202
6. The Bank of United States Closes. Legal Titans Battle.   206
7. The Case of Jules Fink and the Jockey Club.
   A Talk with Bernard M. Baruch.   210
8. The Audacity and Fall of Martin T. Manton,
   Senior Judge, U.S. Court of Appeals.   212
9. Putting Saints on the Façade of St. Thomas Church,
   New York City.   214

10. The Rhode Island U.S. District Court Is
Plumbed for Women Jurors. 218
11. Legalizing "The United Church of Christ."
The Legacy of Dr. S. Parkes Cadman. 220
12. Combat with Louis Nizer in the Case of Victor Ridder,
the Refugee Professor. 225
13. Combat with Louis Nizer in "The War of the Roses." 227
14. Archbishop, Later Ecumenical Patriarch, Athenagoras.
"The Grand Cross of the Order of the Holy Sepulchre." 229
15. The Authority of the Russian Orthodox Church
of North America over Church Property. 236
16. The Removal of the Federal Judge from the
Occidental Petroleum Corporation Suit. 240
17. The United Brotherhood of Carpenters & Joiners of America
and the Anti-Trust Law. 242
18. Foreign Commerce in Liquor by Air and Sea.
The Supreme Court Cuts the Gordian Knot. 245
19. A Trust Company's Strange Façade Leads
to the New York Dock Company Case. 247
20. Eradicating the Poisonous Weed of Apartheid. 248
21. A Taxpayer's Right to Challenge Public Expenditures as
Violative of the First Amendment's Religion Clauses. 250
22. The Right of Corporations to Equal Protection under
the Fourteenth Amendment of the U.S. Constitution. 252

Chapter Nine

CONTINUED PUBLIC LIFE
AFTER THE 1930 ELECTION

255

Section
1. The Board of Higher Education of the City of New York. 255
2. Co-Chairmanship of the Metropolitan Rapid Transit Commission,
1954-1958. A Last Effort at Unified Mass Transportation. 256
3. The First Law in the United States against Discrimination
in Employment for Race, Creed, Color or National Origin. 260
4. Codification of the Cooperative Corporations Law of
the State. Equality versus Privilege. 264

5. Proposals for the Change and Simplification
    of the State Constitution.   266
6. Presidency of the National Republican Club.
    The 1952 Republican National Convention.   268
7. The Judgeships I Declined — and Why.   270
8. A Degree of Doctor of Laws from Syracuse University,
    Chancellor Tolley.   273
9. Some Unforgettable Recollections of an Unforgettable Man,
    Fiorello H. La Guardia.   274

Chapter Ten

SELECTIVE SERVICE CHAIRMAN: WORLD WARS I and II

SELECTIVE SERVICE CHAIRMAN:
WORLD WARS I and II   279

Section

1. Chairman during World War I of Selective Service Board,
    Local 141.   279
2. Chairmanship during World War II of the Selective Service
    Appeal Board.   282

Chapter Eleven

RELIGIOUS AND PHILANTHROPIC ORGANIZATIONS AND ACTIVITIES

RELIGIOUS AND PHILANTHROPIC
ORGANIZATIONS AND ACTIVITIES   285

Section

1. Released Time for Religious Education of
    Public School Children.   285
2. The Protestant Council of the City of New York.
    The National Council of Churches. Help from a Catholic. 290
3. Presidency of Brotherhood-in-Action.
    A Presiding Justice and His Vision.   292
4. Grace Episcopal Church: A National Shrine.   296
5. My First Diocesan Convention.
    Can Conscience Exempt from the Law of the Land?   299
6. Separation of Church and State. Argument before Congress
    Opposing the So-Called "Becker Amendment."   301

Chapter Twelve

LAKE GEORGE. "TOP O' THE WORLD." THE ADIRONDACKS.   305

Section

1. An Excerpt from "One Hundred Years on Lake George":
   The Family Story, 1896–1956   306
2. The Story of "Top O' The World."
   "The Lone Pine" and "The Sentinel Mountain."   309
3. Presidency of the Lake George Association.
   The Bishop and the Bass.
4. A Secretary of War at Lake George in the Nude.   311
5. The Case of the Lake George Water Levels.
   Lake or Mill Pond?   314
6. The Protection of the Adirondack Forest Preserve
   and the Constitution's "Forever Wild" Clause.   316
7. Once More Commissioned for Lake George.   317
8. L.G.A. Citation and a Letter from the Governor.   319
9. My Collection of Titles "Emeritus." St. James Church.   321

Chapter Thirteen

FACING UP TO OLD AGE   322

Section

1. Kindly Accolades in the Sunset.   322
2. The Mayor of New York City Cites
   An "Illustrious Citizen."   325
3. Retirement after Fifty-Three Years as a
   Member of the Board of Higher Education of   328
   the City of New York.
4. A Degree of Doctor of Laws from the College of the City
   of New York and the State Board of Regents.   332
5. Retirement from Full Partnership in Breed, Abbott & Morgan.   335

POSTLUDE 339

Section

1. My Wife. A Last Look Back.   339
2. Our Children.   345
3. A Song Without Words.   346

CHRONOLOGY   Charles H. Tuttle (1879–1971)   348

ACKNOWLEDGEMENTS   Commemorative Edition, 2002   351

APPENDIX A   A Writer's First Letter, 1885   359

APPENDIX B   The Tuttle Boys: "Truly Remarkable"   360

APPENDIX C   The 1930 Election Results:
             Watching for Signals in the Sky   363

APPENDIX D   The Charles H. Tuttle Citation
             of the Lake George Association   364

APPENDIX E   "Patent Attorney" Tuttle:
             NAB vs. ASCAP   365

TABLE OF CASES   With Citations and Page References   370

INDEX   Of Persons and Places   377

Illustrations

1. Charles H. Tuttle, 1949 Portrait   ii
2. Aerial View of Lower Manhattan   xviii
3. Young Charles Tuttle and His Forebears   7
4. St. Luke's Church, New York City   9
5. Hammond Farm House/ Wayside, Lake George   10
6. Henry Croswell Tuttle   11
7. Rockledge, Lake George   17
8. Phi Beta Kappa key   18
9. Columbia Debating Team, *c.* 1898   19
10. Charles Tuttle's 1899 Columbia Class Pin   20
11. Penelope Cook Tuttle   30
12. Charles Henry Tuttle   31
13. Hamilton Terrace, New York City   36
14. Charles and His Fiancée, Hélène Louise Wheeler, 1906   38
15. Hélène L. Wheeler   40
16. Young Charles H. Tuttle   47
17. Charles H. Tuttle at Window   55
18. *Leviathan* (ocean liner)   57
19. Tuttle Family, 1918; Residence at 339 Convent Ave, NYC   78
20. William J. Gaynor, Mayor of NYC, 1910-1913   80
21. Jimmy Walker, Mayor of NYC, 1926-1932   84
22. John Hylan, Mayor of NYC, 1918-1925   90
23. City College of New York *(3 scenes)*   92
24. Seth Low, Mayor of NYC, 1902-1903   94
25. Fiorello La Guardia, Mayor of NYC, 1934-1945   95

26.   President Calvin Coolidge   100

27.   Charles H. Tuttle at the Federal Building, NYC   107

28.   1930 Newspaper Illustration of Charles H. Tuttle   125

29.   The "Big House": Political Cartoon of Charles Tuttle   132

30.   *The New Yorker* Profile: "Saint in Politics"   142

31.   President Herbert Hoover   147

32.   Tuttle–Roosevelt Cartoon Commentary   152

33.   Send-off for the 1930 Gubernatorial Campaign   157

34.   "A Good Man for the Job": 1930 Political Cartoon   158

35.   U.S. Attorney Tuttle and the Tammany Tiger   161

36.   Families of the 1930 Gubernatorial Candidates   165

37.   A Memorable Afternoon Tea: Tuttles and Roosevelts   170

38.   Franklin D. Roosevelt and Charles H. Tuttle   173

39.   The Tuttle Boys: "Tut, Tut, Mr. Tuttle" performance   178

40.   Hubert T. Delany   181

41.   Martin Luther King, Jr.   181

42.   Charles H. Tuttle in New York City   182

43.   Whitney Family Crest   185

44.   Charles H. Tuttle, Advocate   189

45.   The U.S. Attorney at his desk, New York City   203

46.   Statues at St. Thomas Church, New York City   214

47.   "Lift up Thine Eyes" *by Norman Rockwell*   217

48.   Patriarch Athenagoras   230

49.   Charles H. Tuttle with the Grand Cross, 1945   232

50.   The Grand Cross of the Order of the Holy Sepulchre   234

51.   President Harry Truman   235

52.   Josef Stalin   237

53.   Hélène Wheeler Tuttle   239

54.   Statue of Liberty   250

55.   Charles H. Tuttle *by Raymond Perry Rodgers Neilson*   253

56. Governor Averell Harriman   259
57. Governor Thomas Dewey   262
58. Charles H. Tuttle, Illustration *by Eric Glass*   269
59. Charles H. Tuttle on Judgeship   271
60. Fiorello La Guardia and Charles Tuttle, Lake George, 1934   277
61. "Freedom of Worship" *by Norman Rockwell*   278
62. Charles Tuttle, Religious Leader *(2 groups)*   286
63. President Harry Truman in the Oval Office   291
64. Grace Church, NYC, Painting by *Ferdinand Richardt*   296
65. The Honorable John V. Lindsay   303
66. Charles Tuttle on Top O' The World, Lake George   304
67. Halcyon, Lake George   304
68. Top O' The World View, Illustration by *David D. Lloyd*   310
69. The "Island-studded Narrows" of Lake George   312
70. The Adirondacks   316
71. Governor Nelson A. Rockefeller   320
72. St. James Church, Lake George   322
73. Mayor Robert Wagner and Charles H. Tuttle   324
74. "Illustrious Citizen" bronze medal *(reverse)*   325
75. "Illustrious Citizen" bronze medal *(obverse)*   326
76. Senator Robert F. Kennedy   331
77. Dr. Buell Gallagher   333
78. Annual Dinners of Breed, Abbott & Morgan, 1936 & 1967   334
79. Hélène Louise Wheeler Tuttle   340
80. Charles and Hélène Tuttle in 1957 *(2 scenes)*   343
81. The Tuttle Family in 1957   344
82. Charles H. Tuttle, 1879–1971   347
83. The Tuttle Family at Election Time, 1930   362
84. Tuttle Family and Friends Boating on Lake George   386

FOREWORD

IN A SPACIOUS OFFICE on the 55th floor of One Chase Manhattan Plaza, on the toe of Manhattan, eighty-nine-year-old Charles Henry Tuttle, my father, began writing his memoirs in 1968. The wise lawyer and gifted writer had recently stepped aside as the senior partner in the law firm of Breed, Abbott & Morgan, in which he had been a partner for thirty-seven years and became "of counsel," retaining his practice. Such was the admiration and devotion of his partners that he remained in his lofty office with its magnificent view of the confluence of the Hudson and East Rivers into the wide Upper and Lower New York Bays, and beyond into the mists above the Atlantic Ocean.

A *New York Times* article had reported of Charles Tuttle in 1966: "despite his age, his voice is firm and resonant, and his 5-foot-11-inch frame is still erect and trim." It was also evident from his many public appearances, speeches, and writings that he retained his keen clarity of mind, his poetic facility of expression, and the great humor and wisdom that had made him a pre-eminent lawyer and civic leader.

Even at the age of ninety, Charles Tuttle traveled daily by subway between his office and his apartment at One University Place on Washington Square, and did so until a month before his death in January, 1971. Equipped for his writing with keen mental and physical ability, he was also equipped in his Manhattan office with the voluminous records of his sixty-five years of litigation, civic activities, and public service, which assured the accuracy, as well as the charm and spirit, of his account of an extraordinary life.

In this felicitous setting, a fascinating story emerged from the pen of a real-life Horatio Alger character, born in the spring of 1879 on West 23rd Street in New York City. His life's story would be wed to that of the burgeoning city which he would do so much to benefit, and which, in turn, would do so much to honor him in the autumn of his life.

Charles Tuttle's father died when he was only three, leaving the young boy and his mother with slight income, under the supervision of his grandfather, who was an Episcopal rector in the City. Fourteen years later, his grandfather died, just as Charles was entering his sophomore year at Columbia College in the Class of 1899. This loss left the young student and his mother with meager resources.

The possibilities for continuing higher education were bleak. The biographer tells, nonetheless, of continuing at Columbia and graduating with the lion's share of honors in the last year of the nineteenth century, and then graduating from Columbia Law School three years later. The most astonishing event then occurred in 1902, related in dramatic detail in the *Memoirs*. With no legal or social ladder connections, the young graduate was taken in, if only in the "dog hole," by the firm of Davies, Stone & Auerbach, two blocks from Wall Street. That very site later became the location of One Chase Manhattan Plaza, where six decades later he would write his engaging story.

LIFE STORIES, rich in Charles Tuttle's personal history, feature the lively recounting of fifty-five of his thousand or so legal cases — some chosen for their human interest or drama, and others for their importance in the development of the law. In these accounts, our consummate storyteller is at his best. He relished jousting with some of the legal titans of his day — Arnold, Buckner, Hays, Nizer, and Steuer. In many of the cases he is representing prominent people — Richard Whitney, president of the New York Stock Exchange, Aristotle Onassis, the shipping magnate, Billy Rose, the theatrical producer, and Archbishop (later Patriarch) Athenagoras, of the Eastern Orthodox Church. Other stories tell of the undoing of crooks and arsonists, and even of a feloniously inclined federal judge.

Loosening the grip on New York City of the long-corrupt Tammany Hall was Father's great achievement in his three years (1927–30) as United States Attorney for the Southern District of New York, described in a fascinating segment of the memoirs. His acclaim was so great that he was nominated by the State Republican Party in 1930 to challenge Franklin D. Roosevelt's bid for a second term as Governor. Although the challenger did not win that race, his leadership of a City Fusion ticket succeeded in the election in 1933 of Fiorello La Guardia as reform mayor of the city.

Civic reform was far from all that our father contributed to the city he loved. On the Board of Higher Education for fifty-three years, he oversaw phenomenal growth in the institutions of free public higher education. He also recounts the successful efforts of the interfaith organization which he led for the establishment of a "released time" program for the religious education of public school children upon parental request, the constitutionality of which he helped assure in the Supreme Court of the United States.

Throughout his memoirs are luminous revelations of Charles Tuttle's lifelong love affair with Lake George, a beautiful 32 mile-long lake on the eastern edge of the Adirondack mountains in upstate New York. He cherished, at great cost to the impecunious young man, the west shore property he inherited from his grandfather. When a successful lawyer, he and his wife—an even more greatly cherished lifelong love—developed "Top O' The World" resort and farm on historic French Mountain, across the Lake on the eastern shore. As a member of the Lake George Park Commission and longtime counsel to the Lake George Association, our father did a great deal to protect the beauty of the Lake and the clarity of its water, and to facilitate access to the shoreline by the public. He was called by many a "guardian" of Lake George. The lake stories are collected in a latter chapter of the book.

The 500-page typed autobiography, which the author had entitled *A Story of an Exciting Life of Ninety Years from Ox Carts to Jets,* has been cherished and reproduced by the Tuttle family for its members. But we recognize that this treasure should be released from family confines and made available for others to enjoy. The evolution of the family's decision to publish an edited version as a book in 2002 is briefly described in Part I of the Acknowledgements, beginning on page 351.

There is much of special interest in the book to historians and lawyers. But no degree in law or history is needed to enjoy the humor and dramatic anecdotes, the delightful writing, and the strong assertion of the hope and joy to be found in living. The language is molded by the Biblical literature which nurtured the writer, by the wisdom of the classics which he knew well, and by the optimism of the times in which he grew to manhood.

The autobiography is now being published as *LIFE STORIES* in the full text, excepting a few purely personal chapters, by "The Charles H. Tuttle Literary Trust." The trust was established by his three surviving children, my brother, Henry Croswell Tuttle, my sister, Jasmine Tuttle Bryant, and myself, and by the two children of our deceased eldest sister, Evelyn Tuttle Horne. These are Rear Admiral Charles F. Horne, III, U.S. Navy (Retired), and Anne Horne Warder. Anne's son, Frederick B. Warder, III, a New York lawyer, is the trustee. My credentials as Editor, on behalf of the family, are a legal career in public and private practice in Washington, D.C., for some fifty years, following graduation from Columbia Law School in 1934. All of the family participating in this collaborative publishing project have done so with profound gratitude for the lasting legacy of love and resources Father gave to us, and for his example of a faithful, honorable, and happy life.

In this year marking the one hundredth anniversary since the launching of Charles Tuttle's legal career, we are pleased to release this special Commemorative Edition of his vibrant and significant memoirs.

FOR THE TUTTLE FAMILY

Charlotte Tuttle Lloyd Walkup
Alexandria, Virginia • May 2002

PREFACE

NOW THAT I have been upon this stage for nearly ninety years and must soon be moving into the wings, I find a new excitement in stopping a while to review an exciting life, and, if given time, to make for my loved ones and for others who may find it of interest a record of its lights and shadows, its storms and calms, its parts played well and ill, its fellow actors before the footlights. This done, I can better depart with faith that the Ruler of the Human Drama has further exciting parts waiting ahead.

Indeed the very writing of these memoirs is itself a fresh, exciting experience—a way of returning in psychic disembodiment into the shadow land of the Past and re-living its fateful moments, its suspenses and its joys and sorrows, the while my own role was in its playing. Also thereby I find words for the bequest not measured by money to those whom I love and who are themselves still on the stage and playing their own exciting parts in preparation for their own future adventures which lie ahead.

Of course, in the tapestry of an autobiography the personal pronoun must be a frequent thread in the warp and woof. I realize that it is such a thread, and probably much more than a thread, in what follows. But the grim alternatives are either to stimulate (perhaps hire) someone to cloak the writing with his name, or else to have no writing at all. Lord Alfred Balfour is quoted as saying that a "biography should be written by an acute enemy." But my length of years has exhausted the present possibility of such, or at least of one "acute." What then? For me there seems to be no Boswell save myself.

One summer, sitting on the porch of my Lake George summer home with noted colleague Samuel Untermyer as my guest, the warm air and the glitter from the Lake were conducive to relaxed reminiscence and gentle speculation. At one point he said:

> *Tuttle, I sometimes feel that if I had been previously consulted as to the time in which I would choose to be born I would have replied: "Sir, the present." The human drama may never again be so abundant and fascinating with high tragedy and low comedy. It surpasses wonder to be part of it.*

I am tempted to believe I would have made the same choice. Where else could one better place a span of ninety years from an ox-cart on a farm to a jet above the clouds, while world wars thundered by, the human race was the prize between democracy and tyranny, corruption was nesting in government, religion was in ferment?

Indeed the sense of approaching climax has never been so breathlessly real as now. Man's dominating instinct for progress through knowledge has become explosive.

In the beginning, what lay beyond the next ridge? What Canaan might be seen from yonder mountaintop? Does not this sea have another and better shore? And now, are there limits to researching the secrets lying between the infinitely small and the infinitely large? Will the bloodstained path to Brotherhood reach a Shangri-La? Can there be acceptance of the invitation of the Moon ever sailing in the mighty sky? Can man at last fulfill his dream of citizenship in a Commonwealth of the Universe? Can there be penetration of the locked door of Death?

Hence there may be some public and family value in recording my participations, battle scars, and firsthand observations as the exciting years rolled along and entries were made in the Book of History. Everyone's life is something of a textbook. In any event, here is my story.

CHAPTER ONE

FOREBEARS AND FORMATIVE YEARS

———◆◆◆———

SECTION 1

The Rev. Isaac Henry Tuttle, D.D.
Founder, Builder, and Grandfather

G RANDFATHER TUTTLE, who was to shape and guide my youth, was born in New Haven, Connecticut, on February 6, 1811, of Puritan ancestry. His father, Bethuel Tuttle, a merchant of New Haven, was a direct descendant from William and Elizabeth Tuttle, who arrived on *The Planter* in 1635, and took part in the establishment of the Colony of New Haven. His mother, Julia Doolittle, was also of Puritan birth, being the daughter of Isaac and Thankful (Bellamy) Doolittle.

After a preliminary education in New Haven, my grandfather entered Trinity College, Hartford, CT, whence he graduated in the class of 1836. The same year he began his theological studies, attending the General Theological Seminary of the Episcopal Church in New York City. Completing the course in 1839, he was ordained Deacon on the third of July, by Bishop Brownell in Trinity Church, New Haven, and advanced to the priesthood the following year. His first parochial charge was at Bethel, CT, where on his first arrival he was met by a farmer parishioner who remarked, after scrutinizing him from head to foot, "the Bishop sends all his young colts here for us to break."

The process must have been difficult because the young minister remained at Bethel until December 1, 1844, when he was called to the rectorship of Christ Church, Hudson, New York, taking with him a wife, a playmate of his youth in New Haven and a distant relative, Sarah Parmelee Beecher.

He remained at Christ Church until June, 1850, when he surrendered the charge and accepted the call of Saint Luke's on Hudson Street in Greenwich Village. Saint Luke's had lost its previous rector to the Church of Rome, and it required a man of courage to build it up.

In addition to courage, Doctor Tuttle possessed an expansive spirit and a vision that forecast the future. From the very start he became connected with every branch of the Episcopal Church in the city. In addition to being the founder of Saint Luke's Home for Aged Women, the Home for Old Men and Aged Couples, the Church of the Beloved Disciple, the Orphans' Home and Asylum, an order of Episcopal nuns, the builder of the new St. Luke's Church on Convent Avenue and 141st Street, he assisted the Reverend Doctor Muhlenbergh in founding Saint Luke's Hospital. He was also the founder of St. James Episcopal Church in Lake George Village. He became a trustee of

Trinity School, a member of the Standing Committee of the General Theological Seminary, and a member of the Standing Committee of the Diocese.

Influential congregations and important educational institutions sought him; but he refused all offers, even the bishopric of Minnesota. He preferred to remain faithful to the work he had outlined for himself as rector of Saint Luke's and a lover of New York City. In 1862 Trinity College, his alma mater, conferred on him the honorary degree of Doctor of Divinity.

He held firm religious convictions, and his moral courage never failed under trying circumstances.

During the Civil War riots against Negroes in New York City, he stood in the doorway of St. Luke's Church and beckoned into it for sanctuary the passing Negroes desperately fleeing for their lives. When the mob reached the front of the church it saw a man in a white cassock standing there quietly and holding up a cross. The mob wavered. Then it rushed on, seeking its prey further along.

With mental and spiritual strength Grandfather Tuttle combined tender and sympathetic qualities of the heart, which attracted and endeared all conditions of men. He died impoverished because he had given away so much to the causes to which he had also been giving his life.

I was with him when he died. His last words were typical of his life's mastering motivation to press on with the Lord's business:

"I do not want to die yet. There is still so much to do."

On the Sunday following his death on Friday, November 26, 1896, many rectors from their pulpits announced to their congregations that a great soul had passed on from the Church Militant to the Church Triumphant.

I have fought the good fight,
I have finished the race,
I have kept the faith.
— PAUL, *2 Timothy 4:7*

———◆I◆I◆————

SECTION 2

Father and Mother

THE ROMANCE OF my father and mother was the time-honored
story of the handsome young man and the beautiful young girl
next door. Even as my grandfather Tuttle married his playmate in New
Haven, so did my father in New York.

My father, H. Croswell Tuttle, lived in the rectory of old St. Luke's
where Hudson and Grove Streets still meet. My mother, Miss Penelope
Turner Cook, looking from her window in the adjoining home, would
watch him fencing in the Rectory's rear yard with a classmate, Julian T.
Davies, who later had a very decisive part in my life, as will be told
shortly.

Father and mother were married in old St. Luke's by my grandfather early in 1878.

Father was a young lawyer who had graduated from Columbia
College and Law School, and had been admitted to practice in May
1868. The parchments for his, my grandfather's, and my own professional degrees presently hang on the wall of my law office. They keep
me feeling *en famille.*

In those days there were no title insurance companies. Every lawyer
was his own conveyancer and title searcher. Father began specializing in
real estate law. He compiled from the records in the Court Clerks'
offices three printed volumes entitled *Abstracts of Farm Titles in the
City of New York by H. Croswell Tuttle.* They were copyrighted and
published in 1881, totaling 573 pages, plus numerous maps and diagrams. Concluding the Preface, he wrote:

> *The author would state that he has endeavored to secure accuracy
> by comparing every part of the work at least twice with the origi-
> nal records.*

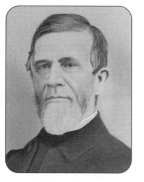

CHARLES TUTTLE

and

HIS FOREBEARS

Center: CHARLES TUTTLE, at the time of his father's death, 1882

Top left: REV. ISAAC TUTTLE, grandfather of Charles Tuttle;

Top right: SARAH PARMELEE BEECHER TUTTLE, grandmother;

Bottom left: HENRY CROSWELL TUTTLE, father;

Bottom right: PENELOPE COOK TUTTLE, mother.

Father also was an accomplished musician and presided at St. Luke's organ Sunday afternoons during the children's service, leading a choir of young boys instructed by him.

After their marriage, my father and mother lived in a small house which he purchased in the Bronx; they later moved to an address in West 23rd Street, the identity of which has long since been lost in the insatiable maw of our great City. It was there that I was born on April 21, 1879.

My father's constant labors on his *Abstracts* in the dusty and dank air of the catacombs of the ancient and now long since gone Hall of Records, rendered him more susceptible to the tuberculosis of which he died on November 10, 1882, at the age of thirty. I have no clear memory of his features until the solemn day of his death when I was brought to his bedside for a parting. I still can see his wan colorless face with his raven-black hair flowing over the white pillow; and I still can hear, as my hand was put in his, his faintly whispered last words: "Take care of your mother."

Mother also became an author and publisher.

During grandfather's last illness he requested her to write a history of St. Luke's Church and his long ministry. When she expressed doubt of her ability, he said: "You are able—if you think yourself to be able"—a motto expressive of his own courage.

Some years later the vestry of St. Luke's repeated this same request. Grandfather's rectorate had spanned nearly half a century of miraculous and eventful growth, both by St. Luke's and by the City of New York itself. The history of the one would intertwine importantly with the history of the other.

Mother finally undertook the task; in 1927 a copyrighted printed volume of 571 pages was published, with 53 illustrations and the reproduction of many important historical documents. The book was entitled *History of St. Luke's Church in the City of New York,* and was affectionately dedicated to the memory of my grandfather. Its obvious importance was such that copies were soon installed in all the principal public libraries of the City and are still consulted by historians as authoritative.

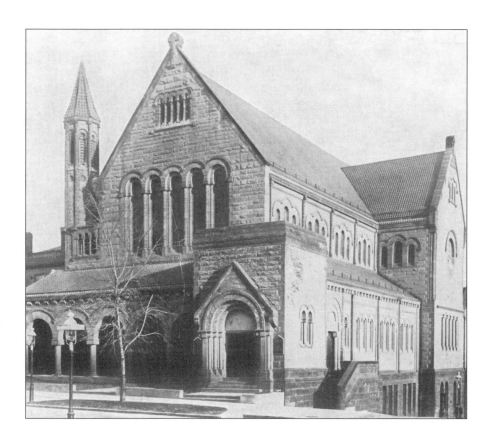

SAINT LUKE'S CHURCH
Convent Avenue and 141st Street
New York City • Erected 1892

This photograph was originally published in the 1927 book, *History of St. Luke's Church in the City of New York, 1820–1920,* a 571-page volume written by Mrs. H. Croswell Tuttle, mother of Charles Tuttle.

HAMMOND FARM HOUSE / WAYSIDE, *Lake George*

SECTION 3

Winter 1881–82 at Lake George.
Effort to Arrest Tuberculosis.

M Y FIRST DAYS AT LAKE GEORGE were in the dreadful Adirondack winter of 1881–82. Tuberculosis was then a prime killer. My grandfather's wife, son and three daughters all died of it. Required to pronounce the words of Eternal Hope beside the five graves of his own family, Grandfather witnessed the death of one after the other in a space of three years.

Medical science had as yet no David for this dread Goliath. The common advice was to prolong the agony in fresh air and open spaces.

As early as 1850 my grandfather had become a summer visitor at the now long gone Lake House in Lake George Village, then known as

Caldwell, on the eastern edge of the Adirondack mountains in upstate New York. In 1856 he bought the "Hammond Farm" on the shore of the Lake, a mile north of the Village. The old Hammond Farm House stood just east of the sandy, unpaved shore road. Water ran to a tub outside from a spring on the west side of the road. Heating was by a wood stove at the beginning of the narrow stairs to the second floor. Sanitation was most primitive. The name of our house was "Wayside."

Notwithstanding the primitive accommodations, that was the place where, pursuant to the best medical advice obtainable, my father was sent to spend the winter of 1881-82. To nurse him through it, he was joined at Lake George by my mother, my granduncle Charles, and, to add to their burdens, my three-year-old self. As I think back to how dreadful that winter must have been, I have always been proud that I have been privileged to carry on with the name of that grand gray-haired old man. Verily, he was of the Order of Love's True Knights.

My memories of those months are very dim. I seem to see the flashing hatchet cutting holes in the ice, which had skimmed over the water tub during the night. I seem to see myself being lifted to ride on one of the ice-cakes cut in the little bay and being drawn by the horse on the stone boat to the waiting sawdust in the icehouse.

But our mission to Wayside was hopeless. In the spring we took my father back to the city to die.

In later years, as I would pass my father's framed portrait on the wall of "Halcyon," our summer home in Lake George, shadowy thoughts seem to come groping for some such words as these:

All that in life was yours to be
You did in death bequeath to me.

HENRY CROSWELL TUTTLE
father of Charles Tuttle

---◆◆◆---

SECTION 4

Life as a Child in Oak Ridge, New Jersey, 1883-8. One Room on a Farm.

AFTER MY FATHER DIED, the physicians felt that in the long nursing of him mother might have contracted the same fatal disease. Fresh air and a change of scene were again the prescription.

Since there was little but the meager royalties from father's *Abstracts,* she and I took up life in a tiny hamlet in the recesses of northern New Jersey, known, so far as known at all, by the name of Oak Ridge.

Our growing country had altogether forgotten Oak Ridge. Nothing was there but a huddle of several old farmhouses staring at each other with unpainted windows across a one-lane sandy road traveled mostly by oxcart. In approaching, one first passed a one-room, one-story, unpainted all-purpose country store, selling buggy supplies, farm clothes, cow halters, mouse traps, and, with the latter, chocolate mice.

Just beyond the huddle was America's traditional one-room backwoods schoolhouse, its white paint only a fading memory. Segregation of the sexes was represented only by the bodily conveniences in the rear.

In the midst was a small Presbyterian church with its stubby wooden steeple hopefully pointing heavenward and housing a bell rung only when the clerical circuit rider came to summon the faithful. Huddled around the church, like frightened chicks sheltering around the mother hen, was a permanent congregation of gravestones at various angles in the unkempt grass and bearing names and dates mainly eroded but, one hopes, recorded more legibly elsewhere.

Mother and I began living as boarders of Farmer Corson in one room in the southeast corner of his second floor. In that room we continued from the time I was three until I became nine. Water came from "the old oaken bucket," cranked up and down in the well. Heat was from the stove in the kitchen and from the fireplace in the parlor. Butter was churned by a large un-pedigreed dog which kept walking to nowhere on the treadmill. Peace of mind was usually recovered in what is universally known in farm patois as the "two-holer," discreetly placed behind some bushes in the rear. At the first hint of light the rooster left his sleepily clucking harem and swaggered conscientiously to the gatepost to crow up the dawn.

Nevertheless, mother recovered her health; and I laid the foundations of the sturdy constitution with which I have been blessed. Tribute I place at the feet of Mrs. Corson, who conducted her kitchen especially for small boys' delight—bowls of hot oatmeal, piles of griddlecakes, doughnuts, jams, and milk fresh from the cows.

Farmer Corson had two boys my own age, Harry and Whitfield. The three of us were the chief problems of the neighborhood and especially of the somewhat elderly schoolmarm—problems usually solved, at least ephemerally, in Farmer Corson's woodshed at the end of a strap.

Education was on the level of rudimentary three R's. I was given a copybook with a word in beautiful Spencerian penmanship at the top of each page, and was told to try to reproduce it on all the vacant lines below. This dreary task was now and then lightened by pulling the pigtail of the little girl in front of me, and then quickly resuming Spencerian absorption as feminine outcry gave joy to the ear.

Education, however, was not confined to the schoolroom. I soon learned to keep a respectful distance from the heavy-necked and unsociable bull in the pasture; the black snake in the brook; and the big turkey-gobbler who warned off mischievous boys with a menacing spread of feathers, and a hoarse volume of profane threat—lessons which added up to the useful knowledge that discretion is the better part of valor.

Across the field of yesterday
He sometimes comes to me,
A little lad just back from play—
The lad I used to be.
— T.S. Jones, Jr., SOMETIMES

Early Life at 218 West 46th Street, New York City, Old St. Luke's.

I N THE SPRING OF 1888 mother and I left Oak Ridge and came to New York City to live with my grandfather at 218 West 46th Street—just west of Longacre Square.

His was a brownstone house, with four stories, high stoop, basement and a yard in the rear. With him were his two elderly sisters-in-law, Mrs. Mary Croswell and Julia Beecher. Mother and I and the maid had the top floor.

The street was paved with cobblestones. Directly opposite was a firehouse with two white horses for the engine. When the alarm rang, I was out as quickly as the firemen and saw some wonderful conflagrations. Horse cars ran through Longacre Square. By jumping aboard I made a little pocket money by selling newspapers to the riders for a cent—the then current price.

My grandfather was very strict in his religious observances. Every morning the family assembled in the living room and, all kneeling, he recited from memory the Morning Family Prayers in the back of the Book of Common Prayer, and likewise before bedtime the Evening Family Prayers. Grace was said at all three meals and occasionally Bible reading. He wrote his sermons and preached them as written. They were often doctrinal and always sternly orthodox.

My schooling began in the apartment of a Miss Hoagland, a single lady who had seen better days and was making ends meet by means of a small "select" coeducational class privately instructed in her apartment.

Soon I qualified for admission to Trinity Episcopal School of which my grandfather was a trustee. Its history ran back to the beginning of the 1800s. When I enrolled, it was located in two dwelling houses on the site later that of the Hotel Astor, around the corner from grandfather's home. Many years later, when occasionally sitting on the dais in the Grand Ballroom of the Hotel Astor, I would speculate whether corporeally I was then in the exact cubic space where, when the moment was safe, my young buddies and I had chanted *sotto voce* our favorite self-composed ditty about two easy-going teachers: *No more Latin, no more Greek; Jones and Perry are asleep!*

The headmaster was a retired gray-bearded clergyman. His pedagogical specialty was securing from the scholars memorized recitation of the Collect for the following Sunday as printed in the Book of Common Prayer. His aid to memory was a rattan across the shoulders if errors were too frequent. Pray correctly or smart ruefully!

On Sundays the whole family boarded a horse car and jogged down to St. Luke's Church then on Hudson Street opposite Grove Street. Occasionally I was sent early enough to attend the Sunday School presided over by Miss Ellen Van Kleeck, who also was the directress of the small parish day school.

The family sat in the Rector's pew near the pulpit. The service was what is Episcopally known as "middle-of-the-road"—candles on the altar, and choir in white vestments, strict rubric observance. The former rectory, where my father had lived, had become a clergy house for the assistant minister and some members of the staff. Mother's former home next door had been sold. Grandfather prevailed on the organist, John W. Carpenter, to try me in the choir. The experiment, thrice repeated out of charity, was a disaster. There was no Orpheus in my make-up.

Gradually in those boyhood days at St. Luke's and Trinity School, I was beginning to sense that there were far wider horizons opening to the eyes of the mind than the encircling hills at Oak Ridge. I began to wander with fascination into the World's Past as into some Museum with countless strange forms, wax figures and showcases along its endless corridors. I also began to be conscious of the Future, with its innumerable pathways leading onward to destinations beyond discernment. I was commencing to be aware that ultimately I must, together with my Destiny, go out from the doorway of the Past and confront the gates into the Future.

Gradually also it ceased to be drudgery to study the contents of the books brought home from Trinity School — to curl up in the big rocking chair under the evening lamp and sip the spring waters of knowledge.

Dimly, a curious question began to nag: Was knowledge power, for good or evil? Was this the real meaning and the challenge of that old, old story about a Tree of Knowledge which grew in a Garden near a Tree of Life guarded by a cherubim with a flaming sword which turned every way?

I wondered.

SECTION 6

Later Life at 218 West 46th Street. Trinity School. A Decision.

LIFE AT TRINITY SCHOOL was shaping up for college, with the question of Career just beyond.

I was in my junior year. Grandfather was anxious for me to prepare for the ministry; but there on the shelf in my room were those *Abstracts of Farm Titles by H. Croswell Tuttle*—a signal of direction from my father.

I vividly recall the day, indeed the moment, of decision. It occurred on a bright Sunday afternoon in the living room of "Rockledge," my grandfather's summer home at Lake George. In those days there was no pension fund for retired Episcopal clergymen. Grandfather always invited them in relays to Rockledge; and on Sunday afternoons they all assembled in the living room with its long French windows overlooking the Lake. Grandfather conducted the service, part of which was antiphonal recitation from the Psalms. There I was, a lad of fourteen, staring hopelessly through

Photo by L.H. Fillmore, Ticonderoga, NY

ROCKLEDGE, *Lake George*

Isaac Tuttle, wife Sarah, and two daughters are seen on the front porch of Rockledge in this stereopticon–photograph, *circa 1877.*

the windows at the waters of the Lake, golden in the afternoon sunlight and stirred by the swirl of fish challenging me to come out and play games with them.

Finally the antiphony between the aged gray-bearded clergy, who at the moment were not at all interested in fish, came to something mournful which sounded like this (Psalm 68:11-12):

> *The Lord gave the word: great was the company*
> *of the preachers; Kings with their armies did flee apace.*

My voice was thereupon heard adding dissonantly: "No wonder! No wonder!"

Obviously, any thought of combining the ministry and me must be decisively dropped. But, if not the Prophets, then the Law! Perhaps father's *Abstracts* were the gateway.

SECTION 7

Life in Columbia College. A New Iliad. Red Flag of Anarchy.

I N THE FALL OF 1895, at the age of sixteen, I entered Columbia College as a freshman. It was then at 49th Street and Madison Avenue. Its site on Morningside Heights was yet to be developed. Seth Low, later Mayor Low, was president.

The curriculum was typically liberal arts and very demanding. For some reason now unclear to me, I kept at Latin until, by graduation day in 1899, I had become able to hold simple conversations in it. With brashness, perhaps not uncharacteristic, I concluded that no adequate Latin classic had been written since Virgil. The void needed to be filled. I elected myself to fill it by composing in rolling hexameter a new Iliad about a hitherto unsung hero of the Trojan War. After a few excellent chapters, I proudly showed my typewritten manuscript (laboriously done with one finger) to Professor Egbert, head of the Latin Department. He read it, and told me: "It's very fine, Tuttle, but a new Latin classic would upset Latin scholars throughout the land. I suggest that for their sakes you do no more of it."

Perhaps by way of amends Professor Egbert later headed a faculty committee which in my junior year (1898) awarded me the key of the venerable Phi Beta Kappa Society dating back to December 15, 1776.

I joined the Philolexian Debating Society and regularly jousted in the verbal arena against the rival Barnard Debating Society, named after the famous Dean of the Columbia Law School in my father's time. Ultimately I became "the anchor man" on the "Varsity Debating Team" and fought for Alma Mater's honor against aggressors in full verbal armor from outlying universities.

I remember one historic battle with Cornell in Columbia's gymnasium packed with supporting Columbia students, admiring parents, girl friends and guerrillas from the enemy. The subject of debate was some dreary economic issue spelled out in large chalk on the blackboard in the rear of the platform.

Everyone was thoroughly bored by the time I arose to close for Columbia. I had not gone far with the lullaby when some movement in the audience broke my thread, left my mind blank, and left me with the problem of how to gracefully turn around and read the subject chalked on the blackboard. Somewhere I read Henry Ward Beecher's maxim that, if you lose the thread of your discourse, rant and tear until you find it again. My classmates never let me forget that suddenly I moved to the edge of the platform and, lifting an arm on high, indignantly declaimed:

> *Ladies and Gentleman, if you adopt the policy which the other side advocates (for a moment I had no idea what it was), it takes no prophet to foresee the red flag of anarchy rising luridly above the horizon.*

FOUR MEMBERS OF THE COLUMBIA DEBATING TEAM, *c. 1898*
"Anchor man" Charles Tuttle is on the far right.

Boy, that was something! The long suffering boredom of the audience exploded into applause, stamping, whistles and catcalls, under cover of which I bowed my appreciation of the tribute, turned around, read what was on the blackboard, and resumed the decorous boredom. In those days the spark word was "Anarchy." "Communism" had not yet replaced it.

During the graduation exercises in 1899 our Class, proud of being "the century's last," staged a three-day gala, part of which was the giving of spoof presents to all its officers. I was treasurer. So, with a merciless recitation of the above story, they unrolled a big red flag bearing "Anarchy," a skull and cross-bones, and the inscription: "This is Tut's"!

There was some salve in the fact that during the same exercises I was awarded the H. C. Brunner Medal, the James Gordon Bennett Prize, the Chanler History Prize, the Philolexian Prize for Best Essay, and final honors in English. My classmates clapped me on the back and laughingly called me "Hog."

Desperately I clung to the warning several millennia old that:

Pride goeth before destruction,
And a haughty spirit before a fall.
— PROVERBS 16:18

CHARLES TUTTLE'S CLASS PIN
Columbia College
Class of 1899

CHAPTER TWO

A CAREER, A HOME, and A WIFE

SECTION 1

Life in Columbia Law School.
Admission to the Bar.

Some say the law's an ass.
Some: it is the tyrant's iron rod.
Some: it is the dictate of the mass.
Some: it is a roadway on to God.
— C.H.T.

SEPTEMBER 1899 conducted me into Columbia Law School as a freshman. The decision had been made. I was to stake my all on a career as a lawyer. My father had prevailed.

At once I found myself put in training to participate in Man's ever unfinished business—to build his World on Justice.

Century after century! One foundation stone at a time—always with blood on it! Animalism, barbarism, superstition, slavery, feudalism, tyranny, assassination, revolt, persecution in the name of God! But always a groping, a reaching upward, a forward pathway discovered here and there, a brave cry in the night "Excelsior," the slow dawn of the inalienable rights in all men!

My studies of constitutional law began with the story of a quiet brook meandering through a lush meadow studded with wild flowers. There had been and always will be many such, but only one will be "Runnymede★."

There the individual man envisioned his birthright endowed by law. Rough-hewn, battle-won phrases for which centuries of human tragedy had been seeking words, were recorded on parchment as inviolable. Once so recorded, the Great Charter became part of the Rock of Ages.

"These liberties underwritten." "No Freeman shall be disseised of his Freehold or Liberties but by lawful judgment of his Peers or by the Law of the Land." "A Writ of Inquisition shall be granted freely, and not denied, and nothing shall be given for a Writ of Inquisition." "We will sell to no man, we will not deny or defer to any man, either Justice or Right." "A Widow, after the death of her husband, shall have her Marriage, and her inheritance." "The English Church shall be free, and shall have all her whole rights and liberties inviolable."

Instruction in the Law School was mostly by "the case system." Our textbooks presented actual judicial decisions in typical tough cases. Open lively dialogue followed between the professor and the class as to whys and wherefores. One soon learned that the daily administration and practice of law, both in and out of the courts, was not reducible to ready-made formulae but reflected and concerned the infinite variety of human life, circumstances and opinion, and that amid these mazes even the most learned and sensitive of judges would differ.

Fascinating also were the far separate sources of our law—"common law" from Anglo-Saxon and Norman customs; "equity law" from the days when the Chancellor as keeper of "the King's conscience"

★ *Editor's Note:* Runnymede is a meadow west of London on the Thames River where King John, confronted by the barons, signed the Magna Carta in 1215.

decided requirements of justice outside the reach of the common law; code laws decreed by legislatures or by authorized executive or administrative departments; and rules of evidence and procedures. As with all knowledge, Justice moves in continuous process from the simple to the complex, from one horizon to a wider.

It seemed that life in the Law could be exciting. I determined to find out.

An occasion soon presented itself when Dr. Keener from Harvard was installed as Dean of our Law School. His sense of public relations was inverse to his knowledge of law. When he founded the *Columbia Law Review,* he staffed its board of editors exclusively with students who had followed him from the Harvard Law School! We Columbia men boiled. Here was aggression at its academic worst. The idea of protest marches, sit-ins, student riots, and pop bottles thrown through academic windows had not yet been born; but nevertheless there was Patrick Henry's famous tweaking of the nose of King George the Third. Immediately I, on my part, began writing avant-garde articles on various current law topics and sending them to the *Albany Law Journal,* a commercial law publication. To my surprise, it published them, called for more, and sent me meaningful checks — my first earnings from the law. But the sweet icing on this cake was sneaking these articles onto the Dean's desk, duly endorsed with my compliments in flowing red pencil.

Justice was lead-footed, but years later it was done. My daughter Charlotte became the first woman officer of the Board of Editors of the *Columbia Law Review.*

Moot Courts were frequent in the curriculum. Students practiced the role of judges, jurors and attorneys for the plaintiffs and defendants. An exciting *casus belli* [cause of war] was chosen from sensational cases in the current news, or was invented by ambitious fiction writers and humorists in the class. An example of the latter: the trial of a suit for damages by a mother-in-law against her son-in-law who, so she claimed, had slapped her hard enough to loosen her teeth because, so he claimed, she was urging his wife to stop getting his breakfast in the morning in order to force him to hire an in-servant.

At times we were honored by having on the bench honest-to-goodness judges in their silk robes, best courtroom manners, and a gavel for enforcement. The air vibrated with: "May your Honor please!" "Objection." "Overruled." "Sit down, or you'll be fined for contempt." Summings-up were always delivered after much burning of the midnight lamps reading examples of oratory set by Rufus Choate, Demosthenes' Phillipics, Portia, Patrick Henry, Abraham Lincoln, and others. Orations were rated E-minus unless interlarded with quotations from the Bible or the patriotic classics. The usual result was "sound and fury signifying nothing"; but those who loved it began to be impatient for the real arenas. As for myself, I recalled the fable of the domesticated lion cub reared on milk, and then getting his first whiff of the smell of blood.

The reaction was swift. In February of my senior year (1902), three months before the hoped for graduation in June, examinations for admission to the Bar were held by the State Board of Board Examiners. Why wait until the Board's later examination in June? Could anything be lovelier than to be admitted in February and then return to the Law School to look down my nose at classmates waiting until June? So I took my own dare!

The examinations were held in the basement of the then new Appellate Division Court House at 25th Street and Madison Avenue. My classmate Loren Wood joined me in the adventure.

The accident of the alphabet seated us together. Three hours in the morning and three in the afternoon! The test was of human endurance, not knowledge. In the middle of the afternoon Loren began taking out his large gold watch, snapping open the back of it, looking intently at what was there, and then scribbling answers on the examination paper. Being desperate and human, I hissed in his ear: "Do you see that proctor standing over there? If you don't share that trot with me, I will call him over." Loren said "Sure." The back of his watch held the best trot in the world—the portrait of a beautiful girl! I immediately divined the answers also. Both of us passed. He married the girl; they lived happily ever after; and they had lots of the best answers in the world—children!

In March 1902, I was approved by the Character Committee, and before the five judges of the Appellate Division took the oath to uphold the Constitution of the United States and of New York and to behave myself honorably as an officer of the Court. The Presiding Justice made a little speech between the lines of which you could read the dismal warning that there were a woodshed and a strap in the background. In short, Oak Ridge again!

Next June I was fortunate enough to pass the Law School examinations also; and my alma mater sent me forth into the world to try my luck, tagged with her B.A. and B.L., and to say "Yes" to Life.

Whence now would come the gift to see
The wisdom of my world to be?
— C.H.T.

➤◆◄

SECTION 2

The First Three Cases.

Case I: THE EX-POLICE SERGEANT

SOON AFTER my admission to the Bar in 1902, Dean Kirchwey suggested that I make my bow in the courts by appearing in the Municipal Court for the defendant in the case of *McCormick v. McCarton.*

The plaintiff was an ex-sergeant of police who had been expelled from the force on charges. McCarton was president of the Police Sergeants Endowment and Benevolent Society, which had a provision in its constitution for the payment of $350 to a member *dismissed* from the force. McCormick sued for the consolation money.

The case came to trial before Municipal Court Justice Francis J. Worcester who called for briefs. I and the dictionary understood "brief" as "short." I shrank my advocacy with the determination of a Papuan head-hunter shrinking the skull of his enemy. Since then the dictionary and I have been irresistibly parting company, notwithstanding that I should have learned that brevity is not only the soul of wit but also of brief-writing, from the fact that Judge Worcester reproduced my brief with almost no change in wording as "the Opinion of the Court," and on March 10, 1903, dismissed the complaint in accordance with my contention that such consolation payment would be contrary to public policy.

McCormick thereupon appealed to the Appellate Term, three Supreme Court Judges sitting. On July 7, 1903, that court, after hearing the arguments of my adversary and myself, unanimously affirmed on "the opinion of Judge Worcester"—to-wit, on my little brief (86 N.Y. Supp. 1140; 95 App. Div. 426, 431).

But even that was not all! The plaintiff next appealed to the Appellate Division, five Supreme Court Judges sitting. That Court, after hearing the arguments of my adversary and myself, unanimously affirmed, and included Justice Worcester's "opinion" with its own opinion in the official report of the case (88 N.Y. Supp. 722 (June 10, 1904) which recited:

Louis J. Grant, for Appellant
Charles H. Tuttle, for Respondent

Thus ended in permanent glory my first bow in the courts and my first "brief."

I should have quit litigation then and there, while my record stood at this 100%. But, having to make a living, I brashly continued, and soon learned the meaning of *sic transit gloria.*★

Over the ensuing years I often turn for the "balm of Gilead" for my wounds by taking from the library shelf *"McCormick v. McCarton"* and retasting the sweetness of my "first."

Someone has said that "Life is just one damned thing after another." So, at least is an advocate's life in the courts.

★ Thus passes away glory.

Case II: WHISTLER'S MOTHER

My second court case was a swift illustration.

The client was a sweet old lady—a "Whistler's Mother," complete with gray hair, lace cap, black gown and angelic face. Any jury would believe against all the world her testimony that she was knocked down by that naughty Gimbel's truck while she was crossing the street under protection of the green light. One of her claims for damages was that, although she was a little deaf before, she was very deaf after.

I carefully schooled her that that wily Mephistopheles, the defense lawyer, would start his cross-examination in a shout close to her face, and then would gradually move away, lowering his voice the meanwhile; and that, if she did not hear clearly, she would help "the damages" by saying so.

Sure enough! Gradually the brute retreated nearly to the room's rear and then asked her a question in an obviously much lower voice. When her silence seemed to me acutely significant, I jumped up and said:

My adversary asked in such a low voice that my client did not hear. Will the court reporter please repeat the question loudly?

Thereupon Whistler's mother turned her sweet face to me and smilingly said:

Oh yes I did! I was thinking of the answer!

With a red face I kept the case going for several days. The ultimate verdict was good, for the laughter at my expense had been forgotten. But it still rings in my ears.

Three morals for fledgling trial lawyers:

- Never try to paint a lily.
- Beware of the guileless.
- If you pull a blooper, keep the case going in the hope that it will be forgotten or covered up.

Case III: "The System"

In those early days, Tammany Hall was ruled by bosses who made no secret of the fact that they were working for their own pockets all the time. The Supreme Court sat in the old "Tweed Court House" in City Hall Park, significantly just behind City Hall. It was a monument not so much to Justice as to Civic Corruption. There were judges who had bought their "elevation" to the Bench by immense tribute laid at the feet of the Boss. There were judges who had their private attorneys general, each known as "the man to see"; and judges who had the reputation of taking "kickbacks" from those favored with appointments to patronage.

The "system" was a rude shock to young lawyers just out of law school with all their shining idealism thick upon them. Not a few resolved to do something about it as soon as they could get the opportunity.

I do not mean that all judges were thus tainted in those days. On the contrary, there were many who revered the thought that the true administration of Justice between man and man was the greatest and holiest prerogative that our State could confer. Their names shine like stars in the Law's Firmament.

But almost immediately I had a brush with the other kind. My client was an elderly widow who could not meet her landlord's demand for increased rent and was faced in the Municipal Court with a suit for eviction. The Judge was notorious. The landlord had employed his "attorney general," who greeted me at the door with the observation that I must be wet behind the ears if I was planning to risk my career there. I told him that I had brought with me a friend who was a newspaper reporter and that I also had with me money enough to purchase the stenographic record. Later I saw him talking to the Judge, and soon he returned with an offer of settlement very favorable to the old lady. I went out into God's pure air.

Liberty under Law we cry!
Without Justice both soon die.
— C.H.T.

SECTION 3

A Great Man Heeds a Long-Dead Friend's Call.
Life in "the Dog Hole" at Davies, Stone & Auerbach.

Who knows what guides an acorn in its fall,
To find a chance to root and grow at all.
– C.H.T.

I HAD NOT GONE FAR in my young life before I began to wonder how much of one's life was one's own choosing and creating, how much was chance, and how much was a kind of mystic guidance and watchfulness not traceable to either choosing or chance. At times I felt as if someone were putting signposts where roads became confused; sometimes as if there were a directing whisper in my ear. I came to call this whispering presence "my guardian angel."

Someone long ago must have had the same inner experience and mused upon it, for he wrote:

He shall give his angels charge over thee,
To keep thee in all thy ways. (PSALM 91:11)

Let me show you an early and very critical instance; and then I will leave to you the propounding of an explanation.

Graduation from Columbia Law School confronted me with a desperate need for "a job." I was twenty-three. Education had left our cupboard as bare as Mother Hubbard's. Mother and I had no "connections" in the great World. I sought the Dean's help. He finally told me that he could probably place me as "a beginner" with a certain prominent lawyer, who had only one client (although a very big one) but who was and always would be a lone practitioner, and that the best I could hope for in the end would be "managing clerk."

The whisper said "wait"; but Mother and I finally decided that we had no choice. I was to see the man the next morning. While we were discussing, Mother casually picked up *The New York Times,* and suddenly said:

> *I wonder whether this can be the Julien T. Davies who was your father's close friend in law school, and whom from the back window of my home I often saw fencing with your father in the rectory's rear yard? The* Times *says that he is the president of the City Bar Association, counsel for the elevated railways and several banks, and head of the large Wall Street law firm of Davies, Stone and Auerbach at 15 Broad Street. I must give you a letter to him. Possibly he will remember your father after all these years.*

I said it would be far more strategic for her to go herself and alone. So next morning, instead of my going to see the lone practitioner with one client, mother decked herself in her "finest" and went down to see the multiple practitioner—the leader of the City Bar. He had her shown in immediately, and with a benign smile said he was happy to greet the widow of his old and dear friend "Croswell Tuttle." After some talk about fencing in the rectory's rear yard, mother told of the need of "Croswell's son" for a job. The great man smiled again and said: *"Send Croswell's son down this afternoon and we will see, what we can do for him."*

PENELOPE COOK TUTTLE
A Mother's Timely Observation

I went and stayed for twenty-five years!

What is your explanation of it all, wise reader? The whispered "wait." The casual falling of my mother's eye on a news article in *The New York Times* at that critical moment which could otherwise have passed forever. A door of opportunity that had been unknown the day before. A great man whose greatness was such that he could hear and answer the call for help from a friend who had been dead for twenty years. I have my own explanation, but it will remain mine.

Next day I was installed in what all large law firms call "the dog hole" — a place where partners keep the young pups from the law schools while waiting to see how well they will bark. A door of opportunity for a meaningful professional career and a rewarding life had suddenly been opened before me.

> *There are more things in heaven and earth, Horatio,*
> *Then are dreamt of in your philosophy.*
> — Shakespeare (HAMLET, Act I)

When I began in the "dog hole" as a novitiate, there were three other pups who naturally had preempted the best desks and the one window. My desk was a superannuated antique in a corner without the adornment even of a blotter. A gooseneck, green–shaded electric lamp provided a modicum of light. There were three drawers at the right side. My knees filled the remaining space underneath. I kept wondering whether "Opportunity" would ever condescend to approach so forlorn a little kennel.

The first call upon me came from the elderly managing clerk, Mr. Roswell H. King, whose timidity and lack of aggressiveness had kept him from a career commensurate with his real ability. The firm, he said, had a lawsuit in which an emergency required a motion in less than the required minimum of five days' notice to the adversary. Roswell asked me to draft "an order to show cause" to be presented to a judge for signature. I quaked at this immediate confrontation with the enormous gulf between the Law School and the Law Office.

Roswell explained that when the required notice time had run out, you asked a judge to sign an order directing the other side "to show cause" in less time why your

CHARLES HENRY TUTTLE
Ready to Practice Law

client should not be granted the relief which otherwise he could have moved for directly. Who was it who mocked at "these sharp quillets of law"? Roswell kindly produced a form, which I laboriously adapted. Sixty-six years later I am still parroting this mumbo-jumbo of "order to show cause." As said by the Prophet Hosea: "Ephraim is joined to idols: let him alone." (4:17).

Then came the great moment! Mr. Davies sent for me! I can still see his awesome face with its crown of white hair as he sat in the rocking chair which Ulysses S. Grant used during his two terms as President. "Tuttle, how would you like to try drawing for me a brief for the Appellate Division?" I stuttered. **Opportunity** had really come to my forlorn dark corner of the "dog hole"!

I tore the library apart in search for judicial gems for that brief. Mr. Davies made few changes, and, with characteristic greatness, he added my name after his at the end. Soon I was carrying his bag when he went to the court house to argue. We lost by a vote of three to two. The official law report of the case is *Mount, as Administratrix, v. Daniel S. Tuttle, as Senior Bishop of the Protestant Episcopal Church* (99 App. Div. 433, Dec. 1904★). The report records (p. 435) as attorneys for appellant Senior Bishop, "Julian T. Davies, Charles E. Hotchkiss and Charles H. Tuttle." Even though I was merely the tail of the dog, that was some dog!

Mr. Davies directed that a motion for re-argument be made. I sweated on that. Under court rules a motion for re-argument had to be on the calendar and submitted without argument not later than the fourth Friday of the month after the decision. When I arrived at the office on that fourth Friday, I found Roswell almost in tears, wailing that he had forgotten to put the motion on the calendar and: "Now it was too late; and what will Mr. Davies say?"

Being brash, I told Roswell to let me handle it. I obtained from the other side a stipulation consenting to add the motion at the foot of the calendar. After the Presiding Justice finished calling the calendar, I arose, respectfully explaining the oversight, and asked that the motion be deemed added to the calendar and submitted. His Honor seemed to

★ *Aff'd 183 N.Y. 358 (1906).*

enjoy the moment, for he said: "Young Man, don't you know the rules?" Not even "Counselor." Just "Young man"! I pleaded the stipulation and the absence of prejudice. Again the reply: "Young man, read the rules." A bright idea then burst upon me. I said I would notice the motion for the following Friday, the fifth in the month. I was unaware that the Court did not sit on the Fifth Friday. "Young man, we do not care if you come then, but we won't be here!" I saw more stars than I ever imagined were in the heavens. Slamming down my papers, I said:

I shall make it a point to be here next Friday, because I will receive from these bare walls more courtesy than I am receiving now!

Roswell grabbed me by the shoulders, and cried in my ear: "Tuttle, shut up or you will be in jail." Picking up my papers, I walked slowly out with my head (I trust) high. All the lawyers in the room were clapping their hands behind the backs of the chairs in front of them.

Back at the office Roswell and I looked at each other. Mr. Davies! I said that that problem had now become mine. When Mr. Davies was reported in his office late in the afternoon I began telling him. The telephone rang. He picked up the receiver, listened intently, and said:

Judge O'Brien, Mr. Tuttle was just beginning to tell me. I know he will be very happy to hear what you are saying. I know that he will join me in thanking you.

Judge Morgan J. O'Brien had been one of the four judges on the bench that afternoon. He was telephoning to say that he and his three associates wish to "apologize" to Mr. Tuttle in the name of the Court for the treatment to which he had been subjected. Roswell King slept well that night. I know I did.

"Opportunity" was soon again at my dingy desk in the "dog hole." Mr. Davies sent for me! This time it was the federal court in West Virginia. He had argued a railroad case there, and the court had felt that the emergency could permit only five days for a brief. Mr. Davies wanted to know whether I had three bright friends who had been my classmates in Law School who would work with me as a team, day and night, at the Bar Association (42 West 44th Street) to get out a complete brief in four days. Expense was no great matter. Hire three good stenographers and a suite of rooms across the street from the Association. Do without sleep. So my three friends of the Law School, Loren Wood, Charles Baker, Henry Molloy and I worked in our clothes for four days and nights. Mr. Davies again had his draft. With a few minor changes he sent it to court—on time! Four young men received dazzling checks.

Shortly afterwards, Mr. Davies again sent for me! A small room in the office had been vacated. Would I like to move in to it?

Cast thy bread upon the waters:
For thou shalt find it after many days.
— ECCLESIASTES 11:1

SECTION 4

A Home and a Fiancée

At last our very own, a home!
To be ourselves, to go and come!
— C.H.T.

MY GRANDFATHER'S DEATH on November 20, 1896 had left mother and me alone. Six years in cramped quarters in various boarding houses followed. Perforce we lived on the brink of a financial precipice with nothing below except for me the dismal gorge of a "drop-out" and loss of a college and professional career.

My grandfather had felt an inescapable obligation to bring to completion the great edifice of the new St. Luke's on 141st Street and Convent Avenue, which with the land had cost over $250,000. He identified it with himself. It was the culminating monument to a long rectorship which had begun in June 1850. He saw in it old St. Luke's on Hudson Street born again.

In the pulpit of glowing brass—his gift as a memorial to his son (my father)—he had preached his farewell sermon on December 18, 1892, in the presence of many distinguished persons, and had stepped down to become "rector emeritus." For the adornment of the new Church he had gathered together the handsome chancel memorials to all his departed loved ones—the beautiful baldachino, the brass lectern, the altar rail, the brass pulpit, and various other impressive furnishings.

He accompanied his resignation as rector with a personal gift of $20,000, and obtained from Trinity Church a matching gift. By his will he established a "Tuttle Fund" of $10,000 to be ultimately applied, with gifts which it might inspire from others, toward payment of the church mortgage debt of $75,000.

In consequence, when my grandfather died, he had very little to leave to mother and me, other than the unproductive and run-down real property at Lake George, burdened with carrying charges greatly exceeding any possible return. It consisted of "the Hammond Farm House" ("Wayside") which had been built in the very early 1800's; of "Rockledge" which my grandfather had built in 1876 and in which he spent his summer vacations; of three other summer cottages which he had built at intervals thereafter in hopes of profitable rentals; of some vague and undeveloped water rights on Prospect Mountain; and a few acres of land, vacant except for an old decayed mill, beside Roaring Brook, east of the shore road then commonly known as Bolton Road. All these buildings were in gross disrepair and were only rentable in the summer for less than the taxes, which were very high because the land was shore property.

In order to give these places some care, I traveled during the boarding-house years to Lake George every three months or so on the Albany night boat, sleeping on the wooden bench encircling the rear deck; and from Albany by trolley to the Lake. My grandfather's super-intendent, Miles Latham, had become very old and had moved to Batesville, north of Lake George Village. He was unable to work. In consequence, for mother and me the going was tough for six years. But my "guardian angel" was faithful in coming down from above and whispering to me to hold fast to a motto which has been my talisman ever since: "Optimism and Serenity." Voltaire once wrote "optimism

is a mania for maintaining that all is well when things are going badly."
But look how Job came through!

The motto began to pay off in the fall of 1902, when I emerged
from Law School and was beginning to have earnings from my profession. At first they were a mere trickle, but even a trickle meant the difference between keeping on or giving up. I remember bringing to my
mother my first pay envelope and saying that my guardian angel had
whispered to me that, small as it was, it nevertheless was the key that
would open the locked door of our Future. It did. "Optimism and
Serenity" forever!

My earnings grew and in 1903 we were able to consider a home of
our own. We sold at a sacrifice price some of the more hopeless Lake
George land, and, with the aid of a large mortgage, we bought our first
home, 10 Hamilton Terrace—a three-story and basement gray stone

10 AND 12 HAMILTON TERRACE, *New York City*

house around the corner from St. Luke's Church and facing in the rear the mansion of Alexander Hamilton whence he went to the fatal duel with Aaron Burr at Weehawken. We furnished the house with a few things from 218 West 46th Street, and with purchases at auctions.

Hamilton Terrace was a quiet short avenue running from 141st to 144th Streets, with the only entrance at either end and with somewhat similar houses on both sides.

There mother lived until she died in 1932. She gave much of her time to gathering material for and writing her *History of St. Luke's Church* which she completed and published in 1927.

During this period I traveled daily from the elevated or subway express stations at 145th Street to the office of Davies, Stone & Auerbach in the old Mutual Life Building at 32 Nassau Street, two blocks north of Wall Street. The site is now occupied by the One Chase Manhattan Building, on the 55th floor of which I have had my present office for many years.

In 1905, John H. Morrison, the senior warden of St. Luke's Church, lived around the corner in 144th Street. He, his wife and my mother were fond of what is now known as "old-fashioned whist." On Friday evenings I escorted mother to their house and we all sat gravely down to cards in their living room on their second floor.

On a fateful Friday evening the maid brought up a card. Mrs. Morrison said that she must go down to meet Miss Hélène Wheeler who was helping at her table at the St. Luke's Church Fair and whose family had lately moved from Oswego into a house a few doors east. We put down our cards and resigned ourselves to patience.

Soon two pair of feet were coming up the stairs. I thought of it only as assurance we could soon get on with the game. Mrs. Morrison brought in Miss Wheeler, introduced her, and, after the usual conventional amenities, escorted her downstairs. The game was resumed; but I had difficulty in minding the cards. The "guardian angel" had come down from heaven and kept fluttering about me, whispering to my heart: *"She is It! Not these cards, but your life is at stake! Go in hot pursuit!"*

While escorting mother home, I asked whether she had noted that girl. She casually replied that Miss Wheeler was very beautiful. I exclaimed: " Mother, she is much more than that. She is going to be your daughter-in-law!"

The "guardian angel" had not failed me. In return, I must not fail the "guardian angel." So, I set about it.

The first thing to do was to take an interest in the Church Fair. I saw to it that the table at which Miss Wheeler served with Mrs. Morrison was bought out; and that Miss Wheeler was carefully escorted home each evening of the Fair. Having got as far as her front door, I soon maneuvered as far as her parlor, where there was a most congenial sofa. What could be more congenial than for both of us soon to be sitting on it?

One thing led to another. Just why or how no one understands.

Once upon a time there was a very wise old man, who liked to think about the puzzling things in life and to write about them in a book.

CHARLES AND HIS FIANCÉE, HÉLÈNE LOUISE WHEELER
At the Wheeler family home in Oswego, NY, 1906.

One day he wrote that there were four things "which are too wonderful for me." Of the four the most mysterious and final one was "the way of a man with a maiden" (Prov. 30:19).

The Fair at St. Luke's soon phased into "dating." Miss Wheeler was in Barnard College. I had been to Columbia College across the avenue from Barnard. She was a Congregationalist, but at the moment she was teaching a boys' class in the Sunday School of the Baptist Church on the corner of 145th Street and Convent Avenue. I was superintendent of the Sunday School of St. Luke's Episcopal Church on the corner of 141st Street and Convent Avenue. She had as background the City of Oswego and Lake Ontario. I had as background the City of New York and Lake George. The Adirondacks lay between our backgrounds as a common bond.

Hence there was much to talk about, intimately. Dressed in our Sunday finery we would walk together along Morningside Heights; visit Grant's Tomb and Madame Jumel's mansion; ramble in the park along the Hudson, or follow fancy elsewhere.

In our free evenings there were parties to be attended together; a theatre occasionally; a dance now and then. She joined St. Luke's; was "received" into the Episcopal Church; became assistant to Mrs. William C. Lester, who conducted the Primary Department in Sunday School, and whose husband had been my Latin Professor at Columbia. Hence, as you see, our lives flowed together as naturally as two brooks flowing toward a junction in a mountain valley. "Dating" phased into "going steady."

One evening I escorted her home from some social affair. We stood a while on the porch, making the kind of conversation that reflects reluctance to part. She was wearing a white evening gown. I reached out my hand to hold hers for a last moment. Suddenly we were in each other's arms. Our lips crushed together in a long lingering kiss. When she finally drew apart, she turned and went slowly through the door, and closed it softly behind her. I groped my way down the stoop. Nothing had been said. But what was there to say? And where could have been found the words to say it?

As I walked home, the fog in my mind cleared enough for me to be aware of the dawning of two urgent objectives. The first was to get immediately a gold ring adorned with a diamond, and personally to slide it on the third finger of that left hand which had just been around my neck caressingly for one enchanted moment. The ring remained there until I reverently drew it off upon Hélène's death sixty-three years later in order that it should become a sacred family heirloom. The second immediate objective was to claw from the practice of the law enough money for an early marriage.

HÉLÈNE L. WHEELER

Years later when I occasionally returned to that neighborhood to act as a lay reader at St. Luke's Church, or to attend a meeting of the City's Board of Higher Education held at City College, I would go and gaze with veneration at the porch and doorway of 453 West 144th Street as a shrine. People whom I did not know would come in and out. They seemed to be unaware that they were passing through the Gate of Heaven.

> *Life's riches oft by toil are given,*
> *A perfect Love is straight from Heaven.*
> — C.H.T.

Editor's Note:

Charles and Hélène were married at St. Luke's on June 1, 1907. They lived with his mother at 10 Hamilton Terrace until 1914, when the identical house next door, No. 12, became available, and they moved there with three small children. About nine years later the family, with four children, moved around the 144th Street corner to a spacious four-story and basement house, 339 Convent Avenue. Eventually, after all four children were married, Charles and Hélène moved to an apartment at One University Place on Washington Square in 1939. Their University Place home was located in the same Greenwich Village area where Dr. Isaac Tuttle had started his New York rectorship in 1850.

SECTION 5

Summer and a Gun in Philadelphia in 1905.

When comes the ringing challenge of the trumpet's call
Can one await to weigh what danger may befall?
— C.H.T.

F OR ME SUCH A TRUMPET'S CHALLENGE came in the summer of
1905.

Mr. Davies sent for me. An election was to occur in Philadelphia
in the first week in November; Mayor John Weaver was running for
reelection on the reform ticket. Civic forces, headed by John Wanamaker, were supporting him. Opposed were entrenched forces of corruption and the underworld. Elihu Root had been retained by the
Wanamaker groups; but in July 1905, President Theodore Roosevelt
had appointed him Secretary of State. Mr. Davies had been retained
in his place. He needed a representative to be a continuous member of
the Reform's legal staff in Philadelphia until Election Day. Would I be
that representative? I would.

Soon I was installed for the campaign in a cubicle in the office of
Judge James G. Gordon, the law champion of Reform. He was a Scotch
Highlander, six-foot-two, with black hair, a Napoleonic forelock, and
deep-set dark compelling eyes in a swarthy face. A formidable lion of a
man!

He placed me in an office for myself, and set me to work as a blood-
hound on the trails of corruption. Those trails ran through high and low
places. I rushed along with the canine eagerness of following hot scents.

One day about a week before election, Judge Gordon sent for me,
closed the door, and ushered me to a chair directly across from his desk.
He gazed at me for a while, and then said he had a necessary job, which

might be too dangerous for any of his staff living in Philadelphia. He asked bluntly, "Are you white-livered?" I said, "First tell me."

He then said that an hour before there had been sitting in the chair I was now occupying an extraordinarily beautiful woman who stated that she was the mistress of a certain X who was a leader of the underworld; that she and X had been offered $10,000 for an affidavit that when she had been going to Europe on the same steamer as Mr. Wanamaker things had happened inappropriate for the Angel of Reform; but nevertheless for $25,000 paid at once she would make an affidavit that nothing had happened.

Judge Gordon then said that this dastardly scheme must be killed at once. There remained but three more days before the election. Mayor Weaver's success seemed probable, but it might be close. The skillful publicizing of such a false affidavit at the last moment could be harmful. Of course, he would not pay a cent; but he had a possible plan for getting the affidavit of disclaimer without payment. The plan required that X and the woman come to his office that very night. He had told her that he would send a representative to X to negotiate. He could not use one of his own staff for they all lived in Philadelphia. Was I willing to be that representative? He was not pressing me to go, but would I?

I asked how he planned to induce them to come. He produced $25,000 in large bills and said that in the last extremity I might have to flash them as bait. I put them in my inside jacket pocket. From a drawer he drew a black revolver and extended it to me. I broke it open, removed the bullets and laid them on his desk. I said I would hope that any vis-à-vis would not know that it was unloaded.

So off I went. X had a headquarters, which in front looked like an ordinary real estate office, but an inner rear room had all the luxurious furnishings of an eastern mogul. What a typical gangster, big with thick neck and hard visage! When I glanced around suspiciously, he laughed coarsely and said he did not need anything hidden. Judge Gordon had no choice but to pay. When I started bargaining at $10,000, he told me to get out. Finally I came up to $25,000, but on the condition that they make the disclaimer affidavit at Judge Gordon's office that very night. He hesitated. I drew forth the bills; gave him an eye-full; and held my breath. Would he rush me? He telephoned the woman to be ready to be with him at Judge Gordon's office at eight.

I left and reported.

Judge Gordon said that only he, I and his stenographer, who was a notary, would be present. He hoped that when they arrived I could separate them, get X into my room, the woman into his room where he had the affidavit ready; and that, if trouble arose, I should give the elevator button in the hall three sharp rings.

I never have been clear just how I succeeded in getting X into the chair in my room. I was in a daze. I do remember flashing the money again and, standing in my doorway, I could hear Judge Gordon talking in his room at the far end on the corridor. X became restless, and jumped up saying he was going in to tell Judge Gordon that he wanted $50,000. I drew the revolver, and ordered him to sit down. At that moment Judge Gordon came along the corridor. When he saw the pantomime, he exclaimed, "Why, Tuttle, what are you doing? Mr. X, you must forgive this young man's thoughtless zeal. She will not sign without your presence. So come right into my room."

As Judge Gordon turned, he motioned with three fingers. I lingered behind and gave the elevator button three sharp rings. It came up immediately and two enormous police officers in the full uniform of high rank stepped out and went into Judge Gordon's room. I followed. The woman was sitting at Judge Gordon's desk, with a typewritten draft of an affidavit beside her hand. X was sitting near.

Judge Gordon towered. "Mr. X, I need not introduce these officers to you or you to them. Madam, when this interruption occurred, you were about to sign this affidavit." He dipped a pen in ink and pushed it against her fingers. As in a trance she signed. The notary softly asked whether she swore to it. She murmured, "Yes." She notarized. It was over within a moment.

Then, addressing X and the woman, Judge Gordon asked if they had any further business with him. Apparently they did not. He told the officers to escort them out. I heard the elevator come up and then down. Judge Gordon locked the affidavit in his safe.

Next morning I went at once to Judge Gordon. I said that I now completely understood why he could not have sent a permanent resident of Philadelphia; that the Hudson River would look beautiful to me. He warmly thanked me, and said he would personally visit Mr. Davies the morning after election and report. On the train, the vision of Mr. Davies, that Grand Old Roman, swelled to prodigious proportions in my mind. I kept hearing over and over again his directions: "Remember, Tuttle, you will be in Philadelphia as my personal representative." Yet I had plunged ahead without even consulting him. Should I immediately report to Mr. Davies, or should I await Judge Gordon's promised coming to report? The Wednesday morning papers announced Mayor Weaver's reelection.

My scout, the front office boy, told me that Judge Gordon had come and was closeted with Mr. Davies.

Late in the afternoon Mr. Davies sent for me. How stern he looked! "Tuttle, Judge Gordon has told me all about it. You must know that my reputation was at stake, whether or not you cared for your own. I have talked it over with my partners and we have concluded that we cannot afford to keep as an employed associate a man who would engage in such hazards."

I arose and said: "Mr. Davies, you need say no more. You and all here have been good to me. I will go." I turned and moved toward the door. The prospect of telling my mother and the beautiful girl who by then had entrusted her life to me was bleak.

But Mr. Davies was speaking again. "Tuttle, you did not hear me out. I said we could not keep you as an employed associate. But here is a one-page document in duplicate. Please look at it, and, if you approve it, please sign both copies." I looked. It gave me a junior partnership as of 1906. Nearly four years previously he had said to my mother: "Send Croswell's son down and we will see what we can do for him."

When at last I returned to my room, I made a telephone call: "Start getting your trousseau together. You will need it soon."

A problem then confronted me. I had lots to say to my guardian angel; but I did not know her telephone number. Perhaps, however, there were other methods.

Bless the Lord, O my soul;
Who redeemeth thy life from destruction.
— PSALM 103

SECTION 6

Admission to the Bar of the
United States Supreme Court in 1906

A great man is the greater for his helping hand
In lifting up a young man to a higher stand.

— C.H.T.

NEXT MORNING I hurried to the little office. I overflowed with the excitement of sitting at a real desk.

Soon "Opportunity" again came to the door holding out a note from Mr. Davies to see him. This was a "big one"—no less than the United States Supreme Court itself!

Mr. Davies wished me to help on a brief for the Court in *Blair v. City of Chicago, et al.,* a case involving nearly all the street railway corporations in the City of Chicago. They had gone into receivership. The battle was about their obligations and the interpretation and validity of their franchises, and their rights under them. Davies, Stone & Auerbach were attorneys for the receivers and railway corporations. The opponent, the City of Chicago, had employed as its counsel the famous Clarence S. Darrow whom we had balanced by employing the even more famous John G. Johnson, the leader of the United States Supreme Court Bar.

The lower court's decision had been made in May 1904 (132 Fed. 848 [CC Ill., 1904]). The size and complexity of the case were such that the Supreme Court's official report of the case (201 U.S. 400 [1906]) covered 106 printed pages. The record and the briefs were enormous. The case was argued for three days. The Supreme Court split six to three.

Of course, among the legal giants who gathered to contest that case, I was but a pigmy four years out of Law School. But I ran among the big law libraries, mining for gold nuggets in the sands of past judicial decisions; running down the legislative histories of the statutes involved; and playing the role of Ganymede★ at the conferences of the gods.

John G. Johnson was Zeus in person. He had the majestic appearance, and the awe-inspiring manner. His arguments resembled the hurling of thunderbolts. I have not since seen his equal.

For three days we were in and out of the United States Supreme Court while Darrow and Johnston wrestled before the Bar. I carried our Champion's bag; took care of his coat and hat; arranged to have ready the papers he would call for; and kept his water glass full. It was like playing the supply man in the corner of a Master Pugilist battling in the ring.

Finally, the third day of argument ended (December 16, 1906). As we all exited I reverently tagged along, carrying the Great Man's bag, coat and hat. In the aisle, he turned to me and said: "Tuttle, how would you like to be admitted to the Bar of the Supreme Court?" I was incoherent. Taking me by the arm, he marched me into the office of the Court's Chief Clerk; said that he vouched for my character and qualifications; filled up a form and signed his name as my proposer. The Clerk took it into Chief Justice Fuller who initialed it. The clerk swore me in, then a few days later I received an engraved scroll bearing the names of the Chief Justice and of John G. Johnson. I have not dared to estimate how much red tape that giant brushed aside for this pigmy. Suffice it that my guardian angel had intervened once again!

Often since then that scroll has been my passport to the podium where the Master from Olympus had stood during those three days of fulmination in 1906.

> *A votive candle in my private Hall of Fame*
> *Displays with constant luster John G. Johnson's name.*
> — C.H.T.

★In Greek mythology, Ganymede is the cupbearer to the gods.

CHAPTER THREE

TWENTY-TWO YEARS as a PARTNER in DAVIES, STONE & AUERBACH

When justice is 'twixt warring parties done,
The good of all may well be also done.
— C.H.T.

T HESE EARLY YEARS preoccupied me with the courts. Tedious indeed would be a detailed narrative. Some cases had public note and lasting consequence. Some had a range of human interest from motley to crepe. Here are a few.

SECTION 1

The Case which Exorcised "The Ghost of Wall Street," Clarence H. Venner

I N THOSE DAYS of economic feudalism baronially ruled from Wall Street by moneyed potentates to whom President Theodore Roosevelt gave the title "malefactors of great wealth," Clarence H. Venner was an institutional barony in his own unique right.

He was the Ghost who haunted Wall Street. No one could be sure that Venner was not lurking in some dark corner of the room where "a deal" of great magnitude was being quietly arranged. Certainly he had the uncanny gift of proclaiming from the top of the courthouse what had privately been confided *sotto voce* to the ear.

He was like an Andes condor sailing on enormous wingspread above the peaks and discerning corporate carcasses from afar.

His technique was simple. When he envisioned a likely victim who might be frightened by conscience or by Venner's fame as an avenging Ghost, he purchased 100 shares of stock in the selected corporation and then brought a stockholder's representative suit demanding the restitution of millions. Later, when the time was ripe, he would sell his stock to the defendants at prices that grossed him a Wall Street barony.

The following is the story of an honest wealthy man with courage to exorcise the Ghost in its own ghoul-haunted den.

In January 1906, Venner and his corporate alias, Continental Securities Company, bought 300 shares of the Interborough Rapid Transit Company, which was constructing New York City's first subway. He then sued its distinguished board of directors for "the restitution" of $4,500,000, which he alleged had been unlawfully diverted to their private gain.

August Belmont was chairman of the board and thus naturally Venner's chief target for his customary technique of opening his assault with examination before trial. Joseph S. Auerbach, the second senior in Davies, Stone & Auerbach, was counsel for the defense, with myself in the supporting role. The examination was held before a referee in a courtroom crowded with newspapermen and Wall Street denizens. The questioning was conducted by J. Aspinwall Hodge, Venner's abusive attorney. Suddenly Mr. Belmont, his voice quivering with indignation at the insinuations lurking in the questions, thundered on the record:

> *Mr. Hodge, your client [Venner] has been designated by the courts as a practical blackmailer. I am really being pursued in that sense and spirit.*

These bristling words immediately appeared in all the press, to the accompaniment of a libel suit by Venner against Belmont for $250,000.

I set to work on an answer that would plead as a complete defense and with particularity the absolute truth of Mr. Belmont's utterance. The resulting document ran to 118 printed pages. It combed through and reproduced Mr. Venner's exploits for 25 years in federal and state courts in stockholders' suits of the above pattern. It particularized the immense sums he had thereby extracted for himself and from whom.

We thereupon moved to feed to the gander the same hot sauce he had been feeding to each selected goose. We obtained an order to examine Venner ("The Wall Street Ghost") before trial, and to unmask him under oath and from out of his own mouth prove that for which Mr. Belmont had truly denounced him. The sauce was too hot for Venner's stomach. He withdrew his libel suit against Mr. Belmont and paid the costs. (158 App. Div. 899, July 1913) We thereupon published in book form the answer from which Venner had fled, and I circulated it in Wall Street. Its Ghost was at last laid to rest.

There followed federal and state legislation of the type creating the Securities and Exchange Commission and state public utilities commissions. Those agencies thereupon took over in the public interest the policing which Venner had been doing in his private interest.

In 1914 Venner's stockholders' suit against Mr. Belmont and other members of the Interborough Rapid Transit Company was tried on the merits and judgment was rendered all the way to the Court of Appeals dismissing Venner's complaint and all his charges (168 App. Div. 483*, affirmed 222 N.Y. 673 [1918]). I confess to some pride in the inclusion of my name as counsel in those official reports.

Many years later, I was speaking in White Plains during my 1930 campaign as a Republican candidate for Governor of New York. At the conclusion of my address, a tall, handsome white-haired gentleman, sartorially perfect, presented himself, and said, "Mr. Tuttle, I am Clarence Venner. I came, not to hear your speech, but to pay a long-delayed tribute to a man who had the guts to stand up to me, toe to toe. Because I admire your courage, I intend to vote for you." In some consternation, I hastily replied, "Thank you, Mr. Venner, but do me one favor. Please don't tell anyone!"

<hr />

SECTION 2

The Racetrack Cases and the Dead Salmon

DAVIES, STONE & AUERBACH were counsel for the famed Jockey Club, and handled much litigation as to horse racing and its accompaniments.

The State Constitution of 1894 forbade the Legislature to authorize or allow any "kind of gambling," and commanded that it "pass

---

* *Continental Securities Co. v. Belmont (1915)*

appropriate laws to prevent offenses." Legislation was subsequently enacted which discriminated between betting *outside* and betting *inside* a licensed racetrack. The former was a crime; the latter carried no penalty except that the loser could recover in a civil court what he had lost.

The constitutionality of such discrimination was sustained by the State Court of Appeals (152 N.Y. 1★). Supplementary legislation was passed from time to time, with the result that there ensued much criminal and civil litigation to interpret the maze of statutes. The principal issues were whether one who received a sum of money in payment of an oral bet at a racetrack between two individuals was guilty of a crime, and whether an oral bet as distinct from a recorded bet was a crime.

The District Attorney of New York County claimed that the oral bet was a crime. The Appellate Division upheld our contention that it was not (128 App. Div. 599★★). The Court of Appeals dismissed the District Attorney's appeal on the ground that his proceeding was by habeas corpus which was inappropriate for "the determination of important issues" (194 N.Y. 556, January 1909).

The official report of the decision records as counsel for the respondent: "Joseph S. Auerbach, De Lancey Nicoll, John B. Stanchfield and Charles H. Tuttle." De Lancey Nicoll was a former District Attorney for New York County, and John B. Stanchfield had been a candidate of the Democratic Party for Governor of the State.

At the close of a conference with Mr. Stanchfield, I asked him what was his definition of "the most desirable client." His reply was: "A very rich man scared to death."

Mr. Stanchfield had had so many of these "most desirable clients" that he acquired "a showplace" on Long Island and stacked the shelves of its library with classic books, the expensive bindings of which were in harmonizing colors all around the walls. He and Mr. Auerbach often went salmon fishing together on the Restigouche River in Canada.

★ *People ex rel. Sturgis v. Fallon (1897).*

★★ *People ex rel. Collins v. McLaughlin (1908).*

One summer he sent down to his caretaker a forty pound salmon packed in a wooden box filled with ice, together with a letter directing the caretaker to send the box to a certain friend. The letter miscarried. The caretaker, thinking that the box held more decorative books, put it in the library and locked the door again.

After thirty hot summer days, Mr. Stanchfield returned, and the library was unlocked. All the expensive and beautifully harmonized books and walnut wainscoting had to be thrown away, together with the caretaker. Some architects, I am told, advised that the house itself be taken down and a new one built.

Shelley has written with distaste of "odours when sweet violets sicken," but that salmon far outclassed sick violets!

SECTION 3

The Titans of the Bar Battle over $25

THE ORGANIZED BOOKMAKERS *outside* the grounds of the Saratoga racetrack, where betting was illegal, then fell back on the strategy of sending a stool pigeon to the track to place a test bet of $25 with a bookmaker *inside* the grounds and **lose it.** The stool pigeon then sued in the Municipal Court to recover the $25. If successful, this strategy would allow the outside bookmakers to bet deceptively on the races, without loss.

To this day I can see the consternation on the municipal judge's face when lined up before him was John B. Stanchfield, De Lancey Nicoll and Joseph S. Auerbach for the defendant and a like glittering galaxy for the plaintiff. Of course, the statute was plain enough. The loser could recover from the winner. But, on the other hand, was the stool pigeon really a "loser" within the statute's intent, and would the jury enrich "a welcher"? The jury would not.

The counsel fees of the Titans on both sides have remained a dark secret.

SECTION 4

Three Men on a Horse

O NE SUMMER some thirty years ago, James Leary, the Republican Leader of Saratoga County, invited my wife and me to his annual luncheon and racetrack party for the judges of the Judicial District.

At the racetrack he provided each lady with a racing form and two dollars for each race. Good luck enriched them. Bad luck cost them nothing.

But to the men he only gave a racing form and an introduction to his bookmaker. I promptly lost $10 on each of the first two races. There must be a better way! In the old Davies, Stone & Auerbach days, one John G. Cavanaugh had been the reputed head of the organized bookmakers *inside* the grounds. He might recall my little part in defeating the organized bookmakers *outside* the grounds.

I quietly went down to the betting center and inquired whether Cavanaugh was still officiating. He was. We fell to rehearsing those ancient battles. He expressed a sense of obligation and his regret that, as he recalled to me, I was not a betting man. I murmured something about the changes wrought by time. He then took my racing form and smilingly marked "x" opposite a horse in each of the next three races.

I rushed back to Leary's box in time to put $10 "on the nose" of the horse so "x"ed in the third race. The eyes of the judges popped when they saw the bookmaker handing me a small roll of bills. How on earth? "I'm psychic," I replied.

So $25 went on the nose of the horse "x"ed in the fourth race. Again the paying bookmaker, followed this time by threats of contempt of court unless I disclosed the secret.

So $50 on the nose of the horse "x"ed in the fifth race. Once more the bookmaker! I met the storm by asking their Honors if they had ever seen the famous play "Three Men on a Horse." Well, I was the Third Man on that Horse.

I have no explanation. I believe that Cavanaugh died soon thereafter. I have never bet on a horse since. But there still haunts me a lilting jingle with which I left the track that day:

I'll bet my money on de bobtail nag —
Somebody bet on the bay

Perhaps a squirrel could phrase the moral, if there be one. Should you want acorns, don't cut down the oak tree, climb it.

<hr/>

SECTION 5

The Case of "My Nose" and the Boss of Baseball

IN 1919 BYRON B. JOHNSON, commonly known as "Ban," was the autocratic "Boss" of professional baseball's American League. Carl Mays was a famous pitcher in the American League, playing for the famed New York Yankees, owned at the time by Colonel Jacob Ruppert, the beer baron.

On July 13, 1919, during a game in Chicago, Carl Mays was struck on the pitching mound by a ball thrown with some force by the catcher. As a result, Mays walked out of the game to the clubhouse. As the court (Judge Robert Wagner, later United States Senator) said:

"What happened thereafter is largely in the obscurity of dispute" (109 Misc. 138, 141★). Two things, however, were certain: (1) Ban fired off a telegram peremptorily suspending Mays until further notice; and, (2) There erupted a litigation *deluxe* which preoccupied the sports world for months.

Ban retained my old mentor, Stephen C. Baldwin, of whom I shall write about later in recounting the libel suit of *Curran v. Gaynor*★★. On behalf of the Yankees, Ruppert retained me. I procured an order for Ban's examination before trial. The examination room was crowded with pressmen and baseball professionals and fans.

Baldwin took me aside and whispered that Ban had learned of our former close professional relationship, and that in consequence he

(Baldwin) was intending to play "very rough" with me. I said "fine"; it would give me a chance to find out whether the pupil had adequately learned from the master.

In the course of my pressing Ban with barbed questions, my face came very close to his. Baldwin interrupted, saying: "Mr. Johnson, in view of Mr. Tuttle's nasty attitude and highly unjustified innuendoes, I advise you that with complete safety in law you may hit him on the nose." I replied that nothing would give my nose more pleasure than being the center of a case against the Boss of Baseball for a million dollars for assault and battery.

★ *American League Baseball Club of New York v. Johnson.*
★★ *See Chapter 4, Section 1.*

Immediately my nose blossomed in pictures on all the sport pages and became a recurring theme among the sports columnist. I became better known for my nose than for my tongue.

In due time the Court granted an injunction against Ban, in part on the basis of his own admissions in that examination before trial (109 Misc. 138, 143). The higher court affirmed (190 App. Div. 932).

Ban was a big fellow—two hundred pounds or more. To this day my nose twitches a bit whenever I think of that moment of suspense. An attendant and interesting point of law is whether Baldwin could also have been sued as an accessory to the assault and battery if my nose had then met with Ban's fist. Stephen and I both wondered.

SECTION 6

The Beautiful Countess and the Marriage at Sea

O N OCTOBER 24, 1925, the luxurious liner *Leviathan,* owned by the United States Shipping Board, flying the United States flag, and registered in the Port of New York, was plowing the Atlantic from New York to Southampton, England, under the command of Captain Hartley, a Commodore of the United States Lines.

On board was Bud Fisher, the renowned cartoonist syndicating "Mutt, Jeff and Sir Sidney" in a hundred or more newspapers throughout the United States.

Also on board was Countess Aedita, renowned for her beauty. Bud so successfully pressed a quick courtship that, when the steamship had progressed only forty miles from New York, Commodore Hartley ceremoniously married them in the excited presence of all the passengers. Unfortunately, Bud was then under a judgment obtained by a former wife in the Supreme Court of New York divorcing him and forbidding him to marry during her lifetime. She was still alive.

The maritime marriage was short-lived. The Countess soon sued in New York for separation because of inhuman cruelty, and for

LEVIATHAN

alimony and counsel fees. I was retained by the Countess. The defense claimed that Bud had married illegally because: 1. New York's prohibiting judgment rendered him ineligible to marry; 2. The law applicable was that of New York; 3. Under New York law the Commodore was not an official licensed to marry; and, 4. The Commodore was not so authorized by federal or international law.

The trial before the referee was extraordinarily popular with the press and public. Commodore Hartley related his role. On cross-examination, Bud's counsel, one by one, took him down the long list of officials enumerated in the New York statutes as licensed to perform a marriage. Are you the Governor of the State of New York? The Lieutenant Governor? A member of the Legislature? The Mayor of a City? And on he went.

As this style of questioning lengthened, the old sea-dog got madder and madder at being made fun of before the grinning press and chuckling public. Finally, the cross-examiner got down to the bottom of the list, and then caught his own fingers in his trap. "Are you a justice of the peace?"

Down came the Commodore's clenched fist on the table, and he roared: "Yes, on my vessel, I am—and I don't allow any lawyers, and there is no appeal from my decisions!"

Ultimately, the case reached the State Court of Appeals. I researched and briefed the international law as to sea marriages back to the ancient days of Greece. I found that from the earliest days the international law was very humane. Better to have marriage on board than illicit relationships. Let the captain tie the knot.

In the Court of Appeals George Gordon Battle and I jousted against each other. I felt the zeal of a Sir Galahad fighting in the arena for a fair lady's honor. After a month the Court announced the following decision (250 N.Y. 313★):

★ *Fisher v. Fisher.*

1. *The decree forbidding Bud to remarry was not a bar because the Leviathan was then outside the territorial limits of New York.*
2. *Under international law the captain of a vessel could perform a valid marriage on the high seas.*
3. *The law which followed the flag was that of the United States, not that of New York.*
4. *And, in any event, the marriage was good at common law because co-habitation had followed.*

The wealth of learning expended by Court and counsel is illustrated by the following excerpt from the Court's opinion (p. 316):

According to common law of all Christendom, consensual marriages — i.e., marriages resting simply on consent **per verba de presenti**—*between competent parties, are valid marriages.* (Wharton's Conflict of Laws, secs. 171-173). *"This view prevailed, and may be said to have been the common law of Christendom, as it had been of the old Roman Empire, down till the Council of Trent."* (Maitland Select Essays in Anglo-American Legal History, Vol. 3, p. 810.) *The canon law declared a valid marriage existed where competent parties should covenant,* "ego te accipio in meam" *and* "ego te accipio in meum" (Wharton, sec. 171). *Consensual marriages were valid in England, Scotland, The Netherlands, Spain, Portugal, Germany and the United States.* (Wharton, sec. 172, 183). *"Marriage is a thing of right, recognized in all countries, in all ages, among all people, all religions, all philosophies. It pertains, therefore, in the highest sense, to the law of nations, in distinction from the law of any particular state or country."*

Two possible morals in all this are: 1. A sudden marriage at sea is likely to be as unstable as the surrounding water; 2. If it tickles the ego of a cross-examiner to tease a lion, let him beware of the reach of the lion's paw.

My observations in litigation have taught me the truth of the lesson which Emory R. Buckner, my predecessor as United States Attorney, once drew from his own observations: "More cross-examinations are suicidal than homicidal."

"The Bird of Paradise" and the Fire Goddess Pele

ICHARD TULLY was a noted playwright, and Oliver Morosco a noted producer. In September 1911, Morosco produced a copyrighted play Tully entitled *The Bird of Paradise*. It was enormously successful.

The theme of the play was the love of a young American man for a royal Hawaiian maiden, the last descendant of the line of King Keme-hameha. She ultimately throws herself into the raging Hawaiian volcano Kilauea in fulfillment of an ancient legend that only by such sacrifice could the angry Fire Goddess Pele be appeased.

In February 1912, Grace A. Fendler, claiming that Tully had cribbed his play from a longhand unpublished manuscript composed by her and entitled *In Hawaii,* began suit for an injunction and accounting. In 1924 a trial court entered judgment for the plaintiff for more than $780,000. The judgment was unanimously affirmed without opinion by the Appellate Division, First Department, in July 1926 (217 App. Div. 791★).

Morosco and Tully then brought the case to me for an appeal to the Court of Appeals. The unanimous affirmance by the Appellate Division made any chance for reversal dependent upon demonstrating error of law.

The plaintiff claimed that while she and Tully were in California she had shown her manuscript to Morosco in Los Angeles, and thereafter Tully must have had access to it and built his play thereon. Tully and his counsel had conceded at the trial that the resemblances and similarities were so striking that "one of the parties must have had access to and appropriated" some of the conceptions of the other.

★ *Fendler v. Morosco.*

On studying the record on appeal, I found that Tully had brought with him to California an elaborate scenario which he had previously submitted to Morosco in New York; Morosco had paid Tully an advance royalty and made a written contract with him for the production of the completed play based on that scenario. Mrs. Fendler's counsel had conceded at the trial that at the time of composing his scenario in New York, Tully could not have had access to the plaintiff's manuscript.

Obviously, therefore, the only chance in the Court of Appeals centered in Tully's early scenario. In my brief, I set up three parallel columns — Tully's complete early scenario on the left, the plaintiff's complete manuscript in the middle, and Tully's completed play on the right. I showed that some of Tully's wordings in his scenario later reappeared in substance in the plaintiff's manuscript. From these paralleled columns, I argued that the similarities between Tully's scenario and the plaintiff's manuscript were so striking and beyond coincidence as to demonstrate conclusively as a matter of law that the plaintiff and not Tully was the plagiarist.

The three parallel columns convinced the Court of Appeals, which unanimously reversed the two lower courts and in an extended opinion unanimously dismissed the complaint with costs in all courts (253 N.Y. 281). The plaintiff's motion for re-argument was denied (254 N.Y. 563). The Court of Appeals said (pp. 291-292):

> *Where decision depends upon a "nice balance" of such factors, then perhaps it may be said that a question of fact is presented. Here, a reading of the record discloses no evidence which could fairly lead to an inference that Tully copied the plaintiff's play and appropriated her literary property. He conceived the basic theme of his play before he had the opportunity to read the plaintiff's play.*

The decision also is an authority for the principle that, although there may be literary property in a particular combination of ideas or in the form of their combination, there can be none in the ideas themselves.

In any event, the Bird of Paradise remained in Tully's gilded cage — a gift from the Fire Goddess.

SECTION 8

The Case of the New York Times' Drama Critic Alexander Woollcott

In 1915 THE SHUBERT BROTHERS controlled many theatres and were producers of many plays. Their house attorney was William Klein. Their counsel was Benjamin N. Cardozo.

Alexander Woollcott was a noted drama critic on the staff of *The New York Times*. The Shuberts felt that his published criticisms were unfair and slanted. They refused him entrance to their theatres. With the full support of *The New York Times* and through its lawyers, Woollcott struck back with a suit for an injunction. Cardozo had become a judge. The Shuberts retained me.

To condition me for the theatrical climate, Klein took me to a night show at the Winter Garden. We sat in the front row, commonly called "The Bald-Headed Row." In due time a chorus line of lightly clad cuties appeared and began waving their long limbs in harmony with the music. They also produced fish poles and dangled glittering tin fish in front of the smirking baldheads. Obviously one was being invited to take hold of the scintillating fish. Will cautioned me not to "bite." Someone else further along the row became the sucker; but quickly let go with a sound between a squeal and a grunt. I do not know what the fish did; but every one laughed joyously at the oldster's discomfiture.

When the last curtain came down at the end of the third act, Will invited me to go "back stage" and "meet" some of the chorus girls. I replied that it had been a fine show, but I had a big day coming up and had better go home. Will laughed and said that when Cardozo had

become counsel to the Shuberts, he (Will) had put him in the same seat
I had been occupying; at the end of the *first* act Cardozo had said the
show had been very fine but he had a big day coming up and had better go home. *I had outlasted Cardozo by two acts!*

But to get back to *The New York Times* and its drama critic. The
case was obviously bizarre. It drew much attention in the theatrical
world and its press. Could a theatre owner exclude a reputable drama
critic, employed by such a reputable mass medium as *The New York
Times,* simply because the owner was displeased with his criticisms?

The legal battle ranged all the way from the ancient common law
rights of the owner of an old-fashioned pub, right through the freedom
clauses in the constitutions of New York and the United States, and
then to the latest legislation on civil rights, and winding up resound-
ingly around the public's sacred right to know.

Although I am not certain how the case would be decided if it had
been brought today, the decision in 1915-16 was unanimously for the
Shuberts (217 N.Y. 212★).

The Court of Appeals said (p. 216):

> *The acts of the defendants were within their rights at the com-
> mon law. At the common law a theatre, while affected by public
> interest which justified licensing under the police power or for the
> purpose of revenue, is in no sense public property or a public enter-
> prise. It is not governed by the rules which relate to common car-
> riers or other public utilities. The proprietor does not derive from
> the state the franchise to initiate and conduct it. His right to and
> control of it is the same as that of any private citizen in his prop-
> erty and affairs. He has the right to decide who shall be admitted
> or excluded.*

In point of policy, I am not sure that the Shuberts were right. Con-
troversy can be good advertising. It may cause the public to feel a call
to go and form its own judgment.

★ *Woollcott v. Shubert.*

SECTION 9

The Hotel Woodward and "Mutt, Jeff and Sir Sidney"

THIS CASE is another from my years of being understudy to Stephen C. Baldwin, the outstanding jury lawyer of his day.

In 1916 the Ford Motor Company bought the south half of the frontage on the east side of Broadway between 54th and 55th Streets in Manhattan. It had planned to erect thereon a tall building, with the lower floors used by Ford for display rooms and office space. The north half of the Broadway frontage was occupied by the large Hotel Woodward.

The Hotel wished to expand. Negotiations ensued for a twenty-one-year lease by Ford to the Hotel of some of the upper floors in the motor company's proposed new building. Later, professing to find the cost greater than anticipated, Ford cancelled with the Hotel. The Hotel then sued in the New York Federal Court for, as I recall, nearly $1,000,000 as damages for breach of contract. Ford claimed as defenses that no contract had been reached or finally authorized; and that, in any event, all the alleged material terms had not been reduced to a signed writing, and hence the alleged contract was unenforceable, not having been executed or manifested in writing as required by the Statute of Frauds.

The Hotel retained Stephen C. Baldwin with myself in the supporting role.

The trial came on before Federal Judge Augustus N. Hand and a jury. We survived all motions to dismiss; and summation began. Ford's counsel speedily lost the attention of the jury by losing himself in the minutiae of the evidence.

Baldwin rose. There then ensued one of the most daring and successful jury techniques I ever heard. The three lawyers at the defense table had at times come in late and kept court and jury waiting. They were of different sizes, personal appearances and special mannerisms. Baldwin began by saying:

> Gentlemen of the Jury: Last night after I was asleep, I had a dream—a strange dream. I dreamt that I was here in this courtroom, which was entirely empty except for his Honor on the bench, you in the jury box, and Mr. Tuttle and myself at this table. No one was at the defense table. No one was moving. The silence was eerie. Slowly the great door of the courtroom opened and in paced Mutt, Jeff and Sir Sidney.

I do not defend. I simply say it occurred. The judge rapped with his gavel—rather lightly, I thought. The jury exploded. They seemed to sense an aptness. Thereafter they hung on Baldwin's every word. A quick verdict of $600,000 for the Hotel was rendered. Ford's motion to set aside the verdict as "evidently the result of passion and prejudice" was denied.

A struggle then ensued in the United States Court of Appeals that ultimately affirmed (271 Fed. 625 CA 2d 1921*).

Ford retained John W. Davis, who had been Solicitor General of the United States, was then the foremost member of the American Bar, and later became the Democratic candidate for President of the United States.

Mr. Davis presented a petition to the United States Supreme Court for a writ of certiorari (i.e. leave to appeal). Baldwin and I filed a brief in opposition. Ford's petition was unanimously denied without comment on May 2, 1921 (256 U.S. 698).

Seventeen days later Chief Justice White died. A New Chief Justice (William Howard Taft) took his seat on the bench in October 1921. Some months thereafter Ford presented a second petition to the United States Supreme Court, namely a petition for a re-hearing of its denied petition for certiorari. This new petition was signed by

---

* *Hotel Woodward Co. v. Ford Motor Co.*

about as formidable an array as the American Bar could muster, to-wit, John W. Davis, Alfred Lucking, DeLancey Nicoll, William J. Hughes and H.H. Emmons.

I was appalled by the big names and the circumstances of the new and unprecedented maneuver. Mr. Baldwin had become ill. After consulting with the Hotel, I visited the Clerk of the United States Supreme Court. He laughed reassuringly, and said that the Justices read only the contents of a brief and not the names signed to it. So Baldwin and I filed in opposition a short memorandum of protest.

On June 5, 1922, Ford's new petition was unanimously denied, again without comment (259 U.S. 588). The Hotel then collected from Ford the full amount of its judgment, with interest and costs.

Now and then a single phrase or two, once uttered, will pull a verdict, as inevitably as the moon pulls the tide. With Baldwin such phrasing was always as inerrant as William Tell's arrow.

SECTION 10

The Forger and "The Merry Maidens"

DAVIES, STONE & AUERBACH were counsel for the former Knickerbocker Trust Company, later the Irving Trust. Its main office was on the corner of Fifth Avenue and 34th Street.

Among its depositors was an elderly and very wealthy gentleman who had no children but did have a niece who was "the apple of his eye." Unfortunately, the niece was married to a young man whose main intention in life was to live on the rich uncle's money.

The day came when checks upon the uncle's Knickerbocker account created an overdraft. The usual polite letter was sent; but the response was far from polite. *How come? The account should have a huge credit balance!*

Investigation revealed forgeries. The uncle wished to protect his niece from the public scandal of a prosecution of her husband. He stated that he would bear half the loss if there was no publicity. I found myself assigned to the task of unpublicized salvage.

Where was the vanished young nephew-in-law? With the aid of a detective agency, I secured the mournful information that he was in Montreal with a theatrical troupe hopefully calling itself "The Merry Maidens," and that he was making whoopee with an open purse.

I could not move for his extradition because that would involve publicity. In consequence, I quietly secured in Queens County an ex parte order for his *civil* arrest for obtaining money by false pretenses. My detective in Montreal reported that "The Merry Maidens" would arrive in Troy, N.Y. on Sunday to give a performance on Monday and then go on to Massachusetts. Obviously any unpublicized salvage must be worked right after midnight Sunday. A civil order of arrest could not be executed on Sunday.

I instructed the detective to travel down from Montreal with the troupe. When they left the train at Troy, he trailed them, and I and the officer of the Bank, who was accompanying me, trailed him.

The troupe went to a shabby hotel in a shabby street in Troy near the river, and we found a waiting place opposite it. When one minute after midnight came, we went across, located from the register the target room, maneuvered ourselves upstairs, knocked on the door and said we had a telegram.

The young man opened the door, and we went through it. There was a form lying in the bed, and a squeal that she would go into her sister's room across the hall. The young man was shaking—probably because of the severe March cold. We put him in bed; told him who we were; and demanded the money. He said he had spent it all in Montreal. We rehearsed to him what George Washington had said on the occasion of the cherry tree. He then broke down and said that what was left of the money was in a bag around the neck of the "Merry Maiden" who had just gone to her sister's room.

That was one of the darkest moments of my life. I had blundered inexcusably. We rushed across the hall, just in time to intercept the bag. It still had about half of the proceeds of the forgeries. We told him how lucky he was to have a wife on whom his uncle-in-law doted; and then we left him with enough cash to pay his fare back to New York City.

Some time later I was told that the young man had again tried his hand at imitative penmanship and had gone "up the river" for it.

◦━◦◦◦━◦

S E C T I O N 1 1

"Exhibit Q," the Poor Russian, and the "Saving Hunch"

T HIS DRAMATIC STORY is told in Francis L. Wellman's *The Art of Cross-Examination*, bearing the sub-title "With the cross-examinations of important witnesses in some celebrated cases."

I will first give verbatim Mr. Wellman's own account[*], and then add some of the dramatic events during the trial.

CROSS-EXAMINATIONS BY CHARLES H. TUTTLE:

THE STORY OF "EXHIBIT Q"

The following narrative will illustrate the value of a "hunch" in the conduct of a cross-examination, and will also illustrate the spectacle of an intelligent man of affairs gradually disintegrating as a witness under cross-examination.

In 1921 there came to trial before Judge Platzek an action by a former resident of Russia to recover from a large domestic corporation, engaged in the production and sale of aluminum, commissions for bringing about certain introductions which were said in the complaint to have led to the sale to the Russian Government of 17,500,000 pounds of aluminum for war purposes.

---

[*] Francis L. Wellman, *The Art of Cross-Examination,* 4th ed., (New York: Macmillan, 1940), 437-453.

The defense was a general denial with special stress on the claim that no introduction or real service had been performed; that no such contract, as alleged in the complaint, had been made; that, on the contrary, the aluminum had been sold to the British Government rather than to the Russian Government; and that the intermediary had been J.P. Morgan & Co. rather than the plaintiff.

At the trial the defense counsel proclaimed dramatically that the British Government had taken the unusual course of interesting itself in establishing the truth as to the issues in this law suit and was making its secret files available for production at the trial. The defense counsel also emphasized that these files could, in consequence, not be impounded or offered in evidence, and that he therefore had caused triplicate typewritten copies to be made—one set for the court, one set for Mr. Tuttle (plaintiff's counsel) and one set for himself. Through a witness called as a representative of the British Government he then produced the original files and caused the original typewritten set of copies to be marked in evidence. He furnished the second set of alleged typewritten copies to Mr. Tuttle, who found the same very voluminous.

In leafing over the numerous copies of letters, Mr. Tuttle noticed one which closed without the usual conventional ending but merely stopped at the end of a paragraph. Ordinarily, in the hurry of the moment and because of the great bulk of the correspondence, such omission might have passed unnoticed, but it aroused a "hunch" that something was wrong. Just before the representative of the British Government left the courtroom with the original files, Mr. Tuttle seized an opportunity to examine them with seeming casualness and looked particularly at the original of the said letter, the alleged copy of which had been marked "Exhibit Q." Recalling the witness for cross-examination, Mr. Tuttle then had marked for identification the two alleged typewritten copies of this letter and had the witness read aloud the full paragraph in each of the three copy sets. That paragraph was, of course, the same in each copy; and it tended to confirm the impression created by the whole correspondence that the aluminum was really being bought by and for the British Government.

He then caused the witness to read aloud the final paragraph in the original letter in the British Government's files. That final paragraph, omitted from the copies, contained statements which showed that the aluminum was in fact bought by the Russian Government for its war purposes but on English credit.

This fatal disclosure and the apparent effort at deception terminated all doubt as to the outcome of the trial. Mr. Tuttle exonerated opposing counsel when it developed that the so-called copies had been made not in his office but in another office. The jury rendered a verdict for the plaintiff in the sum of $175,000.

On the other issues of the case, the cross-examination of the defendant's president, whom we shall call Mr. X, will furnish a striking example of how a chief executive of a large corporation, who had made a favorable impression on direct examination, could go to pieces when confronted with an analysis of inherent and hidden contradictions and inconsistencies in his own story on the witness stand.

To Mr. Wellman's narrative I add some personal highlights.

A friend in the profession who had come to believe strongly in the Russian's story, pressed me to act as trial counsel. His client was an impoverished Russian who spoke English very brokenly and was without any substantial connections. His story was that he had introduced the president of the defendant aluminum company to General Sapojnikoff, head of the Russian Purchasing Commission, with a view to securing for the aluminum company a large order; that the negotiations were successful; but that he was unceremoniously waved away when he requested payment for his services. He had very little in writing.

My opening at trial was brief. Defense counsel stated that his opening would be briefer and would be a single word of six letters which would adequately describe the plaintiff's claim, to wit, " S-T-R-I-K-E." I began to feel a chill of fear that I had let myself in for a professional disaster.

My plaintiff was my only witness. What with his broken English and crude sentences, the jury looked unimpressed. Judge Platzek denied a motion to dismiss—no doubt because he felt that the quickest and surest way to end the suit was to let the jury bring in the expected verdict for the defendant.

Mr. Wellman narrates what followed. He uses the word "**hunch**" to describe what saved the day. I prefer to ascribe it to the cautioning whisper by my guardian angel of whom I have gratefully written so much.

Judge Platzek's charge was one of the shortest I ever heard. "Gentlemen: if you believe the plaintiff find for him; but if not, find for the defendant.

In summation I told the jury that I need not take their time spelling out a six-letter word as my adversary had done in his opening. I needed only four letters to describe the defense: "F-A-K-E."

SECTION 12

The Too-Quickly-Sold Stock and a Woman's Courage

WHEN THE BRILLIANT judicial career of Judge Benjamin N. Cardozo began in 1913 by his election to the Supreme Court of New York, he was good enough to recommend me to some of his clients to replace him in pending matters. Hence, in 1915 I found myself defending on behalf of Mrs. Ida Small a very large verdict which

Cardozo had obtained for her in 1913 in a trial before Justice Joseph E. Newberger.

During Mrs. Small's absence in Europe, and in the midst of a panic in the stock market, her brokers, A.A. Housman & Co. (the defendants), sold out her 1800 shares of Union Pacific at the lowest price of the day. In a few minutes the stock advanced steeply. The buyer was a brother of a member of the selling firm, and also a member of the Stock Exchange and in the Union Pacific crowd on the floor. Mrs. Small's son (her agent) had protested the inadequacy of notice.

The defendant's firm was represented by William D. Guthrie and George Zabriskie, both eminent members of the bar. The Appellate Division reversed for alleged errors by the trial Judge, and ordered a new trial (168 App. Div. 126).

Since a new trial had been ordered, the only means for an immediate appeal to the Court of Appeals was for Mrs. Small to file a stipulation for a "judgment absolute" dismissing her case if the Court of Appeals should hold that the new trial had been rightly ordered.

I told Mrs. Small that I would not advise such a hazard which I regarded as far more serious than the hazard of not getting a second favorable verdict on the new trial. Nevertheless, she courageously wrote me a letter directing the stipulation.

On March 20, 1917, Mr. Guthrie and I clashed in the Court of Appeals. On May 1, 1917 that Court unanimously reversed the Appellate Division and reinstated the full verdict which Judge Cardozo had obtained (220 N.Y. 504*).

The decision of the Court of Appeals has become what is commonly called "a landmark case" as to what notice is required before a customer can be "sold out" and as to what surrounding circumstances the jury can lawfully consider in determining whether the customer had been treated fairly.

The greatest of courage is measured by the greatness of the adverse odds and the greatness of the stake. By that measure Mrs. Small's courage was indeed great.

---

* *Small v. Housman.*

———◆◆◆———

Reading and "World-Blindness"

THIS IS A TALE of a County in Virginia, and its "smart set." A husband and wife, each with money enough to indulge in the luxury of "an estrangement," had two boys. Each parent had custody of one. The boy with the mother was mentally slow. She made a habit of taking him to expensive psychiatrists who advised that his difficulty with spelling and reading was due to "word-blindness," meaning, so they said, that letters of the alphabet and printed or written words did not transform themselves normally into meanings in his mind. They advised her, so she said, to take him out of school and deliver him to the daily ministrations of tutors in consultation with psychiatrists.

The result was, so the father claimed, that this boy was fast coming to believe that he was a hopeless "misfit" and would be incapable of facing life on his own.

His father, who had a business office in New York City, consulted me as to the legal possibilities for rescuing his son before it was too late. I advised that the matter of the boy's training be taken to court.

Accordingly, I obtained admission to the Virginia bar *pro hac vice,* and soon was in a trial before a Virginia judge and an audience consisting of all the feminine members of the County's "smart set" and all the County's bar—six lawyers.

The wife had retained a distinguished member of the Washington bar who was slightly on the solemn and oratorical side. I put on the father and several psychiatrists who testified that all the lad really needed was patience and a chance to discover self-confidence and ambition in normal rough-and-tumble competition with other boys. The wife put on her tutors and psychiatrists, who pictured themselves as the lad's best hope against the permanent darkness of "word-blindness."

Then came the summations. My distinguished adversary dwelt learnedly on all the psychoses of child retardation, and finally launched oratorically into that dismal mental deficiency which again and again he called *"world-blindness."*

As I listened I thought of the occasion when, according to Scriptures, the Lord delivered Sisera into the hand of Jael (Judges 4, 5).

In reply, I suggested as delicately as possible that the lad's trouble could not really be so hopeless as "my friend" had pictured, seeing that "my friend" had himself risen to eminence in the bar of the Capital of the Nation notwithstanding that in the matter of letters and words "word-blindness" and "world-blindness" were to him indistinguishable.

The judge apparently had some difficulty in preserving the outer aspects of customary judicial gravity. When the inner struggle subsided, he said his judgment was that the lad should be given a change of air, and he ordered him sent to the public school, with special help in the evenings by a teacher approved by the judge.

From time to time thereafter the father visited me, and gave me glowing accounts of the boy's progress.

The moral (if there is one) seems to be "Don't discuss another lady's dress if your own slip is showing."

SECTION 14

The Thomas W. Evans Museum and Institute Society: A Judicial Reform

DURING THE REIGN of Napoleon III, an American dentist from Philadelphia, Dr. Thomas W. Evans, served the dental requirements of the Emperor and his court. His gold went into their teeth, and their gold went into his pockets. In 1897 he died, very rich. By his will he left the bulk of his fortune to create in Philadelphia "The Thomas W. Evans Museum and Institute Society." The Museum was to hold his art treasures. The Institute was to provide instruction in dentistry.

His French executors and trustees seemed reluctant to account or to perform. After some years the City of Philadelphia and the Society substituted Julien T. Davies as their attorney. We moved actively to compel an accounting and performance. To these ends we first applied at Special Term of the State Supreme Court for leave to interpose an amended answer.

The executors and trustees, as well as some relatives of Dr. Evans, opposed. They claimed by affidavits laches and an alleged prior agreement for munificent divisions of the estate to themselves. In those days, a party who desired to amend his pleading before trial encountered many frustrating techniques which frequently made justice seem to be a game with justice itself as the likely loser.

I worked for days on affidavits and brief writing. Our application was denied at Special Term, but on appeal was granted by the Appellate Division by a vote of three to two (113 App. Div. 92, May 1906*). By this narrow vote two salutary innovations in the law were established and have continued to this day in both State and Federal courts:

1. A party should have the right at any time to amend his pleadings as his "counsel may advise in order to properly protect his interest"; and,

2. "The court ought not to assume to dispose of such questions upon affidavits."

The further public beneficence of the decision was that Dr. Evans' intended philanthropy came into full being and the service of the Philadelphia public.

For the French "nobility" of Dr. Evans' day it could at least be said that the aches in their teeth worked the relief of aches in teeth in America.

---

* *Muller v. Thomas W. Evans Museum and Institute Society.*

SECTION 15

On My Life's Wall: Some Portraits from Davies, Stone & Auerbach

ON APRIL 7, 1927, I left forever my old home with Davies, Stone & Auerbach, and went forth on my own and alone to become a United States Attorney.

I have never been able to rationalize why. I had been happy there for twenty-five years. I was enjoying my constant life in the courts. I had an assured income and an assured place in my profession. I was already forty-eight. Why roll the dice anew?

Was it because I had already drunk too deeply of the addictive wine of public life? Or was it because of a sense of now or never? Or was it because the still small voice of my guardian angel left me no choice?

But I took with me from the old home precious memories wherewith to furnish my new life. Some of them still hang as vivid portraits along the corridors of the mind.

JULIEN T. DAVIES

First, Julien T. Davies, with his iron-gray hair, his stern strong features softened by kindly eyes. How sane and solid he was in council. How compelling in the courtroom. How naturally born for leadership.

And yet deep down there was an ever fresh well of sentiment. "Mrs. Tuttle, send down Croswell's son, and we will see what we can do for him." He showed me no favoritism, but there always was a kindness and, now and then, some fatherly advice.

His great diversion was fishing. He went afar for salmon and other game fish. Was it mere coincidence, or was it one of life's mysteries, that, as we all stood about his grave for the final farewell, there passed by us an elderly man dressed in fisherman's garb, with creel and long pole, moving down a path into the woods?

Portrait on the wall! Often do I pause in reverent gratitude before you.

EDWARD CORNELL

Next, Edward Cornell, a deeply religious man and known in his Society of Friends by the highest of its titles — "a Weighty Quaker." At home he used the "thee and thou" and observed the brief rituals of silence. He was one of those rare characters with whom it was no effort to exchange loving respect. In the profession, he was wise, practical, unsparing of himself, and an acknowledged master of corporate law.

During my time as United States Attorney, his daughter was to be married at his summer home in Central Valley. He had a special car, on the train, for his guests from the city. My office boy gave me the wrong information as to train time. I arrived at the station on the Jersey side just as the gate closed and the train began rolling. The guard said there would not be another train for three hours, but that the crack Blue Mountain Express, which was not allowed to stop at Central Valley, left in thirty minutes.

I got myself shown to the station's superintendent and agitatedly implored that an exception be made. He laughed and asked: "Are you the bridegroom?" "No," I replied, "but I am easily the best man!" He asked me whether I would jump off a moving train. Of course I would. He wrote on a slip of paper and told me to hand it to the engineer of the Blue Mountain Express. The engineer took the slip and said to me: "Be ready as we pass through the Central Valley Station."

I sat down in the "observation car" at the rear of the Express amid all the plush and brass trimmings, and watched the scenery as we rushed along. The conductor came and told me to be ready. I got myself down on the lowest step. As we came near the station, there was Cornell's train on a siding, waiting for the Blue Mountain Express to pass. I waved hilariously at the Davies, Stone & Auerbach crowd watching from the window of their "Special Car." The conductor said "Jump." I jumped; and the Express whizzed away. I glad-handed all when they finally pulled into the station.

Years passed. One day I read that Edward Cornell had died, and that there would be a Memorial Service for him at the Quaker Meeting House at 15th Street and Third Avenue. I went. An usher showed me quietly to a middle seat. The walls were bare of adornment. There was no chancel. At four o'clock two elderly men and two elderly women moved slowly to a bench facing the congregation. Silence for five minutes followed. Then one of the elderly men arose from the bench. Without notes, he spoke eloquently and reverently of the life of Edward Cornell. With intervals of silence, the other three followed, and were in turn followed spontaneously by persons in the congregation. I began to understand what the Quakers meant by " waiting till the Spirit moved." I, too, arose and told of my great debt.

Afterwards I went to the first elderly speaker and expressed the hope that I had not trespassed. He said that Quakers welcomed all, provided only that they spoke quietly and reverently and observed the silences.

JOSEPH S. AUERBACH

Joseph S. Auerbach was a man of action, quick in speech and decision, and with strong feelings. He was a tough debater in council. Among his notable clients were Charles R. Flint, who had the title of "the Father of Trusts"; August Belmont, who pioneered the subways for New York City; the Jockey Club which ruled the racetracks; and several magnates in Standard Oil. To be with him was like having a fast workout in a gymnasium.

Mr. Auerbach was a vestryman of the Episcopal Church of the Ascension at 19th Street and Fifth Avenue, during the stormy days of the Rev. Percy Stickney Grant (the rector), Mrs. Philip Lydig, and the heresy and scandal charges which filled the press and became of major concern to Bishop Manning. I sat in on some of the conferences when Grant came to the office. Only Mr. Auerbach's strong hand on the helm kept the Church from immediate shipwreck. With Grant's death the storm passed.

Mr. Davies, Mr. Cornell and Mr. Auerbach were strong men of wholly different types, yet their very differences seemed to create the close bond and affection between them. Mr. Davies' motto was: *"suaviter in moto, fortiter in re."** Mr. Cornell's preference was for the *"suaviter,"* Mr. Auerbach's for the *"fortiter."*

> *Still portraits framed and on the Wall*
> *Yet walk alive in Memory's Hall.*
> — C.H.T.

---

* *"softly in manner, strongly in deed"*

TUTTLE FAMILY *(above)* IN 1918; FAMILY RESIDENCE
(below) AT 339 CONVENT AVENUE, *New York City*

CHAPTER FOUR

LIFELONG SERVICE with the CITY'S BOARD of HIGHER EDUCATION BEGINS

———·•◆•·———

SECTION 1

A 1913 Libel Suit Marks the Beginning

How can the sordid law of libel
Have approbation from the Bible?
— C.H.T.

CURRAN V. GAYNOR

THE BEGINNING of my fifty-three years of life on New York City's Board of Higher Education and its predecessor Board of Trustees started "without benefit of clergy."

I cannot believe that my guardian angel could consistently have had anything to do with it. Yet, as I look back upon it now, I humbly inquire of myself: *Who are you, Charlie, to judge angels at the bar of consistency?*

The seed of the story germinated in the soil of a famous libel suit which itself never came to flower.

In 1910 William J. Gaynor became Mayor of the City of New York. Henry H. Curran was an Alderman. Gaynor was the prototype of Robert Moses★ in the spicing of speech with vinegar and in the wetting of pens in gall.

One day the Mayor issued to an eager press an anathema of Alderman Curran, richly spiced with vinegar and gall. The outraged Curran struck back with a libel complaint which demanded immense sums as balm for the personal disparagement and as deterrent for others who also might value spite more than charity.

WILLIAM GAYNOR
Mayor of NY, 1910-13

Courtesy of NYC

Obviously, the legal arena would soon exhibit in combat the top gladiators of the Bar. The press opened its box office with the assurance to the public that in this show no holds would be barred.

In the Mayor's corner stepped Stephen C. Baldwin, the greatest jury-trial lawyer I ever saw in action. Baldwin was a lone practitioner. He had his office in his magnificent home in Brooklyn, fronting the Bay. All the fat cats who foresaw the need of a jury Houdini beat a path to his door.

My connection with Baldwin was that of a devoted servitor in the pantry dishing up briefs on points of law. For the great case of *Curran v. Gaynor,* I compiled an exhaustive treatise on the jurisprudence of libel, and laid it at the feet of the Master.

Early in 1913, the day for the great trial finally loomed. The public began sitting on the edges of their chairs. Suddenly the Mayor issued a public statement that he deeply regretted that his great and good

---

★ Robert Moses (1888–1981), one of New York City's most influential "master builders," served for many years as the City's Parks Commissioner and as head of the Triborough Bridge and Tunnel Authority.

friend, Alderman Curran, had misunderstood him. No reflection on Alderman Curran's personal character or the integrity of his public service had been intended. Their differences related only to certain matters of municipal policy. Thereupon Alderman Curran publicly hailed the handsome apology, welcomed the resumption of friendship, and withdrew the suit.

Hence my compendium on the jurisprudence of libel was like a bride deserted at the altar. Baldwin sent for me, and said that of course neither he nor I would render a bill to the Mayor of the City, but that the Mayor, whom I had never met, would like to see me.

I presented myself at City Hall. The Chief Magistrate was alone in his office moving a pen across paper. When he became conscious of my silent presence, he looked up under his heavy eyebrows, and began speech by saying: "Tuttle, there is a vacancy on the Board of Education which runs our public schools, and there is a vacancy on the Board of Trustees which runs higher education at our City College. Which would you like?" I stammered that the word "higher" appealed to me. His next words directed me to hold up my right hand and repeat after him the words of the oath of office.

I stumbled out into the street, murmuring to myself over and over again the word "higher." Little did I foresee that that word would lead me on for fifty-three years through multiplying municipal colleges, a great City University, two LL.D. degrees, and one of the most rewarding and happiest experiences of my life. But that will be another story for a later chapter.

Let me close this portion with the tribute of my heartfelt gratitude to both Mayor Gaynor and Stephen C. Baldwin for making the story possible. I wonder: *Dare I involve my guardian angel by including her in my gratitude?*

> *Some words can kindle fire.*
> *Can such a word be "higher"?*
> — C.H.T.

The 1926 College Merger.
Encounter with Tammany's Boss.

In 1925 THE BOROUGH OF BROOKLYN, ever restless over alleged dominance by the Borough of Manhattan, began intensive clamor for the creation of a free "University of Brooklyn" to be maintained at city-wide municipal expense. Naturally the City College Board became greatly concerned. It appointed a Special Committee, with myself as chairman.

The minutes of the meeting of the City College Board on April 23, 1926 incorporated a lengthy letter dated November 24, 1925. Written by me as chairman of the Special Committee to Ralph Jonas, President of the Brooklyn Chamber of Commerce, and to Joseph A. Guider, President of the Borough of Brooklyn, the letter set out detailed proposals whereby the Legislature would be asked to create a "Board of Higher Education" for the City. This Board would consist of the nine City College trustees, the nine Hunter College trustees, and three more members from Brooklyn representing a prospective Brooklyn College, the resultant twenty-one members to be apportioned thereafter among all boroughs having municipal collegiate centers for higher learning. My letter closed as follows (Minutes, p. 103):

> If an adequate appropriation could be secured from the Board of Estimate and Apportionment, it would be possible to establish in Brooklyn a large and thoroughly equipped center which would not be a mere appendage or branch of a distant institution, but which from the outset would be complete in itself, having all the advantages of local organization coupled with the advantages of administration by an old organization with fine college

*traditions and with considerable experience in the matter of
curriculum and college education practice. May I hear from you
at your early convenience?*

Respectfully yours,
Charles H. Tuttle

The same minutes contained my report as Chairman of the Special
Committee that on April 11, 1926, the Governor had signed these
proposals into law. The enactment is Chapter 407, Laws of 1926. Its
title is:

> *AN ACT to amend the education law, in relation to the
> consolidation of boards of trustees of public colleges
> which are parts of the public school system in any city of
> a million inhabitants or more, into one board of higher
> education, and the establishment of collegiate centers.*

According to the same minutes (pp. 98, 99) the Board then
adopted on my motion a resolution thanking Ralph Jonas for his
effective cooperation and recommending to the Mayor his appointment to the new Board.

The meeting to organize the new Board of Higher Education was
fixed for May 26, 1926 at City Hall, with Mayor Walker presiding.
Several days earlier Moses J. Stroock, a distinguished member of the
City College Board told me that, in recognition of my service in
bringing the new Board into existence, the members intended to elect
me as the Board's Chairman.

But the day before the meeting he called again in consternation.
He said that George Olvany, then Chief of Tammany Hall, had forbidden my election; but that nevertheless the members of the Board
would persist and elect me. I replied that I was very grateful, but that
I would not contemplate their jeopardizing their public careers or the
future success of the Board in obtaining essential city funds. I wished,
however, to have personal verification from Mr. Olvany himself. An
appointment was arranged through a mutual friend, Supreme Court
Justice Thomas W. Churchill.

For the first and only time in my life I ascended the steps of Tammany Hall. We met privately. I told Mr. Olvany that I had called to ask, if he were willing to say, whether he had forbidden my election. He said that he had. My next question was "Why?" His answer was: "Because we do not intend to build you up politically." I thanked him for his frankness, and started to withdraw. Then he added with a smile that he would think it quite probable that I would soon be elected Chairman of the Board's Executive Committee.

The minutes of the Board's organizing meeting on May 26, 1926 at City Hall in the presence of Mayor Walker, recite (p. 3):

> *Mr. Tuttle placed in nomination for the position of Chairman of the Board of Higher Education, Mr. Moses J. Stroock. . . . The vote for the election of Mr. Stroock was unanimous.*

The minutes of the next meeting of the Board of Higher Education record my unanimous election as Chairman of the Board's Executive Committee (p. 16). I continued in that office for many years.

This charade on May 26, 1926, left me with a mental picture of **two** Halls. One was "City Hall," outwardly a beautiful masterpiece of architecture, and inwardly the stage whereon debonair Jimmy Walker charmingly performed his script as Mayor.

JIMMY WALKER
Mayor of NY, 1926-32

The other was Tammany Hall—"the Power House" wherein the Boss sat beside the levers of control.

Courtesy of FDR Library

———————————◆————————————

SECTION 3

The Case of Lord Bertrand Russell and the Chair of Philosophy at City College.

AT A MEETING of the Board of Higher Education of the City of New York on February 26, 1940, Lord Bertrand Russell, on the acting president's recommendation, was appointed Chairman of the

Department of Philosophy — the principal chairmanship at City College. The minutes record no dissent.

This meeting was one of the very few in my long membership on the Board which I was not able to attend.

The public announcement of the appointment brought to me an indignant telephone call from Bishop Manning inquiring whether I was aware of the teachings and character of the man. He then proceeded to read to me extracts from Russell's publications. He mailed me copies. Several days later a thunderous protest also came from the pulpit of St. Patrick's Cathedral. Like protests fulminated from various civic bodies. Also, Mayor La Guardia telephoned me expressing indignation at the Board's action. I stated to Bishop Manning and the Mayor that I would study Russell's utterances, and that my absence at the meeting would entitle me to move for reconsideration if I felt justified.

I did so move at the Board's next meeting on March 18, 1940. I presented from Russell's books and public addresses many quotations setting forth his approbations and beliefs concerning adultery, extra-marital episodes, pre-marital intercourse, homosexuality, masturbation, nudity, irreligion, etc. — many of which quotations are exampled in the opinion of the Court soon to be discussed. The record of the ensuing discussion fills seven pages of the Board's printed minutes. My motion was lost by a vote of eleven to seven.

Immediately, a taxpayer's proceeding under Article 78 of the Civil Practice Act was brought by Jean Kay (with daughters at City College) for a judicial annulment of the Russell appointment. The petition charged that he was not a citizen, his appointment violated the Civil Service Law, and his teachings and his immoral character disqualified him (173 Misc. 943, 944*).

On behalf of the minority of the Board I was granted permission to file an affidavit, a brief, and speak. I argued that Russell's own mouth had proved the illegality of his appointment.

---

* *Kay v. Board of Higher Education, City of New York.*

On March 30, 1940 the Court (Judge John E. McGeehan) rendered a decision upholding the contentions of petitioner Kay and the Board's minority, and annulling Russell's appointment. The Court's opinion is filled with quotations from Russell, the accuracy of which was not denied.

A few examples from Bertrand Russell's writings:

EDUCATION AND THE GOOD LIFE (p. 221): I shall not teach that faithfulness to one partner through life is in any way desirable, or that a permanent marriage should be regarded as excluding temporary episodes.

EDUCATION AND THE GOOD LIFE (p. 211): The bad effects (of infantile masturbation) . . . are, it seems, wholly attributable to attempts to stop it.

EDUCATION AND THE MODERN WORLD (p. 119): It is possible that homosexual relations with other boys would not be very harmful.

WHAT I BELIEVE (p. 50): The peculiar importance attached, at the present, to adultery, is quite irrational.

MARRIAGE AND MORALS (pp. 165, 166): For my part while I am quite convinced that companionate marriage would be a step in the right direction, and would do a great deal of good, I do not think that it goes far enough. I think that all sex relations which do not involve children should be regarded as a purely private affair. . . . I should not hold it desirable that either a man or woman should enter upon the serious business of a marriage intended to lead to children without having had previous sexual experience.

EDUCATION AND THE MODERN WORLD (pp. 119, 120): I am sure that university life would be better both intellectually and morally, if most university students had temporary, childless marriages.

EDUCATION AND THE GOOD LIFE (p. 211): A child should, from the first, be allowed to see his parents and brothers and

*sisters without their clothes whenever it so happens naturally.
. . . He should simply not know that people have feelings about
nudity.*

To these quotations by the Court, I add two quoted in my affidavit before Judge McGeehan. The first is from a publicized lecture by Bertrand Russell in Philadelphia in December, 1929, at the Oak Lane Country Day School under the title: "Some Aspects of Modern Education":

> *Americans should indulge in marital infidelity to preserve
> their homes. . . . Does it seem strange that I should praise infi-
> delity and yet decry divorce? It really isn't. Divorce breaks up the
> home, and when a home is broken up children suffer.*

> EDUCATION AND THE MODERN WORLD *(p. 122): From this
> confusion there seems only one clear issue, which is that the place
> of the father should be taken by the state — a system which is
> easily possible under Communism, but not so easy to adapt to
> the institutions of private property and inheritance.*

The Court's opinion concluded (173 Misc. 943, 953):

> *The appointment of Dr. Russell is an insult to the people of
> the City of New York.*

At the meeting of the Board of Higher Education on April 15, 1940, a resolution to appeal was carried by the same division, notwithstanding a letter from the Honorable William C. Chanler, Corporation Counsel of the City, spread on the minutes, stating that the appropriation for Russell's salary as a professor at City College had already been stricken from the budget by the city Council and the Board of Estimate, and advising against an appeal.

I accompanied my vote against appeal with the following recorded statement (Printed Minutes, p. 206):

> *I embody as reasons for my vote those entered in the state-
> ment I have already made and the additional reason that the*

*suggestion of superseding the Corporation Counsel and disre-
garding the advice which he had given in his letter, is illegal and
a bad precedent.*

Thereupon the majority of the Board filed a notice of appeal to
the Appellate Division by Emory R. Buckner, as its private attorney.
For the minority I obtained leave of the Court to file a brief and speak
in opposition as *amicus curiae.* The Corporation Counsel moved to
dismiss the appeal as illegally taken since the City Charter required
appeals by any agency to be through the Corporation Counsel.

On June 19, 1940, the Appellate Division unanimously dismissed
the appeal as not taken by the Corporation Counsel, and refused leave
to appeal to the Court of Appeals. This let stand Judge McGeehan's
decision permanently barring Lord Bertrand Russell from the teaching
staff at City College. (259 App. Div. 879).

An addendum to the foregoing has caused me to be celebrated in
song *[see following page].*

In my opposition to the appeal and substitution, I had submitted
an affidavit dated April 24, 1940, in which (among other things) I set
forth more quotations from Russell's writings and said that, contrary
to standing custom, the President of the College when submitting
Russell's name for appointment on February 26, 1940, had not
accompanied it with the usual personal history.

In denying the majority's motion for a substitution, Judge
McGeehan's opinion contained the following (130 N.Y.L.J., 1999;
Record on Appeal, p. 266):

*When a man of the character and standing of Charles H.
Tuttle, who has acquired an enviable reputation for truthfulness
and fair dealings, subscribes his name to an affidavit, such
instrument cannot be readily discounted or its contents mini-
mized.*

This judicial accolade has annually been a theme song at our firm's
yearly dinners at Piping Rock, Long Island. I quote a few verses [sung
to the tune of "O Susanna"]:

CHORUS:

OH, OH, CHARLIE,
WON'T YOU LIE FOR ME
IN A TUTTLE AFFIDAVIT
SO IT WON'T BE PERJURY.

He simply asked the court to hold,
As he told of Bertrand's vices,
"What Charlie tells us must be true,
And that's **stare decisis***."* [CHORUS]

We'll take his word against the Board
Of Higher Education
If Charlie says it, it's a fact.
And not an allegation. [CHORUS]

We hold that Tuttle is as pure
As the pure Lake George's waters,
And there'll be no harm on Charlie's farm
For Mrs. Kay's young daughters. [CHORUS]

Oh, the rule that Tuttle tells the truth
Is Rule of Law the first,
But what happens to our Charlie
If McGeehan gets reversed?

(McGeehan did *not* get reversed.)

Perhaps a final valedictory for this Case of Lord Bertrand Russell is in Russell's own public statement shortly after Judge McGeehan's decision (Record on Appeal, p. 209):

He [Judge McGeehan] is obviously a very ignorant fellow,
and as an Irish Catholic his views are perhaps prejudiced.

SECTION 4

State Control of Salaries of the College of the City of New York

IN 1921 the New York Legislature enacted (Chapter 120) that the College's instructional and administrative staffs should be paid by the City according to a schedule representing substantial increases.

John H. Hylan was then Mayor. He and the Board of Estimate refused to comply on the ground that "the legislature was inhibited by the constitution from compelling the City to pay out moneys for (the City College's) maintenance."

JOHN HYLAN
Mayor of NY, 1918-25

At the time I was a member of the Board of Trustees of the College of the City of New York (later the Board of Higher Education), having been re-appointed by Mayor Hylan when the term to which I had been appointed by Mayor Gaynor expired.

I accepted the Board's invitation to act as its counsel (without compensation), since the City's Corporation Counsel would be acting for the Mayor and the Board of Estimate. I instituted a summary mandamus proceeding to compel the City authorities to comply with the Legislature's mandatory schedule. The peremptory mandamus granted by Special Term of the Supreme Court (120 Misc. 314*) was unanimously affirmed by the Appellate Division (205 App. Div. 372) and by the Court of Appeals (236 N.Y. 594).

---

* *College of the City of New York v. Hylan.*

The principle of constitutional law thus permanently established was vital to the independence of our institutions of higher learning from the vicissitudes and controls of municipal politics. As stated by the Appellate Division (pp. 382-383):

That the legislation is mandatory on the board of estimate and apportionment to appropriate the amount required by the trustees of the colleges to meet the salaries and other expenses cannot be successfully urged against its validity. (Matter of Mc-Aneny v. Board of Estimate, etc., 232 N.Y. 377, 386 et seq.) The object of this provision is obvious—it is to enable the colleges properly to discharge their duties as educational institutions.

Education is of vital concern to the State. That the usefulness of these institutions may not be impaired and the funds needed for their proper maintenance and support devoted to other uses, that they may be free from arbitrary control through the powers of withholding appropriations until some exaction of the appropriating power is complied with, that those hostile to their purposes may not destroy them, it was necessary that the trustees should be given power to fix the amount and the board of estimate be required to make the required appropriation, in order that they might be able to regulate their own affairs and insure proper supplies of money, so that they could discharge their obligations to students and the public. Salaries have been fixed within the maximum and minimum limitations.

CITY COLLEGE OF NEW YORK (CCNY)

When Charles Tuttle received a rare honorary degree from the College in 1966, CCNY President Buell Gallagher praised him for more than a half century of service to higher education. He told Mr. Tuttle: *"There are few, if any, in American life who, as they look back over a lifetime of activity in behalf of higher education, can have the genuine feelings of satisfaction to which you are entitled."*

CHAPTER FIVE

LIFE in POLITICS BEGINS

➤◆◄

SECTION 1

Seth Low... Edward M. Shepard... Fiorello La Guardia... Judge Seabury

M
Y LIFE IN POLITICS began without deliberation or drive of
personal ambition.

The Law School opened my eyes to the long and bitter struggle of Mankind in pursuit of the vision of a society which would be governed by Law and maintained by Justice—ideals forever merely utopian unless institutionalized on the foundation of civic integrity.

In the government of New York City civic corruption and cynicism had prevailed so long as almost to have become an accepted way of life.

The public conscience seemed drugged and amenable to the loss of self-government as long as its rituals were given lip service.

SETH LOW

BUT SEISMIC FORCES were gathering beneath the surface. By 1901 legislative investigations, some courageous and successful prosecutions, and a rising sense of disgust and alarm, brought forth an ad hoc Fusion Party, and its nomination of Seth Low, President of Columbia University, for Mayor.

Courtesy of NYC

I volunteered, and was assigned to be a watcher at the polls in the tough Tammany stronghold known as "the Gas House District." What I experienced was a frightening lesson in how the very forms and terms of Democracy could be used against its reality by an entrenched political machine relying on bribery, ballot-box stuffing and intimidation.

SETH LOW
Mayor of NY, 1902–03

The issue in the election was dramatized by the blatancy with which Devery, Chief of Police, had been holding court nightly at his favorite fire hydrant on Eighth Avenue, where, screened by his tough camp-followers, he was the Mecca for those who wished to exploit the City and its people.

EDWARD M. SHEPARD

BOSS RICHARD CROKER was frightened. He sought to divide the Reform Movement by inducing one of its leaders to accept the Tammany nomination for Mayor. He found such a one in Edward M. Shepard, an outstanding lawyer who, several years before, had successfully prosecuted and sent to Sing Sing a corrupt Tammany leader, John Y. McKane. Mr. Shepard sought to justify his willingness to accept this nomination from Richard Croker by letting it be known that if he were elected he intended "to reform Tammany from within."

But the election was over at the very start of the campaign. In his acceptance speech Low said that, if elected, his very *first* act would be to remove Devery as Chief of Police. He then called upon Mr. Shepard to state publicly what would be his *first* act if he were elected. Mr. Shepard's reply was in substance that it was too bad that President Low had no legal training for otherwise he would have known that the State Constitution made it a crime to buy votes by promising value. The ensuing laugh shook the City. Even in politics a man cannot count on success by attempting to serve two masters.

My experiences in the Gas House District stirred a sense of obligation to learn the workings of American Democracy at the grass roots and to participate therein. I joined the Republican Assembly District Club located at 145th Street and Amsterdam Avenue. Colin Woodward was leader and later was succeeded by Assemblyman Bowles. I came to serve on various committees and soon was making "speeches" in the Club House.

FIORELLO LA GUARDIA

I N 1916 AN EVENT occurred which many years later greatly affected my life and the history of the City of New York.

Fiorello La Guardia had been nominated by the Republican Party for election to the House of Representatives. Many Republicans were less than enthusiastic. They feared both his habit of shooting from the hip on social issues and his leftist leanings and associates.

During the campaign my District Club asked me to make an address at a political rally held at another Republican District Club on East 125th Street. I climbed two flights of stairs to a large room, filled with several hundred people and a heavy haze of smoke.

I had never met or even seen La Guardia. But there he was, sitting on the platform and waiting for the Chairman to finish his opening remarks. When the Chairman ended, I introduced myself as the speaker sent by the sister Club.

The Chairman said that he was first calling up the candidate, who had a very busy schedule and must leave immediately after his address. La Guardia heard, and broke in with these indelibly remembered words which, without either of us foreseeing it, would have an echo in the future of both of us and of the City:

No, Mr. Chairman. I will stay. I want to hear the young man.

Courtesy of FDR Library

FIORELLO LA GUARDIA
Mayor of NY, 1934–45

I made my little speech and La Guardia was presented. He walked to the front edge of the platform, faced the audience, and said nothing. Having got the intended electric effect, he raised his arm, pointed to a lady in the audience, and said: "I want you to pinch me." He then walked solemnly off the platform and presented his arm to the lady. She nervously pinched him. He said "Ouch!," walked solemnly back to the platform, faced the audience, and said:

> Listening to Mr. Tuttle, I was not sure whether I was awake or dreaming, for his was the first **liberal** Republican speech I have heard in this campaign. I felt the pinch in my arm, and knew I was actually awake.

He then plunged into his own address which was so "liberal" that it and others like it caused many to question his Republican orthodoxy.

Seventeen years passed. During that time I had been able, as the United States District Attorney, to make some contributions to those revelations which brought on "the Seabury Investigation" and the resultant resignation of Mayor Walker in 1932, and his self-exile from the United States.

Once again a Fusion Party was in the making for the mayoralty campaign. Judge Samuel Seabury* was its driving force. He wished La Guardia to head the ticket. Where would the Republican Party stand?

One day my desk telephone rang. The voice said:

> Charlie, this is Fiorello. I wish you would be my floor leader at the Republican caucus tomorrow night at the National Republican Club. Former Governor Charles S. Whitman is presiding. He is against me, and favors General Ryan.

I have seldom been more astonished. I protested that I was not a delegate to the caucus and had no experience in such a role. He said that one of his delegates would resign; that I would be substituted; and

---

* Samuel Seabury (1873–1958) served as a judge of the New York State Supreme Court and as counsel to the Joint Legislative Committee investigating Tammany corruption which led to the removal of Mayor James J. Walker.

that his delegates were about to hold a planning meeting and would welcome me.

I still hesitated. But suddenly there flashed into memory that scene in 1916 two floors up in a smoke-filled room on 125th Street, and a voice saying: *No, Mr. Chairman. I will stay. I want to hear the young man.*

Obviously it was now my turn! I accepted and went.

At the caucus at the National Republican Club, sentiment seemed closely divided, and partisanship became extravagant. The Chair (Governor Whitman) made a series of rulings which I deemed slanted against the La Guardia party. Finally I took an appeal to the body. In a teller vote, my appeal prevailed *by a majority of one.*

JUDGE SEABURY

A S A RESULT I became chairman of a committee to join Judge Samuel Seabury and the Fusion groups waiting three blocks away at the Bar Association. A Fusion ticket, headed by La Guardia, was promptly fielded, and in November 1933 was overwhelmingly elected.

No! I want to hear the young man.

SECTION 2

Service as a Member of the State Reorganization Commission.

No weed can choke democracy
As quickly as bureaucracy.
— C.H.T.

I N 1926, ALFRED E. SMITH being Governor, the Legislature appointed me as one of an eleven-member State Reorganization Commission (L. 1926, Ch. 836) to recommend the restructuring of the Departments of the State Government and a drastic reduction of their number.

Charles Evans Hughes was chairman of the Commission. He assigned to me the not too onerous role of chairman of "the Department of State Architecture." We promptly gave it the ax. Its remains now lie interred in the reorganized Department of Public Works.

The Commission's recommendations for consolidations and reductions became part of the State Constitution and the body of State law. The number of Departments was pruned down by four-fifths, to wit, to twenty; and prohibition of an increase in their number was embodied in the State Constitution.

My membership on this Commission gave me the privilege of observing in action two such very great Americans as Charles E. Hughes, a Republican, and Alfred E. Smith, a Democrat—the former from the elm-lined avenues of Glens Falls and the latter from "the sidewalks of New York"—both Governors of the State and candidates for the Presidency of the United States.

As to the Department of Architecture:

A short horse is soon curried.

— COMMON MAXIM

CHAPTER SIX

ADVENTURES as UNITED STATES ATTORNEY for the SOUTHERN DISTRICT of NEW YORK

———◆◆◆———

SECTION 1

April 7, 1927: My Service as U.S. Attorney Begins

Fiat justitia et ruant coeli★.

— *LORD MANSFIELD, in* Rex vs. Wilson

ONE SPRING DAY in March 1927, the Republican Committeeman from New York, Charles D. Hilles, whom I had never met, surprised me with a telephone call. He said that Emory R. Buckner

---

★ Let justice be done though the heavens fall.

CALVIN COOLIDGE

was resigning as United States Attorney for the Southern District of New York, and that President Coolidge wished to appoint me. I was astounded. I had not known that Mr. Buckner, whose record in office met with public approval, was even thinking of resigning. Nor had such a post ever occurred to me. I asked a few days for consideration.

The decision was momentous, either way. The salary was only $10,000, far less than my income from my practice. I was already 48, with a wife, four children, and a promising future in my law firm and profession.

Moreover, the office itself was one of great hazard. There was the Prohibition Law, which was deeply resented by the people and the press of the City. There was the Political Establishment, which would have its own ideas of how the office should be run and for whom. The regime governing the City was openly cynical. Graft, big and little, was an almost accepted way of life. Teapot Dome and other scandals during the Harding Administration had sapped confidence in public morality. The legal staff of the office numbered about fifty. All were paid less than a decent living salary. A breath of scandal could be ruinous. The slings and arrows of criticism, misrepresentation and suspicion would be constant.

On the other hand, the challenge of the great office was like the sound of a trumpet from a peak towering over the common plain of life. Acceptance could be admission to the company of the many who were already enlisted in the fight for civic reform and public advance. At the City College, I had often administered to the graduating class the Ephebic Oath which, on admission to full citizenship, the young men of ancient Athens publicly took that they would strive to leave their City better, nobler and more beautiful than it had been delivered to them. *Was this a graduation occasion when I should administer the Ephebic Oath to myself?*

I listened for my guardian angel. I thought I heard a whisper: "Don't chicken. I'll stick around." My wife and mother agreed, soberly. The children sensed excitement. I accepted, and was confirmed by the United States Senate. On April 7, 1927, I was sworn in by United States District Judge Augustus N. Hand. I had crossed the Rubicon. After all, if one wishes to get rich dividends out of life, one must take the hazards of bold investments in life.

After the ceremony I was escorted to my office by Emory Buckner, whose friendship I had long esteemed. I asked him to sit once more in the great chair of office, and I placed myself across the desk opposite him. I requested his advice.

He was blunt. I must decide whether I would be at all times my own United States Attorney, and not someone else's; and whether I would be the mere manager of the office or the maker of it. My assistants must know that they owed their office and their loyalty to no other individual but me. Above all, I must steel myself to the realization that I was alone — alone in a vast sea of humanity with the ultimate responsibility for upholding the Constitution and laws of the United States, civil and criminal, from the tip of Manhattan to the south lines of Albany and Rensselaer Counties. He made the picture look grim, but it was too late to quail.

When he ended, I pointed to a high file of papers on the desk. He laughed, and said that they were letters which he had allowed to accumulate for me to answer. There stood the grindstone awaiting my nose.

When he left, I pressed a button or two. I had heard that Civil Service was continuing with me Emory's secretary, stenographer and office boy. I had never met them. With an exchange of smiles and handshakes, I told them that I was "the new scholar" and was asking to be taught the office routine. I was warmed by their extension of friendship to a stranger.

When they left I sat alone for a while in the big room in which I was now to live. From the walls portraits of some of my predecessors looked down upon me without expression. *Sic transit gloria.* Through the big windows, I could see the homeward hurrying throngs. There were no albatrosses about their necks.

I drew a pad toward me and wrote on it these words, as best I can recall them:

TO THE PRESIDENT OF THE UNITED STATES
Sir:

I hereby resign as United States Attorney for the Southern District of New York. I feel constrained to do so for the following reasons which I trust you will make public or permit me to do so.

Respectfully yours,

The draft was neither dated nor signed. The space for "reasons" was blank. I locked it in the desk drawer. I never used it; but there came occasions when my hint of its presence spared me the undue pressure of certain high-powered political entrepreneurs. I then went home. *A fence at a cliff's brink is better than the hearse below.*

The next morning I examined the confidential list which Emory had given me, containing the list of his fifty law assistants and his private comments about them. I sent for them all, and when they were assembled, I stated that Emory's selection of them was assurance enough for me; that I hoped they would continue; that our relationship should be that of comrades in an association of common loyalty to the office; that I endorsed Mr. Buckner's rule of no moonlighting in the practice of law; that I was aware of the meager salaries of all of us; and that I would continuously press for a square deal for all of us. I asked that each submit to me a detailed report of his work in hand with such comments and recommendations as he deemed helpful for himself and the office. We shook hands. Then and there were sown the seeds of that unique organization of friends which later flowered under the name of "The Tuttle Boys Association."

I then sent for "the men of the press" who were assigned to the office. I said that I sought their confidence and would give them mine; that I knew how important it was for them to make objective and accurate reports to their editors; that I would cooperate within the proprieties; and that I would give no one a "beat" or an "exclusive."

The next day I spent interviewing available heads of the various administrative agencies of the Federal Government with which the office cooperated—the FBI, the Narcotics Department, the Tax Department, the Prohibition Department, the Post Office Department, the Real Estate Department, the United States Marshall, the United States Commissioner, etc. They were by far the biggest assembly of clients I ever had. They were eager to cooperate and to be cooperated with. I asked for written reports as to ways and means.

Reading matter was becoming a blizzard.

Next day I made the rounds of courtesy calls on the federal judges. I asked each for suggestions as to how my office might cooperatively better its service in the administration of justice. They were a dedicated group, far overworked and far underpaid. Each session of Congress added new laws and hence new burdens.

In the Federal system there were no petty magistrates or justices of the peace. The Constitution then required all crime (felonies and misdemeanors) to be prosecuted by indictment of a grand jury and trial by petit jury. How were such important servants of justice selected, and what were their qualities? I spent much time discussing the subject with the Commissioner of Jurors and the Judges, with some results of which I shall write later.

The following day I felt sufficiently informed to consider the organization of the office. The most important Department was the Criminal Department. Its proper functioning and staffing were vital. I appointed as its head George Leisure, who later became senior member of the huge Wall Street law firm of Donovan, Leisure, Newton & Irvine; as his first and second assistants, I chose George J. Mintzer, for many years afterward Chairman of the State Advisory Council on Employment and Unemployment Insurance, and Edward S. Silver, who later became District Attorney of Kings County and Surrogate of that County.

Next in importance was the Civil Department, which handled all of Uncle Sam's civil law business. I appointed as its head Samuel C. Coleman, who later became a judge of the City's Civil Court and was later assigned for service in the State Supreme Court.

Next was the extremely sensitive Prohibition Department. As its head I appointed Robert B. Watts, who later became General Counsel to General Dynamics Company in California, and still later entered the priesthood of the Episcopal Church and became honored with the degree of LL.D. and D.D. His printed sermons have enjoyed wide circulation in the West.

I also made other appointments for specialized work. When I come to write of "The Tuttle Boys Association," I shall be proud to tell of the equally outstanding record in the public life of the City and State which these appointees also achieved.

On the following morning, I began looking over our office housing. We were in a huge, frowning fort built of massive blocks of granite at the end of the Civil War. It had been placed in City Hall Park directly in front of the beautiful City Hall itself, and was intended to be a center of defense for the Federal government against such civic insurrections as had occurred during the Civil War. Yet crowded into it were my staff, the courts, the jury rooms, the post office and the principal federal administrative agencies. All were agreed that it was an unparalleled horror and a disgrace inside and out. My assistants were sitting in small dark cubbyholes, two and even three to a room. The cleaning was only occasional. I was told that that great god "Bureaucracy," entempled in Washington, was so insulated by Red Tape that prayers from New York never penetrated.

Nevertheless, the limit had been reached. I was not willing to be a lamb sacrificed daily to that blind god. Here, indeed, was an adventure which summoned to an attack as eager as Don Quixote's charge against the windmill.

I began writing and telephoning to "Bureaucracy" that what was good enough at the close of the Civil War had now lost even the right to a courtesy title as "the Federal Building." I intimated that the press of New York might be nudged.

The first grudging response was the installation of weather strips on the scores of drafty windows around our quarters. Some window cleaning followed. A few years later the building itself was torn down without a tear shed. The desecrated land became reconsecrated once more as part of City Hall Park. An imposing new Federal Court House towered in the Civic Center.

But back to the office! Installation was immediately followed by Action's insistent knocking at the door.

SECTION 2

The Book, "The President's Daughter." The Vice Society.

M Y FIRST NON–FEDERAL VISITOR was, as I recall, the director of the New York Vice Society.

He placed on my desk a book entitled *The President's Daughter,* written by Nan Britton. He called upon me to prosecute the author and the publisher for sending "obscenity" through the mails. He said the book was a menace to the morals and ideals of the youth of America and brought disgrace upon the nation.

I had never heard of the book. I requested him to return later. When he did, I told him that however offensive the book, it was not "obscene" within the meaning of the mail statutes. It purported to be a factual, detailed and documented account by the author of her life as the mistress of President Harding (then deceased) and the life of the daughter born of the relationship.

I told the Vice Society director that scandal and falsity (if there were such) were not obscenity in the statutory sense, and that the publisher would value at half a million dollars the free advertising by an indictment, assuming one procurable. I asked him to picture the trial and its consequences if truth were her attempted defense, and the mass media of the world publicized her testimony. I reminded him that those who wished to read of mistresses had plenty of ancient and modern classics to browse.

The director of the Vice Society thereupon denounced me as recreant in duty. It was my first, but by no means my last, experience with accusation of malfeasance in office.

The book sank into oblivion. Quite understandably the American people could wish a like oblivion for the Harding Administration itself.

S T O R I E S

SECTION 3

The Sinking of the "Vestris." International Reforms for Safety at Sea.

THE *VESTRIS* was a British liner under the British flag carrying American tourists from New York to the West Indies.

On November 12, 1928, it sank several hundred miles off Cape Hatteras in a terrible storm and with a death toll of 111. The Captain, true to the tradition of the sea, went down with his ship. Rescue vessels brought the survivors and the dead to New York.

Horror stories, such as eye-witness accounts of ravening sharks, filled the newspapers. Demand for immediate public investigation under *American* auspices and without waiting for the British Board of Trade, became imperative. Many of the dead were from the City; and charges were rife that the vessel had been allowed by our Port authorities to sail in unseaworthy condition and overloaded with persons and cargo.

A grand jury investigation could not be in public and would not satisfy the public demand for the facts. I determined to institute an open "John Doe" inquiry before Francis A. O'Neill, our United States Commissioner for the Southern District of New York.

Such an inquiry had been occasionally held on the State side before a magistrate, but never on the Federal side since there were no corresponding Federal magistrates. Nevertheless, on my request, subpoenas were immediately issued by the Commissioner to the surviving members of the crew, to some surviving passengers, and to Port officials; and testimony in public at once began.

I was aided by two principal assistants noted earlier *(page 103)*: George J. Mintzer and Edward S. Silver. No one instituted court

CHARLES H. TUTTLE AT HIS DESK IN THE
FEDERAL BUILDING AT CITY HALL PARK.

proceedings to challenge my jurisdiction; but the British Board of Trade attorney roared in indignation that an upstart Yankee district attorney should assume to investigate the sinking of a British ship under the British flag on the high seas. A stern diplomatic protest was threatened.

A day or two after the inquiry's start, my boss, the United States Attorney General, telephoned. I opened my desk drawer to be sure of the presence of that letter of resignation in blank which I had (as heretofore told) prepared on my first day in office.

The Attorney General said that the British Ambassador had called our Secretary of State; had stated that the British Cabinet had discussed my unprecedented investigation; and that the Cabinet had suggested that I permit Captain Henry McConkey of the Cunard Line to sit with the Commissioner as "a co-investigator"! I closed the drawer holding the blank letter of resignation. I assented, provided I could also designate a distinguished American naval officer to sit similarly and with the same function. The following day the Attorney General telephoned the British assent. I designated Captain E. P. Jessup, nautical expert for the United States Government.

The New York Times of November 16, 1928, reported:

> *The British Foreign Office had sent instructions to Sir Henry G. Armstrong, Consul General in New York, authorizing him to cooperate with Mr. Tuttle.*

The same issue of the *Times* also reported that Senator Fletcher of Florida, a member of the Senate's Commerce Committee, advocated a Senate inquiry, but "he preferred to await the results of United States Attorney Tuttle's inquiry in New York."

The investigation then proceeded in public before this unprecedented "Board of Three." Early in December 1928, the Board reported that the vessel had been allowed to sail without adequate inspection as to seaworthiness; that the cargo had not been properly stowed; and that the Captain had delayed too long the broadcasting of the SOS.

The report of the Board went on to make certain recommendations for greater safety of passenger ships at sea. As summarized in *The New York Times* December 7, 1928, these recommendations were:

1. *That a method of testing lifeboats for water tightness be inaugurated by the Steamboat Inspection Service, when boats cannot be lowered to the water.*

2. *That all ocean-going steamers be required to carry wireless.*

3. *That all sea connections and piping thereto in ships be located where they may be inspected and repaired at sea.*

4. *That owners be required to furnish full and up-to-date stability data for all passenger vessels using United States ports as bases.*

5. *That owners be held responsible for competence of officers and crew.*

6. *That lifebelts be changed in design so as to keep an exhausted person's head and shoulders above water.*

7. *That the agents, both here and abroad, under whose authority examinations of officers and the issuing of licenses to those officers comes, be urged to study their method of examination for licenses, and to inject into those examinations as large a measure of determination of executive ability of the applicants as possible, this to prevent such appalling lack of competence as has been shown by officers of this vessel.*

In time the substance of many of these recommendations became international law by international conventions. Thus the loss of the *Vestris* had not been altogether in vain. Tragedy conducts a stern school for mankind, but the curricula are lessons for progress.

❦

SECTION 4

Murder on the High Seas. The Double Standard.

THE *KINGSWAY* WAS a merchantman under the American Flag. Returning from Africa, it docked at a Manhattan pier and reported to me that it had a murderer in irons.

Murder was not a federal offense unless committed on United States property or on the high seas under the United States flag. The Southern District of New York had never, so far as my staff and a delighted press could discover, had a murder trial. Here was first page stuff. The penalty was hanging by the neck. Someone discovered (or invented) that in the garret of the Federal Building there was a cob-web-covered gibbet on which the English Army, when in control of the City, hung American patriots.

The Captain of the *Kingsway* told me that after the vessel left Africa the "colored" cook (whom we will call "John") came into his galley in the dark of the night and discovered (or claimed to have discovered) his wife and one of the crew in what the law discreetly calls *flagrante delicto*. John went for and got his razor; returned; and, reaching down, nearly slashed his wife's head from her neck.

Whatever "the unwritten law," an indictment for murder had to be and was found. Because our Federal criminal calendars were congested, judges from other Districts were invited. John's case was assigned to a visiting judge from the South. He sent for me and expressed surprise that the indictment was for murder in the first degree. Had I given consideration to "the unwritten law?" He thereupon assigned as John's attorney a noted Southern lawyer in the City whose eloquence made frequent references to the stars of heaven and the Founding Fathers.

John's defense from the witness stand was the famous "dementia Americana," which won an acquittal for Harry K. Thaw when tried for killing Stanford White. A shock creates a mental blank! John could recall nothing between the agonizing scene in his galley and the moment when he found himself in irons.

On cross-examination John and I became friendly, and his rehearsed story faded. Finally, very gently I asked what he intended to do when he went for his razor. Smiles wreathed his face. "You see, boss, when one of our women go wrong, we use a razor to make an X on her cheek, so she will see the mark and remember not to do that again."

I gave a signal, and FBI men brought in a little Puerto Rican girl. John's eyes popped. Gradually I led him reluctantly down a narrative of the night when he had shore leave in Puerto Rico, met this girl, and spent the night with her.

"In the morning, John, did you take your razor and make an X-mark on **your** cheek as a reminder not to that again?"

"No, boss, you see that was only pastime."

The roar of laughter shook the old stone fort. The age-old double standard!

My intention to ask for a first degree verdict vanished. The jury made it second degree. The Judge imposed the minimum.

The old Federal building's first murder trial was also its last. Several years afterwards it was torn down. Later I heard that John had been granted a commutation. He had had the sanction of very ancient masculine Law. Let the woman be stoned!

SECTION 5

The Conduct of Federal Judge Winslow and its Tragedies.

W HEN A PILLAR in the Temple of Justice falls, the whole structure of free government trembles.

In January 1929 my office and the press became occupied with serious rumors questioning the judicial conduct of Federal Judge Francis A. Winslow who had been on the Bench in this District since 1923.

It was being said (among other things) that he: (a) had been sending almost all his receiverships to one David Steinhardt; (b) was apparently allowing a lawyer, one Marcus Helfand, to advertise himself as "Judge Winslow's attorney general"; and, (c) was allowing a stepson named Eaton to receive property from bankrupt estates. Winslow had appointed Steinhardt receiver thirty-six times.

I first asked Judge Knox, the senior district judge, to convene privately in his chambers all district judges, including Judge Winslow, and afford me an opportunity to talk frankly to them, since what was looming might concern and affect the Court itself. He did so. I narrated fully, and said that I thought my inescapable duty, however unpleasant, was to proceed and get for the public as quickly as possible the whole truth "no matter where it led or whom it hurt." Unanimously they requested me to do so (*The New York Times,* February 15, 1929).

I opened a grand jury investigation, summoned Steinhardt, Helfand, Eaton and others, and subpoenaed the bank accounts of Judge Winslow, Helfand, and others.

Judge Winslow retained as his counsel Martin Conboy, a distinguished lawyer who years later became one of my successors as United States Attorney. Mr. Conboy ultimately called and told me that Judge Winslow felt that he wished to go before the grand jury to vindicate himself. I said that was his right, provided he waived immunity, testified under oath, and was willing to answer questions by me after he had made his own statement.

Never before, so far as I could ascertain, had a federal judge in this District ever come before a grand jury in defense of his own judicial conduct.

When the day came (February 5, 1929), the grand jurors asked me in some concern whether when the Judge entered they should stand up and bow as if in a courtroom. I said: "Certainly."

The Judge then read a lengthy and carefully prepared statement covering matters which had appeared in the press. I then asked him, with the aid of some records, including the bank accounts, as to his relations with Helfand and some others above named. When I finished, I told him that he was entitled to tell his counsel, Mr. Conboy, all that had occurred and to let me know if he or his counsel wished a further hearing.

Later the Judge issued a public demand that the grand jury file a public presentment vindicating him. (See *The New York Times,* February 6 and 13, 1929.)

On April 1, 1929, Mr. Conboy telephoned me that Judge Winslow was sending to the President of the United States a letter of immediate resignation (*The New York Times,* April 2, 1929).

Almost immediately after the grand jury began, George J. Mintzer, chief of the Criminal Division, informed me that Steinhardt had disappeared, and that his office was beginning to teem with creditors concerned about receivership assets. Since property and records involved were in immediate danger and were not the private property of Steinhardt but were property of the law and constructively in its possession, I did not stop to prepare and procure a search warrant. Mr. Mintzer hired a van and soon brought back all records belonging to the receiverships.

They showed embezzlement and more. I sent at once for a court bailiff named Max Pinner who was often serving in Judge Winslow's court. When he was seated, I asked him to look at the clock on the wall and tell me the time. He registered great astonishment. "Why ask?" I responded:

> *Because, Mr. Pinner, unless you wish a lawyer or claim constitutional privilege against self-incrimination, you will be talking for some two hours about this large bundle of large cancelled checks from Steinhardt to you and cashed by you.*

Pinner turned white. He asked to go to the toilet at once. Mr. Mintzer accompanied him to my private washroom. Soon we heard loud groans. Pinner was bloodily cutting his neck with a pen knife. A police ambulance took him under guard to a hospital where he remained in the police ward during a long recovery (*The New York Times,* March 8 and April 10, 1929).

Search revealed that Pinner, who received a salary as bailiff of only $1,800 a year and paid rent of $1,400 a year, had received at least $100,000 in checks from Steinhardt in a single year, and had in his apartment and in two safe deposit vaults gilt-edged securities of a value of $53,000. We took possession of the securities pending investigation as to their possible owners (*The New York Times,* March 8, 1929; January 14, 1930).

Steinhardt was promptly indicted, and the search for him was pressed throughout the United States and Canada. We placed in all post offices his photograph and an offer of a large reward for information leading to his arrest.

Next there was Stuart Eaton, Judge Winslow's stepson. One E. Bright Wilson, a former Speaker of the Tennessee House of Representatives and also favored by Judge Winslow with receiverships, was receiver in bankruptcy of the Goody Shop chain of candy stores. Wilson had appointed Eaton as appraiser of the Goody Shop properties despite the fact that Eaton had no experience whatever as such. Wilson also had appointed as attorneys for the bankrupt estate Marcus Helfand, Archibald Palmer and Edward Corcoran, whereas one attorney would have been sufficient.

Eaton had become possessed of a Packard automobile which had been an asset of that estate. Eaton claimed he had bought it from a man he did not know.

We found no record of an order for the car's sale to Eaton or payment for it. Wilson claimed that his stenographer had received by telephone a verbal order and a verbal statement of payment of $350, and had recorded it in shorthand in her notebook. I sent for her and her notebook.

The entry was not in a natural place and seemed to me very recent. Gathering from her name that she might be Roman Catholic, I asked her to consult her priest and return with the notebook in the morning. When she returned she burst into tears, and said that she had been told that a verbal order and statement of payment of $350 had come and that she should make a shorthand note thereof in some blank place in her notebook.

The public furor became intense. Helfand, Wilson and Eaton were severed from the Bar. (*The New York Times,* March 16, 17, 21, 26, 1929.) The City's Bar Associations and members of Congress began calling for examinations of bankruptcies and bankruptcy administration in this District and a restudy of Bankruptcy Law. Public commercial bodies were appointing committees on the subject.

On February 27, 1929, the grand jury voted "a presentment" which it requested the District Court to make public. The court filed the presentment as a public document, and it was printed in full in the press. (*The New York Times,* February 28, 1929.)

The presentment reviewed at length the jury's findings to that date and promised further investigation. The portion which related specifically to Judge Winslow read:

We conceive it to be, however, our duty to say—particularly as an expression on our part has been expressly invited—that, while there is no evidence before us which we are willing to accept as proving personal corruption in judicial office, there is much evidence that serious indiscretions were committed, and that some of these tended to cause identification with the name of a particular lawyer practicing in bankruptcy and receiving appointments as receiver, and thereby caused unfortunate and injurious impressions to become prevalent. In addition, the evidence as to the conduct of the attorney justifies its immediate presentation to the court, and the United States Attorney purposes to do so tomorrow.

We also feel that the affairs of the receivership in the bankruptcy of Costis Takis, trading as the Goody Shop, should be presented to the court for its summary consideration. Property under the receivership has not been accounted for, although the accounts of the receivers were judicially approved in the middle of 1927. The circumstances under which three separate attorneys for the receiver were simultaneously employed and paid out of this comparatively small estate (out of which no dividends have as yet been paid to creditors) also demand, in our judgment, summary consideration. To this end, the United States Attorney is about to present the facts to the court. Parenthetically we add that in our opinion Mr. Edward T. Corcoran, one of the attorneys for the receiver, was throughout diligent in performance of duty....

We believe that, pending completion of further inquiry, Mr. Max S. Pinner should continue to be regarded as a material witness and that all legal steps should be taken to assure his presence when needed.

On March 6, 1929, I petitioned the judges of the District for authority to pursue, as recommended by the grand jury, an investigation into the malpractices in bankruptcy and "bankruptcy chasing." The authority was granted, with leave to the local bar associations to participate. On March 12, 1929, this phase of the investigation was

opened by me before Federal Judge Thomas D. Thatcher. I narrated
what had occurred, and again described it as an "Arabian Nights Tale."
Witnesses were examined.

On March 15, Judge Thatcher entered an order removing Wilson
as receiver, annulling the prior judicial approval of his accounts, holding that Wilson had made "a gift" of the car to Eaton, discharging
both him and Eaton from Federal courts, and sending testimony to
the Grievance Committee of the City Bar Association with a view to
the severance from the State Bar of Wilson, Eaton and Helfand — a
severance which promptly occurred. (*The New York Times,* March 16
and 17, 1929.)

And how about Steinhardt? Early in April 1929, the editor of the
Brooklyn Eagle called upon me and said that he had information about
Steinhardt which he would disclose if I promised not to rush him before
the grand jury. I said I could not obstruct justice by withholding what
he knew. He then told me that through an intermediary who withheld
his name, he (the editor) had been promised for $25,000 Steinhardt's
"Confessions" in longhand and had been told that "they would blow
the works." What should the editor do?

I said that the "Confessions" could be of no legal or probative
value for they would be unauthenticated, from a corrupt source, and
only hearsay; that I would have nothing to do with them; but that he
could help the cause of Justice and perhaps the *Brooklyn Eagle* if he
would send back word through the intermediary that if Steinhardt
wished to surrender and cooperate he would be doing a recognizable
service.

In a few days the editor was back. Steinhardt was ill and tired of running. He would surrender next day at noon in a designated room in the
Robert Morris Hotel in Philadelphia where he would register under the
assumed name of "Stuart Miller of New York." Mr. Mintzer and Mr.
Silver, chief assistants in the Criminal Division, went with some arrest-
ing officers.

When Mr. Mintzer telephoned me the next day at noon, I sensed at
once from his voice that something horrid had happened. Mr. Mintzer
said that when he and the officers opened the door of the designated

room, Steinhardt was sitting on the bed. As they approached he swallowed a large dose of potassium cyanide and fell over *dead.*

An intensive and prolonged investigation to find whether he had been pressured to commit suicide ultimately failed.

With the foregoing grand jury presentment, the resignation of Judge Winslow, the suicide of Steinhardt, the prolonged hospitalization of Pinner, the disbarment of the three lawyers, and the removal of Wilson and Eaton from the administration of the bankrupt estate of Goody Shops, Congress dropped consideration of the pending impeachment proceedings against Judge Winslow and the grand jury suspended its investigation of him.

Within a short time thereafter Judge Winslow died.

But my investigation of the bankruptcy maladies continued with the aid of the grand jury and the proceeding before Judge Thacher. Charles Evans Hughes, President of the City Bar Association, wrote me a letter contributing the aid of the Association's Bankruptcy Committee.

One result of it all was the revision by federal judges of this District of the Bankruptcy Rules, and their appointment of the American Exchange—Irving Trust Company as a standing single receiver in bankruptcy (*The New York Times,* May 8, 1920, and January 12, 13, 15, 17, 1930).

As I now look back upon those first four hectic months of 1929, I marvel anew at the miraculous wisdom and courage of the Founding Fathers in including the freedom of the press in the four preeminent rights on which they staked their all at the very outset of their Bill of Rights.

Desperate indeed during those four months were the efforts to keep the foregoing scandals under the rug, but the determined press raised such a wind of public opinion as to blow the rug right off.

A free and civic-minded press is the chlorophyll which supplies the public air with the freshness without which good government and free society would smother.

SECTION 6

County Judge W. Bernard Vause— "The Hanging Judge"—Hanged.

I N 1923 W. BERNARD VAUSE became a County Judge in Kings County (Brooklyn). He resigned when our investigation grew hot.

While on the Bench, Vause was a frequent speaker at public occasions, advocating the hardest sentences "as the best cure for crime"— *a hanging judge!* Actually, he was a hard core and unscrupulous scoundrel.

In 1930 we indicted and convicted Vause and his confederates on twelve counts for using the mails to defraud. His conviction was unanimously affirmed by the United States Court of Appeals (53 F. 2d 346★) and leave to appeal was unanimously denied him by the United States Supreme Court (284 U. S. 661). The whole story, unequalled in my experience for sheer sordid robbery of the poor, is detailed in the opinion of the former Court.

The trial commenced on June 17, 1930, and lasted a month. I have never been through a rougher one. It began with his counsel's presentation of doctors' certificates that Vause was too physically and mentally unwell to cooperate for his defense. In the courtroom he maintained, with the aid of drugs, the image of slobbering and eye-rolling inanity. I produced counter medical proof and witnesses who testified that when out of the courthouse, feeling unobserved, he speedily became normal.

A continuous theme in his defense was that (to quote the appellate court) he was the innocent victim of my "flair for publicity and political ambition."

Vause's scheme was worked by means of a pretended financial corporation called Columbia Finance Corporation, serving as a false front and as an issuer of gaudy certificates and mailed circulars (product of the

---

★ *United States v. Vause (CA 2d 1931)*

brain of Vause) and promising extravagant returns. These were peddled in its name among the poor and credulous. For a time, payments thereon were ostentatiously advertised, but were made out of incoming new moneys from new suckers. The old Ponzi scheme!

The Judge's confederates were unsavory characters, one of whom, to the Judge's knowledge, was an ex-convict and had been a fugitive from justice under charges of fraud. In order to give this confederate an enviable public image, Judge Vause seated him beside himself on the Bench in open court.

The following is a highlight from the opinion of the Court of Appeals (53 F 2d 346, 353):

At the trial Caroline Timm was produced by the government and sworn as a witness. She was eighty-six years old, and Judge Vause was the trustee of her husband's estate of which she was the beneficiary. She was permitted to testify that she had never signed the note on which Vause got the loan, knew nothing about it, and at one time blurted out, "And he took the money." The court immediately struck this out and then denied a motion for a mistrial. That was all that was necessary to be done. The incident created by an indignant, and very old, lady's comment called for nothing more. . . .

Witnesses were permitted to testify that after the Columbia was closed, Vause told them to keep him out of it; not to mention his name; that they told Vause they were shielding him; and that he told them not to talk too much, to keep cool, and not say anything about him.

The Court also noted (p. 349):

Vause was not an officer nor did he appear to be interested except as an investor. He was always behind the scenes, however, giving advice, knowing the facts, urging the visible actors on, drawing his salary in the name of his brother, and encouraging the others with the thought that the failure of a business so conducted would amount to nothing but ordinary commercial bankruptcy from which all would emerge with no other legal entanglement.

Vause was sentenced to six years in jail.

"A hanging judge" hanged!

✦ ✦ ✦

Supreme Court Justice Joseph F. Crater Vanishes.

I N APRIL 1930 Governor Roosevelt appointed Joseph F. Crater to
fill the vacancy in the Supreme Court created by the retirement of
the highly respected Joseph M. Proskauer. As a lawyer Crater was
unknown except to Tammany Hall and its Chief, John F. Curry. Soon
there was disclosure that immediately following his appointment he
had raised in cash $25,500 — the exact salary of a Supreme Court
judge for one year.

Crater's appointment had occurred during the period when my
investigation of bankruptcy frauds had forced the resignation of Federal Judge Winslow *(see Section 5);* and I had submitted to the proper
state prosecuting authorities evidence that certain judges in the City's
courts had paid out large sums in cash immediately following their
appointments; and that County Judge W. Bernard Vause, before his
judicial appointment, had received $250,000 for "negotiating" certain
pier leases from the City. Vause had not reported this receipt in his
income tax return, "explaining" that he was a mere "conduit."

After his resignation from Kings County Court and our conviction of him for mail fraud in the Columbia Finance Corporation case
(see Section 6), Vause chose to undergo his full sentence to Atlanta Penitentiary without revealing to me or later to Judge Samuel Seabury the
name or names at the other end of the "conduit." He told me, and I
believe Judge Samuel Seabury also, that revelation would imperil his
life.

Four months after his appointment and against this background,
Judge Crater walked out of his courtroom and vanished. His flight was
on the day after I wrote a public letter to the District Attorney of New
York County reciting the foregoing investigation as to other judicial
appointments. Simultaneously Crater sold all his stocks, closed out his
bank accounts, and erased all traces into the thin air.

A few days before Crater's disappearance, a prominent lawyer with whom I had had friendly relations, asked for a private meeting. The question, diplomatically put, was whether, as in the case of the other judges, I was contemplating subpoenaing Judge Crater's bank accounts. My reply, equally diplomatically put, was that I was not saying.

Like Vause, Crater found that the price of silence, however high, must be paid.

⎯⎯⎯⎯▰◆▰⎯⎯⎯⎯

SECTION 8

The Alien Property Custodian and the $50,000 Bribe.

D URING THE PRESIDENCY of Warren G. Harding (1921–23), his Attorney General was Harry M. Daugherty and his Alien Property Custodian was Thomas W. Miller.

Under my predecessor, Emory R. Buckner, both Daugherty and Miller were indicted and brought to trial, charged with defrauding the United States by taking bribes. On the first trial the jury disagreed as to both defendants. On the second trial the jury convicted Miller and disagreed as to Daugherty. In consequence the indictment was dismissed by Mr. Buckner as to Daugherty. Judge Knox sentenced Miller to eighteen months in the penitentiary and a fine of $5,000. The scandal ranked with the contemporaneous Teapot Dome as a national moral disaster.

The whole sordid story is starkly detailed in the ten-page unanimous opinion of the United States Court of Appeals, Second Circuit, in 24 F. 2d 353★ (1928). In essence, Miller as Alien Property Custodian had seized German assets of a value of more than $7,000,000, and had

---

★ *Miller v. United States.*

later accepted a bribe of $50,000 for a fraudulent authorization for their release to the German claimants.

Resistance of Miller's appeal became my responsibility. The Honorable Samuel Seabury and Robert S. Johnstone argued for Miller; I argued for affirmance. David W. Peck, who, under Buckner, had participated in the trial, was my chief aide in seeking affirmance. In February 1928, the conviction was affirmed. In the following April the Supreme Court of the United States denied Miller's petition for leave to appeal (276 U.S. 638).

My brief in the Court of Appeals summarized the case thus (pp. 73-74):

> The close and familiar relations between King, a powerful politician, Miller, Jess Smith and Daugherty are conceded in the appellant's brief and are familiar history (pp. 125-7).
>
> Merton (the German agent) was getting nowhere with his claim until he employed King, paying him $50,000 and promising five percent of any recovery if the claims were allowed and paid in two months.
>
> Then suddenly the Merton claims, which had been tentative and timidly advanced as debt claims of $3,600,000 (the amount of the Swiss Company's debentures), magically evolved into ownership claims of $7,000,000, which were allowed overnight, without investigation into their truth, without consulting the files of the Custodian's office as to the subject matter, without any inquiry of the many persons who would have important information, and without references to the contradictions and irregularities on the face of the claims themselves.
>
> Miller was in touch with the claims throughout their brief flight through his office and that of the Attorney General; he immediately seized the checks and hurried with them to the rendezvous at New York; and he even delivered them to a person to whom they did not belong without obtaining receipts and releases. He at once received $50,000 par value of the very Liberty Bonds he had rushed up from Washington; and proceeded to hide the bonds behind the name of dummies.

The Court of Appeals' opinion was written by Judge Manton and closed with these words (24 F. 2d 353, 362):

> *He (Miller) has been convicted of a conspiracy which brands him as unfaithful to a trust imposed upon him in high office, where his government had the right to expect fidelity and conscientious performance of duty.*

By tragic coincidence Judge Manton himself was years later convicted of exactly the same offence — bribery in office (107 F. 2d 834★, 309 U.S. 664).

The Miller case, along with that of Albert Fall, Secretary of the Interior and his Teapot Dome, and other scoundrels known as "the Ohio Gang," made the Harding presidency one of the worst in American history. Harding himself was a perfect empty effigy of a statesman. The rumor of suicide yet clings to his sudden death in San Francisco, three thousand miles from the White House.

━━━━◗◆◖━━━━

SECTION 9

The Snaring of Daniel P. O'Connell, "the Boss of Albany."

IN THE MIDDLE OF MY TERM, evidence accumulated that a criminal lottery, called the Albany Baseball Pool, was operating with political protection in Albany.

Although Albany was not in my jurisdiction, the pool came within my reach by its use of the mails and its distribution of tickets through conductors on New York Central trains.

The grand jury indicted some of the conductors. Daniel P. O'Connell was subpoenaed to attend as a witness. His non-compliance

---

★ *United States v. Manton (CA 2d 1939).*

caused me to obtain a body execution. After a legal struggle, he was brought before our grand jury for questioning.

Accompanied by distinguished Albany and New York City counsel, he at first refused to be sworn or give his name "on the ground it may tend to incriminate or degrade me." The court overruled. Finally the grand jury orally presented him to the court as "willfully obstructing its investigations." After argument by his counsel and by me, the court said that the contempt was "perfectly flagrant," and sentenced him to three months in jail or until he purged himself.

O'Connell then appealed to the United States Court of Appeals where, on April 7, 1930, the judgment was affirmed (Learned Hand and Swan concurring, Judge Manton dissenting) (40 F. 2d 201*). The majority said (p. 205):

> *Such conduct, coupled with his refusal to answer some questions at all, under a claim of privilege which the court had previously instructed him to be inapplicable, furnishes a typical example of recalcitrance. His attitude was clearly obstructive and contemptuous of judicial authority.*

On May 28, 1930, the United States Supreme Court granted O'Connell leave to appeal (281 U.S. 716), but his appeal was later "dismissed per stipulation of counsel" (296 U.S. 667).

Several days later after O'Connell's sentence to imprisonment, I was told by my secretary that he was in the anteroom asking to see me. She begged me not to see him alone, because he was much bigger than I. I said that since he was calling alone, I would see him alone.

He was indeed impressively large. He said his call was solely to see personally the man who had done what he thought could never be done, namely, drag him from Albany and put him under jail sentence of ninety days in New York City. I thanked him for his tribute, but cautioned him to remember that Uncle Sam was the biggest man around.

Since I left the office in the following September, the Albany Baseball Pool passed to my successor, except for the convictions which I had obtained. My understanding is that the exposure of the Pool was lethal to it.

---

* *O'Connell v. United States (CA 2d 1930).*

GUARDIAN OF GOVERNMENT'S LAW HERE

ILLUSTRATION OF CHARLES H. TUTTLE
in the NEW YORK TELEGRAM, August 9, 1930.

(Shown at actual size; artist: Seymour Marcus)

SECTION 10

The Bishop's Warehouse and the Double "O"

FIRES HAD BEEN occurring in storage warehouses. There was a certain similarity in their pattern. The Honorable Thomas P. Murphy, Chief City Fire Marshal, the New York Board of Fire Underwriters, and the Board's counsel, Abraham Kaplan and Samuel A. Berger, began intense investigation.

On June 24, 1927, at four o'clock in the afternoon, a fire started in the Bishop's Warehouse at 52 and 54 Greenwich Street, New York City. Insurance companies had policies of insurance upon the contents for about a million dollars. So rapid was the fire that within a few minutes the building was a roaring furnace; three alarms had been sent out; and a large part of Manhattan's fire apparatus had been assembled.

Members of the Fire Underwriters' Board and its counsel called on me. They said that the County District Attorney felt himself fettered by the New York rule of law that prosecution could not proceed on the testimony of a co-conspirator (assuming there was a criminal conspiracy) without independent corroboration on material matters. They had been advised that the federal law made no such absolute restriction. I told them that, while there was this difference, arson was not a Federal crime unless Federal property was involved.

But the words "mail fraud" occurred to me. I asked whether the claims for the fire losses came in the mails and whether they thought they could find any containing envelopes bearing canceled postage stamps.

Several days later they brought in a sheaf of such envelopes. We at once began working with the City Fire Marshal and the Board's counsel. My chief assistant was Carl E. Newton, later a member of the firm of Donovan, Leisure, Newton & Irvine, 2 Wall Street. He was in turn assisted by Hubert T. Delany, later to become a Justice of the City's Court of Domestic Relations.

The claims for more than $300,000 were for the loss of very expensive furs and other valuable merchandise. In the wreckage the Fire Marshal later found a charred but empty five-gallon can of benzene, the presence of which reminded one of the ominous description in the Book of Daniel of "the abomination that maketh desolate" (12:11).

The task was, in the conventional phrase, to find "the mastermind" and his confederates—the spider in the center of the web. The web had been so carefully woven that no one in any of the outer strands had close knowledge of those in the next inner strand. Slowly confession was added to confession. And circumstance added to circumstance. Finally an indictment was found and filed against the spider himself, Socrates Moscahlades, and seven confederates.

Moscahlades retained my predecessor, Emory R. Buckner, who protested to me that I had indicted an "innocent man." I replied that "innocent men" were the only ones who could be indicted since the law presumed everyone innocent until proved guilty by trial. Emory asked a month for preparation.

In the interval the proof tightened and tightened until we in the office thought it airtight. A detailed narrative would consume too much space. Emory's own investigation must have similarly convinced him.

On November 9, 1927, all the defendants appeared before a federal judge. A panel of one hundred talesmen were waiting to be called for jury service. I was ready. Our witnesses were on hand. All the defendants elected to plead guilty.

I thereupon addressed the Court for two hours, giving in detail the marshaled evidence. In closing I said that my experience had convinced me that, just as there was in roulette a double "O" which in the long run tipped the game in favor of "the bank," so in the order of the

universe there was a double "O" which in the long run tipped the
scales of justice in favor of the moral law. The conflagration at the
Bishop's Warehouse was, I said, an apt illustration.

Following the pattern of the other fires, very expensive furs and
merchandise had been brought in and fire insurance policies obtained.
Then some of Moscahlades confederates would remove the valuable
and substitute worthless material. Two hirelings, known as "the
torches," would then enter with benzene, saturate the worthless merchandise, pour a trail of benzene across the floor; put a lighted candle
at the far end of the trail; and escape before the candle burned down to
the benzene.

That was done in this case. Just as the lighted candle was being
planted at the end of the trail of benzene, the double "O" befell! One
of the "torches" tripped over the edge of the saturated furs, and the
lighted candle fell into the benzene. The uprush of flame was so immediate that both "torches" were burned and barely escaped from the
flames and acrid smoke.

I added that Moscahlades was fortunate in that he was before a court
which had no jurisdiction to try him for willfully jeopardizing the
human lives in the adjoining buildings.

The attorneys for the respective defendants then undertook the difficult task of pleas for clemency.

Judge Goddard sentenced all defendants to the Atlanta Penitentiary.
He gave Moscahlades the maximum—eight years.

Immediately after the sentencing, the following colloquy as
recorded in the official transcript occurred between Judge Goddard and
myself:

>THE COURT: *Mr. Tuttle, it is quite proper for the court to
state that through the very efficient handling of this case by
yourself and your assistants, and the gentlemen who have been
associated with you here, the Fire Department of the City of
New York, the Fire Commissioner and the Fire Marshals, that
you have succeeded, without any trial, in ridding this community of men who are a real menace to life and property of this
City. I congratulate you.*

MR. TUTTLE: *I, of course, appreciate deeply what your Honor says, but I think I should say in justice, that while it has fallen upon me to play the part of spokesman, and therefore in that sense to be conspicuous, the active work of this matter has been done by Mr. Carl Newton and by my other assistant, Mr. Hubert Delany. They, of course, have been most ably assisted by counsel for the Board of Fire Underwriters, Mr. Samuel A. Berger, and ex-Senator Abraham Kaplan, and the Fire Marshal of the City of New York and his assistants, I might observe, have been helping constantly.*

It is a matter of satisfaction to know that probably the worst arson ring ever known has been broken up, and I believe that the good effect and influence that will obtain from the results relating to that fire will be far-reaching in this community. I thank your Honor.

The moral of the Bishop's Warehouse case seems to be that "the perfect crime" is like a perfect doughnut. There's a hole in it.

The "Doctor for the Elimination of Business Ills" who Loses His License.

ON JULY 8, 1929, THERE WAS A FIRE in the place of business of Lerner & Greenberg, Inc. at 214 West 29th Street.

On July 29, 1929, shortly after midnight, there was a terrific explosion in a warehouse at 213 West 27th Street. Almost immediately flames engulfed the building.

Three men had left the warehouse at 9:30 p.m. that night. Total destruction had been guaranteed by them. They felt that the guarantee had been safely fulfilled.

The ground floor of the warehouse was occupied by Louis Dachis, dealer in raw and dressed furs. Investigation disclosed that these two fires were of the same pattern. Greenberg was a brother-in-law of Jacob Dachis, the brother of Louis Dachis.

The cases were brought to me for possible prosecutions for mail frauds. Working with me were my assistants, Thomas J. Curran, later Secretary of State of New York; Chief City Fire Marshal, Thomas P. Brophy; and Abraham Kaplan and Samuel A. Berger, counsel for the New York Board of Fire Underwriters.

The firebug was Joe Eisenstein, a professional arsonist, who advertised himself as a "Doctor for the Elimination of Business Ills." He guaranteed a complete destruction or total loss job. He said that his methods never failed. Later the evidence connected him with similar fires in other cities. His fee in the present instance was $3,000.

Before the confessions of all had been obtained, lawyers for some of the principal defendants staged the traditional court battles. Thus, after Jacob Dachis had made false statements to the Federal grand jury about what had become of some highly material records, I moved to punish him for criminal contempt. His lawyer countered with a motion for dismissal of the indictment. On December 30, 1929, Judge Goddard rendered a decision (36 F.2d 601*) dismissing the defendant's motion and setting for a hearing my motion to punish for contempt. Jacob Dachis also moved for an order directing the return to him of certain books and records which he claimed had been illegally seized. He also moved to prevent cross-examination of him by claiming self-incrimination. Both motions were denied.

Finally, the Dachis brothers, Lerner, and Greenberg confessed to hiring Eisenstein as a "Doctor for the Elimination of Business Ills." When the story became public, it was carried as front page material in principal newspapers across the country. For example, *The New York Times* of March 17, 1930, carried a banner headline the full width of its front page, reading:

---

* *United States v. Dachis (SD NY 1929).*

4 HELD IN $1,000,000 ARSON RING, BARED BY TUTTLE

Inquiries poured in from almost every large city requesting information which might be helpful to officials prosecuting arson within their own jurisdictions.

In telling what followed, I am paraphrasing from a book entitled *The Dachis Case,* composed and published by Abraham Kaplan and Samuel A. Berger, counsel for the New York Board of Fire Underwriters. The book is far more fascinating than the usual "whodunit," for the latter is fiction, while *The Dachis Case* is reality.

The District Attorney of New York City, Thomas C.T. Crain, took cognizance of the published confessions; without difficulty he obtained indictments by the County Grand Jury.

An unusual situation then arose. On the Federal side the defendants stood indicted for **mail fraud**, and on the state side they stood indicted for **arson**—both sets of indictments being the same basic facts.

I had conferences with the County District Attorney. As a result, on April 16, 1930, both the Federal and State courts simultaneously convened in the same room in the Federal Courthouse. Seated in Room Number 337 were United States Judge Henry W. Goddard, on one end of the Bench, and Max S. Levine, Judge of the State Court of General Sessions, on the other end—both with their robes, clerks, marshals and bailiffs and seals of office. The defendants came forward and pleaded guilty to both sets of indictments separately. I then narrated the evidence, and my counterpart, the County District Attorney, did likewise. At the close of his address he said:

> As to any service rendered to Mr. Tuttle, we would consider it in the imposition of sentence by our court as a service rendered to us.

The attorneys for the defendants then addressed the two judges, who thereupon retired to confer together. On May 7, 1930, they reconvened. Judge Goddard then sentenced Louis Dachis to three years and Jacob Dachis and Lerner to one year and a day in Atlanta Penitentiary. He then turned the defendants Eisenstein and Greenberg over to Judge Levine, who sentenced Eisenstein to twelve-and-a-half to 25 years and

Greenberg to three to ten years in State Prison. Each Judge thereupon adopted the other Judge's sentence on a concurrent basis.

Perhaps the moral is that there is no such thing as a perfect crime, or a guaranteed successful arson.

I have since received from my friend and collaborator, Samuel A. Berger, a complimentary copy of his entrancing book *The Dachis Case,* with the following inscription on its flyleaf:

> *To the Honorable Charles H. Tuttle, without whose interest and help as United States Attorney, the results set forth herein could not have been accomplished. Mr. Tuttle was of great service to the business community, not only in the Dachis case, but in the other successful prosecutions, which he directed with distinguished legal ability. I am proud to call him my friend.*
>
>   — SAMUEL A. BERGER

The "Doctor for the Elimination of Business Ills" had permanently lost his license to practice.

NEW YORK AMERICAN, JULY 28, 1930

Often cited in the press for his effective campaigns against corruption, Charles Tuttle was the subject of many newspaper stories and cartoons during his service as U.S. Attorney.

SECTION 12

The Tong Wars in Chinatown. "Peace or Pack Up."

THERE WAS A WAR in Chinatown. The battle was between the Hipsings and the Onliongs. Mott Street became the no-man's land. Murder had to be matched by murder. The lethal feud began to spread to other cities. The *casus belli* was jurisdictional rivalry over illicit traffics.

The Chinese Consul General visited me, expressed the concern of the then Government of China, and suggested that I might help. Why? Because the leaders of the warring Tongs had one great fear — that of being charged with unlawful entry into the country and consequent risk of deportation. After notifying the Police Commissioner of my intention, I agreed to meet these leaders in the evening at the Consulate.

The Consul General was a handsome and impressive man, a graduate of Harvard, and spoke the English of culture. His Consulate had a wealth of beautiful oriental furnishings.

The meeting was to be held in the conference room. He seated me at one end of a long table and himself at the other. Soon there arrived five Hipsing leaders dwarfed by hulking and doubtless well-equipped bodyguards. The bodyguards were parked in another room. The five leaders were seated on one side of the long table. Soon their Onliong counterparts arrived, and were seated on the other side. Across the table they shook hands unctuously and broke out in broad smiles and Chinese chatter directed at me. The Consul General said they wished me to understand that they were terribly misunderstood; that they were philanthropists; that their Tongs were fraternal organizations in Chinatown; and that they knew nothing about these bloody murders. I replied through the Consul General that, if that were so, they should be willing to draw up and sign a pledge of peace then and there.

Consternation followed, to which I hope I contributed by proclaiming that the alternatives were: "Peace, or pack up and be sent back to China!"

After some thirty minutes, they were convinced that I meant business. Two long rolls of red paper were produced by the Consul General and spread along the table. Ink and small paint brushes followed. Duplicate lettering began. I asked why two duplicates. The Consul General smiled wryly— "one for each side of Mott Street, so that no Tongman need risk death by crossing over to read."

Finally, the lettering ceased and clamorous conversation broke out across the table. The Consul General again smiled wryly, and said that these "philanthropists" were discussing how much time must be allowed to get word of peace to their respective gunman in other cities. I stood up and said, "Tell them 'I guess it's pack up.'" Ten signatures were hastily affixed. I left saying that I would ask the Police Commissioner to inform me of any further Tong trouble.

Soon each side of Mott Street displayed the peace treaty. I heard of no further Tong war homicides here or elsewhere in the country. Murder had ceased to be an ingredient of "philanthropy" in Chinatown.

SECTION 13

The Theatre Tickets Tax Frauds.

ON MAY 25, 1927, I opened before United States Commissioner Garret W. Cotter a public "John Doe" investigation into frauds upon the revenue in the sale of theatre tickets.

My complaint alleged:

> I am informed and believe that none of the said agencies has filed returns purporting to report the sales of tickets at prices exceeding by more than 50 cents the established price,

and that the returns filed by them throughout the said period since 1918 (with several slight and temporary exceptions) have, so far as they reported sales at all, reported them as if made at prices not exceeding the established price by more than 50 cents, whereas during the said period the agencies made multitude of sales at prices greatly in excess of a 50 cent advance. As a result the United States Government has lost in taxes, which are still unpaid, millions of dollars.

Of course the complaint brought forcefully to public notice the widespread agency practice of selling tickets to clubs, groups and patrons far in excess of the price on the face of the tickets; and it immediately raised public interest as to how far (if at all) theatre owners and producers secretly shared in these excess charges thus hidden from taxation.

There were wholesale cries of ignorance and astonishment from the ticket agencies, theatre owners and producers, and efforts were made to make individual employees "the goat."

Nevertheless, when the evidence thus gathered was reproduced before the grand jury there were indictments of the Alexander Theatre Ticket Office and numerous other agencies and some of their officers on fourteen counts for making false tax returns for fourteen consecutive months, commencing March 1926.

I brought the defendants to trial before a jury and Judge William H. Atwell, a visiting judge from Texas. The defendants were represented by Louis Marshall of Untermyer & Marshall and other distinguished counsel. They were found guilty on all counts, and promptly appealed to the Circuit Court of Appeals where, on December 12, 1927, their conviction was unanimously affirmed (23 F. 2d 44★). The Court said:

> *There was sufficient in the proof to require submission to the jury of the question of whether or not the defendants below had, by fraudulent means and subterfuge, evaded and defeated the tax and prevented the government from ascertaining the truth as to this obligation.*

★ *Alexander Theatre Ticket Office v. United States (CA 2d 1927).*

All the defendants then pleaded guilty and (to quote *The New York Times* of February 21, 1928) "bound themselves, under bond of $40,000, to abide by any rules established by Mr. Tuttle."

The final result was thus stated in *The New York Times* January 2, 1928, under the significant heading "ONE SET OF GOOD RESOLUTIONS":

> *A happy new year for patrons of New York theatres may result from the "good resolutions" of ticket brokers. District Attorney Tuttle has not relaxed his pressure toward compulsory obedience of the law in the past six months of his insistence on taxpaying. The twenty-four agencies convicted last July of fail-ing to pay half their profit on tickets sold for more than the fifty cents advance permitted by law have now joined in a voluntary agreement to pay their arrears and not to incur similar debts. Heavy fines and jail sentences for one agency making a test appeal has had a salutary effect.*

"Good Resolutions" are always more likely to be kept if backed by law and penalties.

To supply this mandate, I drafted, and the Legislature enacted (L 1928, ch. 600), an amendment to the General Business Law " in rela-tion to the sale of tickets of admission to theatres and places of amuse-ment." Its drastic nature is shown by the subtitles of some of its sections, to wit: "reselling of tickets of admission," "licenses," "bond," "revoca-tion of licenses," "supervision of secretary of state," "printing price on tickets," "posting of licenses or certificate," "records of purchase and sales," "commissions to employees of tickets."

This statute is still on the books *(General Business Law: Article X-B — Theatre Tickets)*.

Some years later I took Mrs. Tuttle to the matinee of a Broadway hit. The box office man routinely said that the only seats left were in the back row. Looking up as I pushed in the money, his face changed and he quickly said: "On closer look, I see I have two forward orches-tra seats reserved by the management for visiting VIP's." I laughed, paid the additional price, and enjoyed the show.

SECTION 14

The End of Bail Bond Gouging.

SOON AFTER TAKING OFFICE I found that there was "a bail bond racket" which imposed upon poor defendants in criminal cases. The Federal Building was infested with bail runners for suppliers of bonds who made a practice of exacting a fee in excess of three per cent allowed by law.

In November 1927, I laid these abuses before the federal judges and received their full authorization for a housecleaning. I then filed a complaint on November 22, 1927, with United States Commissioner Thomas A. O'Neill in a "John Doe" proceeding, and obtained many subpoenas for a public hearing before him.

As summarized in *The New York Times* of that day, my complaint alleged that in addition to the gouging of poor defendants, the runners would steer the defendant to "a good lawyer," and the defendant would be taken for a fat fee "for services which frequently are purely nominal." At times there were hints of "knowing" the judge or the prosecutor. Indeed, witnesses openly testified at the public hearing that they had paid in the belief the money would be used to "fix" "the prosecutor," or "the police lieutenant," etc. One "elderly woman testified she was mulcted by bondsmen and lawyers till impoverished." (*The New York Times*, Dec. 2, 1927)

The result of the hearings and the public airing of the abuses was thus stated in *The New York Times* of February 2, 1928:

> *There have been hearings and progress has been made in sustaining the charges, but the biggest step came yesterday when fourteen of the agents appeared before United States Commissioner O'Neill and agreed to be bound by conditions accepted by the Equitable Surety Company. These conditions were that only bondsmen and bonding agents acceptable to Mr. Tuttle be employed in the*

Federal Building, that no attempt should be made by bondsmen to induce defendants to employ particular lawyers, and that not more than three per cent should be charged for writing bail bonds.

Mr. Tuttle told Commissioner O'Neill that the Equitable Company did more than 90 per cent of the bonding business within the Federal Building, that this company had agreed to have only one agent stationed in the building, and that any rules made by Mr. Tuttle for the conduct of the business would be observed.

And to quote from the *The New York Times* of March 7, 1928:

Mr. Tuttle said United States Commissioner O'Neill has been charged by an order signed by Federal Judge Knox to make recommendations concerning the regulation of the bail-bond business.... Mr. Tuttle said that the Surety Association of America, representing the principal surety companies doing business in this city, had appointed a bail bond committee which had adopted a resolution offering to cooperate with State Authorities in solving bail bond problems.

The halls of the Federal Building ceased to be stalking grounds for predators seeking whom they might devour.

SECTION 15

The Founding of the Grand Jury Association and the "Run-Away" Grand Jury.

MY CONTACT WITH the Grand Jury System began at once. I found that the Grand Jury had become a somewhat perfunctory body. It tended to regard itself as a mere rubber stamp for the desires of the United States Attorney's office. Too often it was used as a sanctuary from the more arduous petit jury service.

In consequence, I visited each new grand jury and impressed upon its members the solemn function that each had to inquire and determine on his oath and conscience whether the evidence established reasonable cause to believe that a crime had been committed and a specified person or persons had committed it; and that while his duty was to regard the advice of the United States Attorney on the law, determination of facts was his prerogative alone.

To the same end, after consulting with the Senior District Judge, I initiated "The Federal Grand Jury Association for the Southern District of New York," and drew for it a set of "By Laws." The organization meeting was held on December 15, 1927. The officers elected were Olin J. Stephens, President; Charles S. Sargent, First Vice President; Alfred P. Perkins, Second Vice President; William D. Harper, Treasurer; and Eugene J. Cantin, Secretary.

I also prepared — and the new Association printed — a "Handbook for Federal Grand Jurors, Southern District of New York." Thereafter a copy of it was given to each new grand jury when sworn in.

This Handbook was 36 pages in length. It told at length the history, functions, powers and duties of the Grand Jury; its procedures; its relations to the Court and to the United States Attorney; the receivable evidence and the manner of obtaining it; and the methods of selecting and impaneling the body itself.

The Association made me an honorary member, and printed in the Foreword of the Handbook the following:

We acknowledge with thanks the invaluable aid given by Charles H. Tuttle, United States Attorney, in the preparation of this handbook.

The relations of my staff and myself to our grand juries were always cordial. Official business was so voluminous that at times we had as many as three grand juries sitting at one time.

"Run–Away" Background

The story of what came to be known as our only "run-away" grand jury is interesting.

When Prohibition entered its death agony, its advocates got through Congress an enactment raising the penalty from misdemeanor to felony. In the City all possibilities of enforcement immediately ceased.

One morning a bailiff told me that the Grand Jury wanted to see me *at once*. I reported.

"Mr. Tuttle! Mr. Tuttle! Did you read in this morning's Times *that a Congressman who helped to change whiskey from a misdemeanor into a felony was caught by the customs inspectors with a bottle of whiskey in his baggage? We are indicting him under his own law. Send us in a form."*

"But, gentlemen, the Times, *however credible a newspaper, is not legal evidence."*

"Mr. Tuttle, this is no moment for technicalities. We have learned how to draw an indictment. We will take the responsibility. Just give us half an hour alone."

"But, gentlemen, why not proceed right? Let's get the customs inspectors and the bottle."

Next morning the inspector came, red-faced. The bottle had *disappeared!* Twenty-three voices chorused angrily:

"Well, you smelled it, didn't you?"

"Yes, it smelled like whiskey."

"Mr. Tuttle, that does it. Send us a form of indictment."

The moment was dark. "Gentlemen, you may not understand it, but the law requires a body, a corpus delicti. *You have no bottle."*

There was a pause. Down came my guardian angel. Hastily I said that Judge Harry Goddard was in charge. "Let's go to his courtroom, and you ask his advice on the law. I'll tag along but say nothing."

Down we all trouped. Judge Goddard listened patiently to the foreman. "But gentlemen, you have no bottle — hence no *corpus delicti!*"

"Bravo, Harry!" I said to myself. There were tears and, out in the hall, some sulphurous words. But my neck had been spared a dead albatross.

Several lessons are plain. The first is that, as a snake sheds its skin, the public sheds laws prohibiting personal habits deemed under regulation of conscience. The second is that the quickest way to render a law unenforceable is to include an unconscionable penalty.

SECTION 16

A New Yorker "Profile"

HE MAGAZINE *The New Yorker* bolstered its reputation for humor by occasionally publishing under the title "Profiles" a cartoon portrait of someone in the current news and framing it with gentle burlesque.

Its issue of March 23, 1929, contained such a "Profile" of me entitled "Saint in Politics" and accompanied with "a history of a model boy who became a model man." Portrait and burlesque were "a scream." The town's laughter was led by myself.

Space has room for only a few typical extracts:

> *Five years ago he began to develop a craving for public office, a disease which sometimes attacks successful men at middle age. The fact is that Mr. Tuttle already held every possible private office and could increase his collection only by going after public offices. He started two years ago with the United States district attorneyship.*
>
> *There was some doubt whether Mr. Tuttle, after all his years of civil practice, would make good as a prosecutor of crime; it was questioned whether he had the presence. He is a spare man of medium build, hatchet-faced, with sandy hair parted in the middle, quiet in dress, unassuming in manner. He had hardly been in office a week, however, before he exhibited his trick of dominating a courtroom. . . . It [his voice] had something ventriloquistic about it, the speaker catching the ear much more quickly than he caught the eye. Jurymen peered this way and that with uplifted eyebrows. Vibrating with rectitude, the voice began to cross-examine defense witnesses who suddenly went all to pieces, unable to face the music. Long before the verdict of guilty was rendered, it had become clear that Sam Koenig did not exaggerate when he said, "In the appointment of Charles H. Tuttle, the government gets a hundred-thousand-dollar man for ten thousand dollars."...*

^{x x} PROFILES
^x

SAINT IN POLITICS

Charles H. Tuttle

THE history of United States District Attorney Charles H. Tuttle is that of a model boy who became a model man. The high hopes which he aroused in kindergarten have been steadily fulfilled, without any of those backslidings at adolescence or maturity to which lads of abnormal excellence are peculiarly subject.

As a boy he won a gallery of lithographs for Biblical scholarship and a collection of medals, stars, buttons, scrolls, and pins for temperance and deportment. At Trinity School he gathered all the trophies for learning and righteousness; at Columbia he took the Chandler Prize in American history, the James Gordon Prize in English prose, the Bonner Medal in English literature, and the Phi Beta Kappa key. He was a born valedictorian. At ten years, heels together, toes turned out, tawny hair tossing wildly, he would rail in falsetto at the abuses of the age. Forty years have passed, but almost nightly, at public gatherings, he strikes the same valedictorian stance and arraigns in a rich baritone an equally formidable set of abuses.

He formed the presidential habit in childhood. The class elections and Sunday-school *coup d'états* always swept him into posts of honor. On leaving school, he became Sunday-school superintendent and vestryman at St. Luke's Episcopal Church in Convent Avenue. He is president of the Hamilton Grange Association, a community organization in the Washington Heights section where he winters, and president of the Lake George Association at Lake George, where he summers. He is president, chairman, or executive committeeman, of the Board of Religious Education of the Greater New York Federation of Churches, the International Council of Religious Education, the United Neighborhood Houses, the Daily Vacation Bible Schools, and forty other religious organizations. He is a trustee of City College and a member of the Board of Higher Education of New York. The Republican County Committee window-dresses all its important committees with Charles H. Tuttle, and several different bar associations do the same. Dr. John H. Finley is the only man in America who can sit down

with Mr. Tuttle and match him chairmanship for chairmanship and presidency for presidency.

After being admitted to the bar, he was successful both as a trial and office lawyer. In twenty years with Davies, Auerbach & Cornell, he wrote one hundred and ten fat volumes of briefs. Five years ago he began to develop a craving for public office, a disease which sometimes attacks successful men at middle age. The fact is that Mr. Tuttle already held every possible private office and could increase his collection only by going after public offices. He started two years ago with the United States district attorneyship.

T HERE was some doubt whether Mr. Tuttle, after all his years of civil practice, would make good as a prosecutor of crime; it was questioned whether he had the presence. He is a spare man of medium build, hatchet-faced, with sandy hair parted in the middle, quiet in dress, unassuming in manner. He had hardly been in office a week, however, before he exhibited his trick of dominating a courtroom. The government was being routed in a bankruptcy fraud case, which was being prosecuted by a young assistant district attorney, when the new D.A. slipped quietly into the courtroom and listened for a while. Suddenly the courtroom was surprised by a grave, melodious voice of extraordinary color and richness—a voice that had been developed by nearly fifty years of hymning, carolling, and psalming. It had something ventriloquistic about it, the speaker catching the ear much more quickly than he caught the eye. Jurymen peered this way and that with uplifted eyebrows. Vibrating with rectitude, the voice began to cross-examine defence witnesses who suddenly went all to pieces, unable to face

the music. Long before the verdict of guilty was rendered, it had become clear that Sam Koenig did not exaggerate when he said, "In the appointment of Charles H. Tuttle, the government gets a hundred-thousand-dollar man for ten thousand dollars."

On taking office Mr. Tuttle faced a serious problem. As a conservative lawyer of the old school he shuddered at the thought of seeking newspaper notoriety, but recognized that a man embarking on a political career needed it. Mr. Tuttle could not bring himself to blow his own horn and yet he disliked the idea of ruining himself by an excess of good taste. The situation was saved when a clever and aggressive press agent was hired so that the Tuttle ballyhoo is efficiently carried on in spite of the Tuttle reticence. No man in public life has ever been more thoroughly rescued from the consequences of his own modesty.

At the same time, Mr. Tuttle realized that, in order to be a successful public servant, he must learn to mix with the boys. He must conceal the high-mindedness and refinement that stood out all over him. A hail-fellow-well-met in the vestry-room, a boon companion at a men's Bible-class rally, he had a natural endowment of wholesome well-regulated animal spirits. All that was necessary was to develop this gift along more robust lines, and although there is still something synthetic about his camaraderie, he is gradually eliminating the false note from his jovial baritone "Ho, ho." Sometimes, after having his little joke, however, he becomes abruptly solemn by way of preventing the other fellow from having one. A nervous dread still lurks that somebody will take advantage of his bonhomie by uttering a coarse word or an improper epigram.

M R. TUTTLE speeded up the administration of justice. During

In the case of Earl Battice, cook of the schooner Kingsway, *who killed his wife because of her obvious preference for the mate, Mr. Tuttle achieved a curious blend of his two favorite sciences, theology and law. Introducing the fundamentalist Satan as the mastermind in this homicide, Mr. Tuttle alleged in the indictment that Battice, "not having the fear of God before his eyes, but being moved and seduced by the instigation of the devil," had committed the crime—this ancient form of words having been resurrected by a man eager to put Christian piety back into our courts.* (See Author's Note below)...

Later, Mr. Tuttle warmed up to the work and became determined to expose and punish all rogues...

Though a militantly wholesome member of society, Mr. Tuttle is not a Puritan. He is a wizard at bridge and plays a good game of tennis for a man of his years. Mr. Tuttle is almost dissipatedly fond of his Lake George farm where he rears prizewinning fowl. He is a friend of the theatre-goer and the prizefight fan, and conducted a vigorous though unsuccessful crusade to keep the ticket speculators from gypping them. He entertains the Federal Building boys at memorable dinners at which some say hard liquor is sneaked in without his knowledge and everybody sings, "For he's a jolly good fellow."...

Mr. Tuttle's reverence for judges is whole-hearted. Commenting last year upon the conduct of those who had aided him in clearing the calendar, he proclaimed that one judge had worked every day...

He has been fighting hard to eliminate abuses and cut out red tape. On the whole he has administered the office with so much energy and success that he is an unquestionable asset to the Republican Party and to the community.

AUTHOR'S NOTE:

Surely "the Fairness Doctrine" entitles the burlesqued to bite his burlesquer.

An acute profiler would have discerned that the inclusion of God and Satan on the indictment of the *Kingsway* cook was not to satisfy a personal passion for combining theology and law but, with tongue in cheek, to stir a reform. Forms of indictment had become monstrous ritualisms. What better than to mimic them with a beauty from the time of Edward the Confessor?

The effect was electric. Indignant editorials and bar association resolutions poured forth. The Legislature quickly responded with a "form of simplified indictment," effective July 1, 1929 (Code of Criminal Procedure, sec. 295-d). Now a good indictment for murder or other crimes may be in one vernacular sentence.

All of which fortifies my preachment that, however disadvantageous to the lucre side of practicing law, the conservation of paper and the English language in legal documents would be a public blessing. Samuel Tilden, Governor of New York [1875-77] and one of the greatest lawyers of the State, so adorned his Will with the luxury of words that the greatest Will contest in the State's history kept the courts and the profession busy for nearly a decade.

Editor's Postscript

Rajah the Cat in the News

ON AUGUST 9, 1930, the *New York Telegram* ran a story headlined "CHAS. H. TUTTLE, TAMMANY'S FOE." Accompanied by an artist's sketch *(see page 125)* with the bold caption, "Guardian of Government's Law Here," the article ended with this amusing story:

> *Of all the things that have happened since Charles Tuttle entered public life three years ago, none has impressed him more than the episode of his lost Persian cat, Rajah. Rajah disappeared a few days after he took office. He telephoned the want ad department of a New York newspaper, and, as suddenly as did Lindbergh arriving in Paris, discovered his new public importance.*
>
> *"Why, do you know," he says, "they immediately transferred my call to the city editor? And the next day Rajah was all over the front page. And I didn't have to pay a cent."*

And Rajah was happily reunited with his family!

CHAPTER SEVEN

NOMINATION FOR GOVERNOR. THE ENSUING CAMPAIGN. MY DEFEAT.

———◆◆◆———

SECTION 1

Gubernatorial Nomination on September 25, 1930. Stand for Repeal of the Prohibition Amendment.

B Y JULY 1930 THE DISCUSSION of my possible nomination for Governor became so frequent that I issued to the press the following statement:

> *I desire to make it clear that I am concerned solely with the duties of my office as United States Attorney. There are now pending here a number of important cases which require and are*

receiving my undivided time and attention. In no way am I seeking any other office, and any references to me as a candidate are wholly without any action or authority on my part.

In other words, as long as I was the United States Attorney, I held the office in trust for all the people, and felt bound to keep it and myself out of politics and polemic issues.

Nevertheless the discussion became more intense. By early September, Republican leaders and organizations were pressing me to become a candidate to oppose the Governor, Franklin D. Roosevelt, who was seeking a second term. Confrontation with an inner personal decision was before me. Only if I could be square with myself could I be square with the Party and the voters.

Prohibition had become a political furor and would increase in frenzy as the Convention approached. Republican voices in high places urged caution, pussy-footing, and dissimulation. The Anti-Saloon League and its allies demanded allegiance. President Hoover had been elected in 1928 on the platform that Prohibition was "a noble experiment." But by 1930 it had been in the United States Constitution for ten years. Was it still an "experiment?" Was it "noble?"

My face-to-face experience with Prohibition as a citizen and an official had finally convinced me that it was neither—that it had proven to be a misuse and corruption of government and that it had become a malignancy, a breeder of open disrespect for law, and a stimulant to the power of the underworld. Could I honestly run for Governor without saying so? The Eighteenth Amendment commanded the state governments as well as Congress "to enforce" Prohibition "by appropriate legislation."

The Party's leaders were in confusion. Efforts to write a plank, which could be read both ways, were occupying long hours in smoke-filled rooms. One prominent upstate leader said publicly and with truth that "the drys will fight to keep repeal out of the platform even if it entails the sacrifice of Charles H. Tuttle as the candidate—absolutely."

The National Administration was also reported to oppose any positive stand by the Convention on the subject of Prohibition.

But all the cacophony seemed to leave out of the reckoning the moral independent decision of just one person—myself. In consequence, I could neither run from the nomination nor run on an equivocation. I must make my personal position clear, and in sufficient time to leave the Convention with a free choice.

Accordingly, on September 16, 1930—nine days before the Convention—I issued a public statement in which I said that I was keenly aware of the many proposals of my name; that I had not the slightest desire to dictate any selection or any stand on Prohibition or its repeal; but that duty required me to state openly my own personal convictions. My statement continued:

> *The essence of the issue lies deeper than the sincerity and quality of the effort at enforcement, presenting rather a question of successful and practical government.*
>
> *National Prohibition goes beyond the question of abolishing the saloon and even beyond the grant of power to Congress to cooperate with States wishing enforcement and prevents any State adopting any other system. Out of this has grown the recognized evils.*
>
> *Real temperance and respect for law cannot be maintained by means of compulsion unless the means are such as local sentiment approves. No one is satisfied with things as they are. The dangers of the present system are obvious. We cannot indefinitely ignore conditions in favor of theories.*
>
> *The good in Prohibition lies in outlawing the saloon and granting Congress power to cooperate with States that wish to maintain a Prohibition system. The evil lies in compelling States which do not accept the national law to observe it. . . . To sum it up, I favor the repeal of the Amendment.*

Of course this public announcement required me to resign as United States Attorney, and I immediately so notified President Hoover.

Courtesy of NARA

HERBERT HOOVER
Prohibition:
"A Noble Experiment"?

There followed furious threats by organized Prohibitionists and their allies not only in New York but throughout the country. To quote the *New York Sun* of September 17, 1930:

> The ultra drys who have terrorized the Republican party for years by their threats of bolting, are on a rampage today, threatening to put up an independent candidate as they did in the Wadsworth campaign and bring certain defeat to Tuttle. That threat seems to have lost some of its effect.
>
> The county leaders insist they had rather run up their standard of independence and take a beating at the polls than knuckle down to the Anti-Saloon League and its auxiliary associations. They say they will have broken from that extreme dry group at any rate, which means something. Dr. Robert P. Carroll, member of the faculty of Syracuse University, is being put forward by the Anti-Saloon League group to run independently if Tuttle is nominated.

On the other hand, to quote the same issue of the *New York Sun:*

> Tuttle's statement together with his resignation has made a strong appeal. Even those not agreeing with him expressed admiration for his stand and said his courage would win him support. His statement that he "does not wish to be considered" adds strength to his position. He is not asking anything nor seeking to dictate. He simply defines his attitude on the prohibition issue, most troublesome of all political questions, and steps aside while waiting for his party to decide whether it wishes to summon him as leader. If the call does come, he will be far better off than if he had participated in a scramble for the nomination.

The threats of political homicide also took form in a flood of denunciatory letters, many calling for Congressional investigation of the manner in which I had enforced the laws—meaning the Prohibition Law. Where such letters came from persons and not mere cranks, I used a form reply the contents of which I quote:

Dear Sir:

I have your letter of the 9th instant. Let me say at once that whatever I say will be an expression of my personal conscience and independent judgment with the view solely of serving the cause of temperance and good government.

If you permit me to say so, I do not think I will be influenced by threats of either side. I am not seeking any office and have not sought any. The fact that numerous Republican leaders were making declarations which they did concerning myself, compelled me out of a sense of self-respect to make my own personal views known in order that no one may be misled. Those views I shall not seek to press upon anyone else. I think you are in error in assuming that I am under any illusion or delusion. My sole purpose is to make an honest and sincere contribution, if I can, to public thinking irrespective of the consequences.

I do not know whether you will be interested in the results of the work of this office under the prohibition law during the fiscal year ending June 30, 1930 in comparison with the preceding years. On the chance that you will be I make the following quotation from a summary of that report:

As to the prohibition law, the number of padlock decrees was the highest in the history of the office as shown by the following comparisons, to wit, for the fiscal year ending June 30, 1928, the number of such decrees was 143; for the fiscal year 1929, the number of padlock decrees was 482; whereas for the fiscal year of 1930, the number of such decrees was 620—the greatest number in any district in the United States. This figure represents an average of three such decrees for every court day in the year. The government lost no padlock action which was tried on the merits.

As to jury trials under the prohibition law, the record for the past year is the maximum in the history of the office as shown by the following comparison, to wit, in the fiscal year of 1928 there were 27 jury trials under the prohibition law; in the fiscal year 1929 there were 50 such trials; and in the fiscal year 1930 there were 62 such trials. The cases so tried are the major cases under the prohibition law, whereas the minor criminal cases under the law usually result in short jail sentences or fines.

As the Convention approached, the Anti-Saloon League and the Women's Christian Temperance Union began openly to field a separate ticket of candidates pledged to every jot and tittle of the Eighteenth Amendment. Part of the purpose was to frighten me into a refusal to be considered. But the determinative, as I saw it, was not personal victory or defeat. Rather it was the opportunity at hand to advance freedom of decision for the states in deciding their own liquor policies.

That opportunity was advanced when the Convention's Platform Committee drafted a plank for the repeal of the Eighteenth Amendment. The Plank was read to me over the telephone and I agreed that it was unequivocal. The plank was later adopted by the Convention by a vote of 733 to 258.

That morning I traveled alone to Albany by a New York Central train. I wished to have free time to consider my address, since nomination seemed certain.

At the afternoon session the roll of the delegates was called. What followed was thus stated in the *New York Sun* of that evening:

> On the call of the delegates for candidates for Governor, Albany yielded to New York and Major-Gen. James G. Harbord was recognized. As he walked to the platform he was given one of the biggest ovations of the convention. He made the nominating speech for Charles H. Tuttle and put the delegates in good humor at the outset by remarking: "Before I start I wish to waive immunity for anything I might say."
>
> At the mention of Mr. Tuttle's name, the convention blew up. New York started off with Sam Koenig grabbing up the New York standard and leading the parade. The counties flocked into line.
>
> Every delegate had a flag, rattle, a horn and husky lungs, and all were used to their capacity in noise-making. Every county fell

into line. It was a real demonstration, the biggest and realest outburst of Republican spirit witnessed in a convention for many a year. "What price judges." "Turn out the crooks," the delegates shouted.

I trust I may be forgiven for human weakness when I quote the following from General Harbord's gracious nominating speech:

> *Here, Republicans, is a man and a fighter. His progress through life has not been a bed of roses. He was born with no silver spoon in his mouth. He worked on a farm, he sold papers in the streets, he toiled at night and endured many sacrifices to win an education. Every step up the ladder of achievement has been a fight. Now, after three and a half years of campaigning on a hostile battleground, where the enemy held all the strongholds, and the cards were stacked against him, he emerges triumphant.*

My own address to the Convention as its nominee was too long for useful reproduction here. It covered many political matters which have been swept away by the River of Time. Its tenor and its focus are presented by the following quotation:

> **My Fellow-Citizens: You are about to perform the central function of American citizenship. In addressing you I want to lay aside my role as candidate and speak to you merely as a fellow-citizen and fellow-voter.**
>
> **I want to do this because government is the business of each individual citizen. Your ballot is the symbol of personal responsibility and personal power....**
>
> **Mr. Roosevelt states that the controlling issue is to keep marching onward progressive and liberal thought in government. But that thought expresses no difference between us at all. I yield no place to him in the matter of making government perform its full part in the great human task of building a better social order. No one desires more than I do the full application of the traditional American principle of equality and opportunity. I believe as strongly as he claims to in the obligations of society to care for the poor, cherish the indigent sick, promote the public health and foster a wider culture and outlook in every home in town and countryside....**

TUTTLE–ROOSEVELT CARTOON COMMENTARY

This 1930 editorial cartoon in the *New York Herald Tribune* echoed the sentiment of candidate Charles Tuttle, who proclaimed on the campaign trail: *"Unless this moral crisis in government is boldly and adequately dealt with, any appearance of progress in other directions is a sham."*

So far as I can see the only important difference between us in this campaign is that I see and he does not see a great moral crisis in government and that I contend that his failure to see it and to act with the boldness and strength which the crisis requires has aggravated the crisis itself, has encouraged the forces of corruption and has tended to strengthen the sinister system which is undermining the foundation of government itself. I contend that unless this moral crisis in government is boldly and adequately dealt with, any appearance of progress in other directions is a sham, because there can be no real progress in government unless the character of government itself is first preserved. One cannot build a secure house on a foundation of sand....

Surely if this policy of inaction in the face of such a crisis wins tomorrow, the only gainer will be Tammany Hall and the loser will be the State and all its citizens who need the protection of clean and honest government. Flushed with victory, Tammany Hall would not only treat the city of New York as a conquered province but would reach out for the conquest of the whole State. The system which it represents would speedily pervade the whole State Government....

As a candidate for the Presidential nomination in 1932 he [the Governor] would need the ninety votes which Tammany Hall will control. He has acted on legislation as Tammany has desired; he has appointed its men to office without a scrap of written recommendation; he has evaded demands for speedy action to uncover graft in the Tammany government. In short he needs Tammany Hall and Tammany Hall needs him....

This, my friends, concludes my analysis of the issues, the program for which I stand and the record already made by my party. I submit it to you with the utmost confidence in its soundness and in the verdict which it will receive from your judgment. That program will destroy corruption, correct abuses, promote progress and encourage liberal thought. It has as its ideal of government the giving of a square deal to every man, woman and child. It looks forward to a better social order, the assurance of a wider culture among all our people, the making of happier homes and the preservation of those moral and civic standards without which our proud American institutions cannot stand or function.

———◦◆◦———

SECTION 2

The Declaration of All-Out War by the Anti-Saloon League and the Women's Christian Temperance Union.

A fanatic is a closed individual who fashions a god
out of his own obsession, and then in its name
pontificates in the vocabulary of anathema.
– C.H.T.

A T A LATE HOUR after the Convention's adjournment, my family and I went to the Hotel Ten Eyck. I said that it would be my last chance for a good night's sleep until Election Day. But even that was not to be.

Shortly after midnight a messenger brought a summons that I meet certain of the Dry Officialdom in their apartment. Unlimited denunciation of me was to begin. Nevertheless postponement for a few hours was pointless.

I opened the encounter by saying that the meeting would be futile unless mutual sincerity was assumed. The amazing reply began a conversation which, as I look back upon it, strains credibility.

Its substance was: Sincerity is not the issue, Mr. Tuttle. You, who have had so many church connections, have now "laid a sacrilegious hand on the religion of America. We intend to defeat you."

What religion, I asked, are you referring to? "The Christian religion, of course." Then am I to understand that you regard the Eighteenth Amendment as part of the Christian religion? "Yes, we do, and we shall prove it to you at the polls." Doubtless, I said, you may be decisive at the ballot box; but, I ask, if you regard the Eighteenth Amendment as part of the Christian religion, and opposition to it as "sacrilege," what do you do with the Founder of Christianity? There was a pause. Doubtless events, beginning with the wedding feast at Cana, came to memory. "But that was only grape juice."

I arose and left. The Declaration of War against me and its character had been delivered.

That Declaration followed me all through the State and every day of the campaign. Details would be profitless; but one or two incidents relieve the memory of them with the balm of humor.

One day in Malone, a political citadel of Prohibition, I was making an address from the balcony of a hotel facing the public square. In addition to the usual heckling, I was interrupted by a tipsy voice directly below me which kept solemnly repeating: "But you sent Boys to Atlanta [Penitentiary]!" When patience ran out, I angrily denied that I had ever done so.

After my address was over, my friends rushed to me in consternation for what they termed "an awful booboo." Up here, they said, "boys" means "bootleggers"; and you have just denied to this "dry" audience that you ever sent a bootlegger to jail! Alas, I had not realized how the Eighteenth Amendment could turn even the English language upside down!

In the course of the campaign, I was honored with a large dinner in the Ballroom of the Astor. My "advisers" had become greatly concerned that my "image" was burdened with too much rectitude. There must be more of the "common touch." Since Prohibition barred my taking a drink, how about a little smoking? I had never smoked a cigar. But why not? It could be more conspicuously photographed than a cigarette. So, in the course of the dinner, the photographers of the press were lined up. I stuck a big lighted cigar in my mouth. At the signal, I blew out a cloud of "common touch" smoke. My "advisers" were delighted with the ensuing picture in the following morning's press. Alice in her Wonderland met no stranger adventures than Charlie in his Politicalland.

Perhaps to the foregoing several postscripts are appropriate.

In 1932 President Hoover himself came out for the repeal of the Eighteenth Amendment. A plank for its repeal, similar to that in the New York Republican State Platform of 1930, was then included in the Republican Party's National Platform.

On February 20, 1933, Congress proposed to the State Legislatures the Twenty-first Amendment repealing the Eighteenth. I was thereupon elected by the people of the State of New York to be a member of the State Convention to consider and act upon the ratification of the repeal. On June 27, 1933, the Convention voted for the repeal unanimously (Chap. 143, L. 1933). On December 5, 1933, the repealer became part of the United States Constitution.

SECTION 3

Campaign for Governor. The Fun. The Insurmountable Obstacles.

PART I

AFTER THE CONVENTION, I returned to New York. The pleasantest day of the ensuing campaign was its first.

I found awaiting me a gala homecoming party by the whole official family of my former office—greetings, best wishes, cheers, some tears, offers to help, and an ornate pen presented by Robert E. Manley, then the acting United States Attorney, to be used later (so they said) in signing the lease on the Mansion House in Albany. During the festivities the following letter from President Herbert Hoover was read aloud:

> I beg to acknowledge your telegram requesting that your resignation as United States Attorney for the Southern District of New York be made effective at once instead of the date which you had previously requested.

SEND-OFF FOR THE 1930 GUBERNATORIAL CAMPAIGN

With "greetings, best wishes, cheers, some tears, offers to help," the staff of the United States Attorney's office bid farewell to their recent "Chief" the day after he returned from the Albany convention at which he accepted the Republican nomination for Governor of New York. Charles Tuttle recalled that he was presented with an ornate pen *"to be used later (so they said) in signing the lease on the Mansion House in Albany."*

"A GOOD MAN FOR THE JOB"

Depicting Charles Tuttle's strong record as U.S. Attorney against Tammany Hall corruption, the *New York Tribune* offered a hopeful editorial cartoon regarding his gubernatorial bid of 1930. *The New York Times* later described Tuttle as "a vigilant crusader against corruption."

In accepting your resignation I take the opportunity of expressing my personal appreciation and that of the administration for the faithful and efficient service you have rendered the government as the representative of the Department of Justice in the largest and most important district of the country, and in maintaining the high standards which have been traditional in the office of the United States Attorney in your district. You have indeed established a high record of accomplishment.

I am, sincerely yours,

HERBERT HOOVER

At the close of the reading, I said:

Whatever words of approval this letter from the President contains are due to all persons in this office. Those about me are not only friends, but in many respects closer than relatives often are.

Part II

There followed the stern business of the campaign—incessant conferences in person and by telephone with Republican leaders from all over the State, and the planning of a personal caravan which would take me into every county. Organizing a staff, fact-gathering, press relations, news conferences, fund raising, listening to conflicting advice, public appearances, radio talks, speech writing and speech making—all these soon put me on fifteen-hour days. But even more demanding days soon came—the personal rallies and hand shakings throughout the State.

The political history of the campaign has had a scholarly description in a book published by Columbia University Press in 1955 entitled *Franklin D. Roosevelt as Governor of New York*. The book was written after extensive research by Professor Bernard Bellush, then Assistant Professor of History at The City College of New York.

In order to be as objective as possible, I summarize by quoting from
Professor Bellush's account (pp. 158-9; 163-5):

> Walter Lippmann, who two years earlier had urged Roo-
> sevelt's nomination upon the Democratic convention, was now
> extremely critical of the Governor's handling of Tammany. He
> maintained that Tuttle's record as United States Attorney had
> earned him the respect and gratitude of the people of New York
> and would make a powerful appeal to that section of the voters
> known formerly as "Al Smith Republicans" who, since 1922,
> had held the balance of power in gubernatorial elections.
>
> Lippmann was referring, amongst other things, to the case in
> which Tuttle had produced evidence that the wife of Magistrate
> George F. Ewald, an appointee of Mayor Walker, had "loaned"
> Tammany district leader Martin J. Healy $10,000 on the day
> of Ewald's appointment, on an unsecured note which had sud-
> denly "disappeared." Eventually the evidence in the Ewald case
> was turned over by Mr. Tuttle to Tammany District Attorney
> T.C.T. Crain, who, not unexpectedly, was unable to secure
> indictments.
>
> The Republican party, in the meantime, was planning a
> campaign which would bring Tuttle to more than 130 upstate
> towns, hamlets, and cities. Though increasing numbers of rural
> citizens had come to view Roosevelt as above reproach on the
> issues of graft and corruption, the Republican candidate insisted
> on hammering away at Tammany corruption, Tammany waste,
> and Tammany governors.
>
> Both campaigns sought a direct appeal to the people. The
> charges hurled by a candidate in one town were rebuked by the
> other close by. This situation enabled the voters to become inti-
> mately familiar with the appearance, speech, and personalities of
> their political choice. This was quite an achievement for Statewide
> candidates in New York before the era of television. The thor-
> oughness with which both men wove through the State served as a
> stimulant to political interest among apathetic citizens.

"YOU DON'T HAPPEN TO KNOW WHO GOT THE $10,000, DO YOU?"

U.S. ATTORNEY TUTTLE
INTERROGATES THE TAMMANY TIGER

George F. Ewald, a New York City magistrate appointed by Mayor Jimmy Walker, was charged with paying $10,000 for his judgeship. The Ewald case was spearheaded by U.S. District Attorney Charles Tuttle, described by the press as "Tammany's foe."

At his first campaign rally in a crowded Brooklyn hall, Tuttle set the tone for his entire campaign when he charged Roosevelt with reluctance to interfere with Tammany until obliged by public opinion. Tuttle said:

> On the one hand the Governor needs the support of Tammany Hall in the current campaign and in preparation for 1932. On the other hand, the state needs a Governor that leads rather than follows public opinion and is bigger than Tammany Hall.

Tuttle further charged that Roosevelt had been indirectly responsible for the refusal of Tammany chieftains to waive immunity and appear before the grand jury through limiting the jury's scope so that it could not make an issue of the refusals of Tammany leaders. Tuttle then catalogued the succession of scandals that had contributed to the Governor's dilemma: the sewer graft, notorious and unsolved murders, the enforced retirement of several judges from the bench, the City Trust Company failure, payroll padding in the Street Cleaning Department, and graft in the County Clerk's office. The Republican spokesman contended that this condition had compelled the legislature to enact a bill authorizing the Governor to appoint his own commission to investigate the administration and certain local authorities in New York City, which Roosevelt had vetoed. Tuttle then asked why, on the other hand, the Governor had authorized investigations into the Republican counties of Westchester and Saratoga.

Tuttle later insisted that Roosevelt give a fuller explanation of his judicial appointments, hinting at the purchase of judicial posts by citing cash withdrawals made by Justices Crater and Bertini soon after the Governor had appointed them. He derided the note the Governor had sent Mayor Walker urging city officials to wave immunity, because it had referred only to investigation into their "official acts," not their personal acts. This had given Tammany Hall the necessary loophole.

At Syracuse, Tuttle blamed Roosevelt for the prison riots of 1929, and in Plattsburg dared Roosevelt to deny that Tammany

*had dictated the appointments of Crater and Bertini. In Ogdens-
burg, Republicans heard Tuttle denounce the Governor for
neglecting to consult the Bar Association before appointing
Bertini to the General Sessions bench.*

*Roosevelt opened his upstate campaign in Binghamton with
Eleanor Roosevelt, Herbert Lehman, and Morris S. Tremaine.*

*Speaking in four counties that same day, Tuttle continued to
score Tammany corruption while charging that Roosevelt was not
using all available funds to ease the effects of unemployment.
Trailing Roosevelt into Binghamton, the Republican nominee
reminded his audience that the farm relief bills Roosevelt referred
to had been adopted by a Republican-controlled legislature. At the
same time he renewed his challenge to the Governor to "stand up
and fight" on the Tammany issue.*

PART III

But what Professor Bellush described as "Tuttle's vigorous campaign" availed nothing as against **three factors** impossible to over-
come:

1. The organized "drys" were fanatically determined to defeat me
at all cost. Only by my resounding defeat could they hope to prevent
President Hoover from abandoning in 1932 "the noble experiment"
and then swimming with the fast-rising tide for its repeal.

A Holy War was declared. Crusades against me were organized in
churches, in church councils, in women's organizations, and in political
groups, particularly upstate. Whatever battles I may have fought and
won for good government in other fields, availed nothing. I was "a traitor" to the only cause which counted in their eyes—the Sacred Cause
of National Constitutional Prohibition.

2. To all this gathering darkness there was added the black shadow
of the deepening Economic Depression—soon poisonously to be
called the Hoover Depression. The landslide which had swept President
Hoover into the White House in 1928 was now sliding rapidly the other
way. The stock market was crashing. Bankruptcies were proliferating.
Breadlines were forming. The Democratic Party was being hailed as the

David who alone could surely slay the Goliath of the Eighteenth Amendment, and conversely as the Hercules who alone could reverse the slide toward economic disaster, and usher in a New Deal for all.

3. The third insurmountable factor has been thus stated by Professor Bellush (p. 171):

> *In addition, too many Republican voters realized a Republican party of national oil scandals, of a Boss Vare of Pennsylvania, and of corrupt upstate county machines could not be morally superior to Tammany, no matter what the honesty and integrity of the Republican gubernatorial candidate.*

PART IV

Mercifully, the physical strain of the campaign was lightened by the many devoted supporters, the cordial crowds and wonderful people it became my privilege to meet. There were numerous lively incidents to fend off fatigue.

In "going upstate" my first stop was a huge Republican Dinner at the Nelson House in Poughkeepsie. My daughter Charlotte was then at nearby Vassar College. She was given a seat at the speaker's table. I saw the eyes of the newspaper men sparkle with anticipated opportunity. Charlotte had already had publicity as a devoted disciple of Norman Thomas, who (as usual) was also running for Governor—on the Socialist ticket! Laughingly I said to Charlotte that the Boys of the Press were planning to make her a headliner in the morrow's story.

Sure enough! As soon as the dinner and the speeches concluded, they gathered around Charlotte like bees around honey. "Miss Tuttle, we know that you belong to the Norman Thomas Club at Vassar. Whom will you vote for—Norman Thomas or your father?" I held my breath. Her answer went through the State as a classic: "Since I am not twenty-one I am not voting for anyone, but I do commend my father as a most wonderful man."

Another incident still finds me laughing. Tammany Hall could not afford to have me win. Accordingly, true to its methods at the time, it busied itself with skillfully floating rumors wherever ignorance and

Photo by P & A Studios, NY; Inset: Evelyn Tuttle in 1930

**FAMILIES OF THE GUBERNATORIAL CANDIDATES:
THE TUTTLES** *(above)* **AND THE ROOSEVELTS** *(below).*

Courtesy of Franklin D. Roosevelt Library

prejudice would furnish circulation. One such floatation was in the
form of an unsigned leaflet charging that I was "anti-Semitic." Thereupon two things happened. My former staff at once published a list of
their own names. One-half of them were Jewish. Next Samuel
Untermyer, who was Tammany Hall's chief adviser, published the classic bon mot:

> There are so many reasons for voting against Mr. Tuttle that
> one need not lie about him. He is not anti-Semitic!

Not to be outdone, the *Jewish Morning Journal,* which was supporting me, thereupon appeared with a banner first-page headline:

UNTERMYER COMES OUT FOR TUTTLE!

Just one more! I finally came back to the City from walking to and
fro all over the State, usually making two major and a half dozen minor
addresses a day. My blood pressure had almost disappeared. Thinking
and walking had gone on strike. Yet the next day there was to be a huge
welcoming luncheon in my honor at the National Republican Club,
with all the press present. A major speech was *de rigeur.*

That morning I crawled down to headquarters and tried to lock
myself in. I needed a little quiet in order to find out if I could still
think, and, if so, about what? But iron bars would not have held back
the interruptions. Finally the limousine to take me to the National
Republican Club was announced. I was on the verge of panic.

Just then word came that Meier Steinbrink, the Republican leader
in Brooklyn, was on the telephone, urgently.

> *Charlie, I regret that I must warn you of some very bad news
> about to happen. The Republican member of a Brooklyn law
> firm of which the other member is a Tammany Hall Democrat,
> has just whispered to me that his partner has ready a complaint
> against you for $250,000 damages, charging you with the false
> arrest of so-and-so when you were the United States Attorney.
> The complaint will be served right after your speech today. Of
> course the complaint is nonsense; but its object is to out-headline
> what you will say at the luncheon.*

When Meier rang off I stared blankly at the wall. Suddenly my guardian angel was descending. " There's your speech," she whispered in my inner ear. I could not get to the limousine fast enough!

The luncheon was crowded. My address flowed easily. Near its end, I said I had a warning to make public. Tammany Hall was readying one of its low blows, standard fare just before election. The blow would be delivered as I would be leaving the building!

The newspaper boys literally howled for enlightenment. No, in view of what I have already said, you will easily identify the low blow when it comes.

Nothing happened. When I returned to headquarters, Meier Steinbrink was again on the phone. "Charlie, what did you say at that luncheon?" "Why, Meier?" "Because the Republican partner has just excitedly told me that something you said there caused Tammany Hall to countermand the service of the complaint."

———◄◆►———

SECTION 4

The Three Days After the Election in 1930. Up from the Bottom of the Well.

O N ELECTION DAY Mrs. Tuttle and I remained at headquarters until midnight. Roosevelt had been elected by a statewide plurality of 725,001. I have often wondered what voter had cast that lonely "1".

Acknowledging his victory, I sent the Governor a telegram of congratulation and received thanks in reply.

On the way home I established myself as a poor prophet by telling Mrs. Tuttle that I had at least achieved secure eminence in the State Republican Party's political history by losing by an unexcellable plurality.

Early next morning my home telephone rang. A voice which I immediately recognized said gleefully, "Charlie, I want to cheer you up by being your first client." All night I had been mulling the thought of going away for a vacation. This mulling instantly stopped. "Good," I said with equal gleefulness, "but for the moment I have no office or staff. So meet me for lunch at the Lawyer's Club."

His was a real piece of law business. It helped relieve the gnawing question: *At the age of fifty-one had I thrown my life away?*

After the luncheon we came down to the front steps of the building. My first "client" walked off briskly. He had a place to go. I had none. At the curb was a sight familiar in those days — a shabbily dressed man with a crate of apples and a doleful sign: PLEASE HELP THE UNEMPLOYED. I said to him: "Brother, you do not know the bond of union between us, but in honor of it I now will buy one of your apples." He looked startled.

Then I and my apple mechanically started toward the Federal Building. There I could at least have someone to talk to. As I passed St. Paul's Chapel, my low blood pressure overtook me. I had to sit down. I tottered into the Chapel's graveyard. It seemed such a natural place for me. The rear door of the Chapel was open. I went in and was soon asleep, sitting up in the back pew. The sun had been high when I entered. When I woke up the electric street light was shining through the windows. I went home and said to Mrs. Tuttle:

> *My dear, this is a red-letter day for me. Today I struck bottom.*
> *I cannot go lower. So I am now on my way up!*

The next morning I went down to the United States Attorney's office. Then and there the mystic fraternal order of "The Tuttle Boys' Association" was born, destined to go from strength to strength for four decades.★

That afternoon William C. Breed, the senior member of the large Wall Street law firm of Breed, Abbott & Morgan telephoned an invi-

---

★ In 1952, the Tuttle Boys composed a lyrical spoof of the 1930 election campaign for their annual celebration. It is reproduced in Appendix B, p. 361.

tation to lunch the next day. I left that lunch as a member of his firm, and went to work at once.

Mr. Breed was an aggressive business go-getter, counsel to some large institutions, soon to be president of the City Bar Association, and socially prominent. When he died on December 3, 1951, I succeeded him as the senior member of the firm. For me, the firm has always been more than a law partnership. Within these walls, there has been a continual sense of teamwork, mutual esteem, and deep respect for each other's ability. The firm has truly served as a warm professional home—for the duration of my life.

As I think back to those first three days after the 1930 election, I thank my guardian angel for her part in shaping their events.

Postscripts

1. I was soon tumbled from my eminence as the worst beaten Republican gubernatorial candidate in the Party's history. In 1932 William J. Donovan lost by a plurality of 847,439. In 1934 Robert Moses lost by a plurality of 808,091.

2. In 1932 I attended the Republican Convention in Buffalo which nominated Colonel Donovan. In the hotel lobby I met my old political archenemy, the president of the Anti-Saloon League. I greeted him by saying I was sorry to see him looking peaked and worried. He said that he had reason to be so because his "dry" associates were calling him "traitor" for supporting President Hoover for reelection notwithstanding Hoover's recent advocacy of the Eighteenth Amendment's repeal. I replied:

> *Mr. President, can it possibly be that they are calling* **you** *"traitor"? Here is a broad sympathetic shoulder for you to cry on and be comforted by me!*

As of December 5, 1933, the American people purged their Constitution of the Eighteenth (Prohibition) Amendment. The control of liquor was, as I had advocated in 1930, left to the various states.

NYC and Roosevelt photos courtesy of FDR Library

A Memorable Afternoon Tea

After the contentious gubernatorial campaign of 1930, Franklin and Eleanor
Roosevelt invited Charles and Hélène Tuttle for a friendly afternoon tea at
their home on East Sixty-fifth Street in New York City. Years later, that
building, and the adjoining home of Mrs. Sara Roosevelt, served as a student
center for Hunter College's student association. Charles Tuttle, who became
chairman of the Association's board of directors, recalled with amusement:
*"I found myself presiding at board meetings in the very room in which Mrs.
Tuttle and I had had that memorable 'cup of tea.'"*

SECTION 5

A Cup of Tea with Governor and Mrs. Roosevelt. Its Sequels.

I RECORD THIS HERETOFORE UNPUBLISHED EVENT as a tribute to Governor (later President) Franklin D. Roosevelt and to Mrs. Roosevelt. I believe the event unique in American politics.

It began with a letter from Governor and Mrs. Roosevelt to Mrs. Tuttle and myself cordially inviting us to a private afternoon tea at their home on East Sixty-fifth Street.

We were warmly received in their living room on the second floor. The Governor led the conversation through interesting and delightful channels, with only a pleasantry or two about our recent campaign against each other. Mainly we talked about various civic and public causes in which we and our wives had had a part. There were personal and humorous anecdotes on both sides. No sense of stiffness or artificiality occurred. We stayed for an hour.

After we left I said to Mrs. Tuttle that only a very great and noble couple could have thought of offering such personal hospitality to a late and strenuous opponent. I was happy to recall that, although the campaign had been toughly and robustly fought, neither of us had impugned the other's character. The "cup of tea" was assurance that the door to personal friendship had not been closed.

The hour thus uniquely spent had sequels of large and lasting proportions.

There later came a time when certain Catholic, Protestant and Jewish groups drew together to devise ways and means for an interfaith religious center for the students in Hunter College, 68th Street and Park Avenue. At the request of the group, the Legislature created a special non-profit membership corporation named the Hunter College Student Social, Community and Religious Clubs Association and authorized it to raise tax-exempt funds to acquire a suitable building off the Hunter College campus which would provide separate facilities for the respective Faiths and also major rooms for use in common and by organizations cooperating in support (Laws of 1943, chapter 140). The board of directors was equally divided among the three religious groups. I was honored with the chairmanship and have been continued in that office to the present day.

The three groups thereupon secured adequate funds and purchased from Franklin D. Roosevelt (then President) his aforesaid house on East Sixty-fifth Street and also the adjoining home of his mother. The two houses were then united to become the home of the corporation, and a center for religious life and training among the students of Hunter College, without violation of the basic constitutional principle of separation of Church and State. I found myself presiding at board and committee meetings in the very room in which Mrs. Tuttle and I had had that memorable "cup of tea" with Governor and Mrs. Roosevelt a month after the 1930 election. Into what admirable designs the shuttle of Time often weaves the threads of coincidence!

But that was not all! On the day when President Roosevelt died, I had a professional engagement which had kept me uptown until seven o'clock in the evening. When the matter concluded, I dimly remembered that I had accepted an invitation to a very large dinner, but I could not recall by whom or where. My office was closed and my secretary had not reached her New Jersey home. There was no time to get into evening clothes if dinner was of that quality.

The word "Waldorf" kept intruding. I went on the chance that the dinner was there. An enormous crowd was in the Ballroom's foyer. Timidly I presented myself to the beautifully gowned and coiffured young woman sitting under the banner blazoned with "T." Alas, my name was not on her list.

How, thought I, might a detected gate-crasher slip away? Just then Supreme Court Justice Edgar Nathan took my arm and said: "Charlie, what's the trouble?" I explained my mortification. He laughed and said that the only trouble was that the young lady had not looked at the list of the dais guests. The occasion was the United Jewish Appeal. As a symbol of good will, a Catholic layman was to sit at one end of the dais, and a Protestant at the other. I was the latter. My default in the matter of evening clothes would work no forfeiture.

In the middle of the dinner, Sam Leidersdorff, who was presiding, told me that he understood that B'nai B'rith had scheduled a business meeting at the Roosevelt House for that evening; he hoped that as chairman of the board I would suggest that they make it a memorial meeting. I was hustled into a taxicab while still expressing wonderment that he himself had not conveyed the suggestion by telephone.

On arrival, I asked the directress of the House whether there was a rabbi in the neighborhood. One soon came, and an impressive and moving memorial meeting began. At its conclusion, they asked me to speak. What more fitting than to tell the story of "the cup of tea" in that very room a month after the 1930 election. When I ended the story, many eyes (including my own) were being softly wiped.

The room still hears repetition of the story. "The cup of tea" lingers there as a tradition *in memoriam*.

SECTION 6

The Tuttle Boys' Association.
Lifelong Friendships.

L ITTLE THAT I HAVE WRITTEN causes me more joy than what I am
now about to write. Perhaps some day the story will be almost as
luminously legendary as the Knights of the Round Table.

The saga began just two days after the Election in 1930.

Being unemployed and officeless, I wandered for some companion-
ship into my former home in the Federal Building. I had become an
outsider there. I had nothing to offer. I could distribute no patronage.
But I could at least thank the boys with a full heart for their united and
devoted help during the lost campaign.

To my surprise and joy, I was received as a long lost elder brother
who had wandered afar and had at last returned to the domestic circle.
When Good Fortune leaves, good friends come.

The family must continue together! Fraternity had been too close to
be loosened! Nothing but a permanent association would do! "The
Tuttle Boys," of course!

And so a lifelong circle was born that day and adopted as its heraldic
motto: *"All for one, and one for all!"*

Since then, "The Tuttle Boys" have annually staged a celebrating
banquet on my birthday, with "the Chief" as "the fall guy"—complete
with music and songs, toasts for all, wisecracks exploding, wives
adding grace and enthusiasm, and a cake and handsome gifts for "the
Chief"and his Lady.

When "the Chief" was approaching his 70th birthday, the Tuttle Boys told him to go to Raymond Perry Rodgers Neilson, the most expensive portrait painter in town. Mr. Neilson sat around with me casually in his studio for half an hour discussing our summer places. After thirty minutes, he told me to return in thirty days and judge the portrait. I registered surprise, for I had not seen any painting being done, or any pastel, or any paint daubed gown. Mr. Neilson smiled and said: "I told your Boys that, if you did not like the portrait, I would not charge them anything; but, if you did, I would charge them plenty!"

I grinned and said challengingly: "You evidently are a daring sport. How about making that gamble depend on Mrs. Tuttle's liking it or not?" "Done!" he said.

Thirty days later, I took Mrs. Tuttle to his studio. When he unveiled the portrait, she cried: "How wonderful!" I wrung his hand. "Charge them plenty!" The portrait has since had a proud place on my office wall *[see page 253]*.

The last of these annual birthday banquets was on my eighty-ninth, April 21, 1968. "The Boys" are now themselves moving into or past their seventies. But how they went to it! The quartet in full throat! The ringing piano! The jibes and wisecracks hurled around! The photographer's bulbs flashing!

They had written a special song, the last verse of which read:

Gee but it's great to meet each year
Those old boys of mine
Within me well those memories
Now that I'm eighty-nine.
And when I see you, to tell the truth,
A certain something helps bring back my youth,
Believe me.
Gee but it's great to meet each year
Those old boys of mine.

I responded with a special song which I had written for the occasion, the first and last verses of which read:

> *Merrily we roll along!*
> *Roll along from Wonderland!*
> *That ancient fortress grim*
> *which frowned at City Hall.*
> *'Twas there we met and*
> *formed our merry band*
> *And made our mutual pledge:*
> *"All for one, and one for all!"*
>
> *And now and then there comes a*
> *distant hail*
> *From mates beyond where sky*
> *and ocean meet and now ashore:*
> *They've laid aside their oars*
> *and furled their sail,*
> *Awaiting us as merrily we*
> *roll along still bending at a stalwart oar.*

And who are these "Tuttle Boys"? They are all truly remarkable men with outstanding lives and careers in their own right. Here are the names of some, arranged in no intentional order:

GEORGE S. LEISURE, my first chief of the Criminal Division, who later became the senior member of the Wall Street law firm of Donovan, Leisure, Newton & Irvine.

GEORGE J. MINTZER, who succeeded Leisure as Chief of the Criminal Division and later became Chairman of the State Advisory Council on Employment and Unemployment Insurance *(See postscript)*.

EDWARD S. SILVER, Mintzer's immediate associate, later District Attorney and Surrogate of Kings County *(See postscript)*.

SAMUEL C. COLEMAN, Chief of my Civil Division, and until his retirement, a judge of the City's Civil Court and serving by assignment in the Supreme Court.

EDWARD J. LUMBARD, later Senior Judge of the United States Court of Appeals, Second Circuit.

DAVID W. PECK, who served for many years as the Presiding Justice of the Appellate Division of the State Supreme Court, First Department, and later as a Senior member of the law firm of Sullivan & Cromwell.

HARRY G. HERMAN, who became County Attorney and later Surrogate of Westchester County *(See postscript)*.

THOMAS J. TODARELLI, who became a member of the law firm of Sabbatino & Todarelli *(See postscript)*.

PORTER R. CHANDLER, who later joined the leading law firm of Davis, Polk & Wardwell, and became Chairman of the Board of Higher Education of the City of New York.

EARLE N. BISHOPP, who for many years served as United States Commissioner, Southern District of New York.

HUBERT T. DELANY, who became a Justice of the Domestic Relations Court of the City of New York *(See postscript and Editor's Note)*.

ROCCO A. PARELLA, who became a Judge of the Civil Court of the City of New York and a member of the Judicial Conference of the State of New York.

HAROLD A. FELIX, later a Judge of the Family Court of the State of New York, City of New York.

ARTHUR H. SCHWARTZ, who became a Justice of the State Supreme Court and a member of the State Law Revision Commission.

LOWELL WADMOND, subsequently a member of the distinguished law firm of White & Case, and Chairman of the Appellate Division's Committee on Character and Fitness of Applicants for Admission to the Bar *(See postscript)*.

THE TUTTLE BOYS

Above: Serenading "the Chief"; *right:* Program for the Tuttle Boys' lighthearted 1952 musical "Satirony": *TUT, TUT, MR. TUTTLE.*

THE TUTTLE BOYS

present the first and last performance of

"TUT, TUT, MR. TUTTLE"

A Musical "Satirony" in One Act

Written and Staged

by

TOM TODARELLI

THE CAST

Court Crier	George Leisure
A Lawyer	Tom Crawford
An Attorney	Sam Coleman
A Barrister	Hubert Delany
A Member of the Bar	Ed Silver
A Mouthpiece	Lowell Wadmond
A Counsellor-at-Law	Reuben Carlson

Time: 1879 to 1952. *Place:* New York, City and State.

MUSICAL NUMBERS

1.	Overture:"*Charlie, My Boy*"	The Cast
2.	"*A Lawyer's Lot Is Not a Happy One*"	Ed, Hubert, Lowell and Sam
3.	"*From the Hills of Old Oswego*"	Ed
4.	"*If You Knew Charlie Like I Know Charlie*"	Tom
5.	"*Clients Are a Lawyer's Best Friend*"	Hubert
6.	"*I Am the Very Model of the Modern Ely Culbertson*"	Sam
7.	"*Tut-Tuttle*"	Ed, Tom, Reuben and Hubert
8.	"*He Ran Thru the State With the Greatest of Ease*"	Lowell
9.	"*Old Man Tuttle Had a Farm*"	The Cast
10.	"*Breed, Abbott & Morgan*"	Lowell, Hubert, Tom and Sam
11.	"*Happy Birthday to Charlie*"	The Cast and the Audience

At the Piano — Elmo Russ

MAXWELL SHAPIRO, who became a Justice of the Civil Court of the City of New York.

LAWRENCE J. RITTENBAND, my efficient secretary. Later he moved to California, and became a Judge of the Superior Court of California, sitting in Los Angeles.

ALVIN McK. SYLVESTER, counsel to the New York State Liquor Authority.

THOMAS J. CRAWFORD, a Justice of the New York Supreme Court.

THOMAS J. CURRAN, Secretary of State of the State of New York.

MARCO G. DI PIRRO, a Justice of the Civil Court of the City of New York.

HERMAN T. STICHMAN, court-appointed trustee of the Hudson & Manhattan Railroad and the holder of other important offices by appointment of Governor Rockefeller.

BERNARD TOMPKINS, a Senator of the State of New York.

CARL E. NEWTON, George Leisure's partner, has been our Houdini reincarnated—the incomparable Master of Illusions at our parties. At the wave of his wand, reality transmogrifies. (A lot of us have clutched our pocketbooks tightly!)

RICHARD BALDWIN, LEONARD BRONNER, FRANK CATINELLA, FRANK W. FORD, HENRY GERSON, ISAAC GUTMAN and THOMAS KERWIN, who continued with distinction under my successor GEORGE Z. MEDALIE, as well as in their subsequent private practice of the law.

But I could go on with the names of many others. I repeat that they all became men of distinction and highly esteemed publicly. I have been greatly honored to have had through the years as friends and comrades men of such outstanding character, ideals and achievement.

Postscripts

1. The Tuttle Boys, and I in particular, are deeply indebted to TOM TODARELLI for his longstanding role as master of ceremonies, songwriter and general promoter for our annual festivals. He is our "Broadway" producer. Closely associated with him in this role has been Benjamin R. Raphael, who almost from the beginning has been a Tuttle Boy by adoption and affection. Each year they bring "The Sound of Music" and their trainees — "the Judicial Quartet."

2. GEORGE MINTZER, EDWARD SILVER and I were jocosely known in the office as "THE THREE IRON MEN," possibly because of often being together in the forefront of battle.

3. LOWELL WADMOND will always be enshrined in my memory as one to whom I owe an unpayable debt of gratitude. Throughout my entire campaign in 1930 he devotedly gave all his time to accompanying Mrs. Tuttle and me in our caravan travels throughout the State. He saw to her comfort and was my personal guide, philosopher and friend. He always had a bag full of poultices for my wounds.

4. HUBERT T. DELANY became one of my bridge cronies. I made it a frequent point to tell him that he was a better judge on the Bench than at the Card Table. *(See Editor's Note on next page)*.

5. HARRY HERMAN got his job with me because he had the iron nerve to walk in one day without an appointment and tell me to my face that I had no assistant from Westchester and that he was just the man to fill the void.

As of this [early 1969] writing, the whole band is now licking their lips, spraying their vocal chords, composing their doggerel, whetting their knives, and icing the champagne, in anticipation of the upcoming (God willing) ninetieth birthday of "the Chief." *You ain't seen nuthin' yet!*

Editor's Note

HUBERT T. DELANY (*left*, 1901-1990) was both typical and unique among the remarkable "Tuttle Boys." He was typical in his distinguished legal career and broad public esteem, and unique in his heritage and family. The son of a former slave who later became an Episcopal bishop, Mr. Delany was the brother of the celebrated Delany sisters, Sarah and Elizabeth ("Sadie" and "Bessie") who, when both were over 100 years old, authored the best-selling 1993 book, *Having Our Say.*

Hubert Delany's legal ability, noted admiringly by friend and colleague Charles Tuttle, was also highly praised by Martin Luther King, Jr. Recalling a case in which he was represented by Delany, the civil rights leader described his New York attorney as one who "brought to the courtroom wisdom, courage, and a highly developed art of advocacy …[and an] indomitable determination to win."

"Defeat seemed certain," wrote King of the 1960 case in his autobiography★, "and we in the freedom struggle braced ourselves for the inevitable. . . . [but] I learned that truth and conviction in the hands of a skillful advocate could make what started out as a bigoted, prejudiced jury, choose the path of justice." To King's relief, the jury returned a verdict of acquittal.

MARTIN LUTHER KING, JR.

Hubert Delany's place of honor among the Tuttle Boys is one of many notable examples of the remarkably diverse racial, ethnic, and religious backgrounds of the group of fifty which enjoyed such profound lifelong comraderie, mutual esteem, and dedication to the law.

Spontaneously created by his former staff two days after Charles Tuttle's election defeat in 1930, the Tuttle Boys Association continued to gather together annually until the death of their "Chief" more than four decades later. Hubert Delany, longtime law colleague, political comrade, and "bridge crony" of Charles Tuttle, was a key player—in the law office, at the bridge table, and at the annual Tuttle Boys events.

★ *The Autobiography of Martin Luther King, Jr.,* Clayborne Carson, ed. (New York: IPM/Warner Books, 1998).

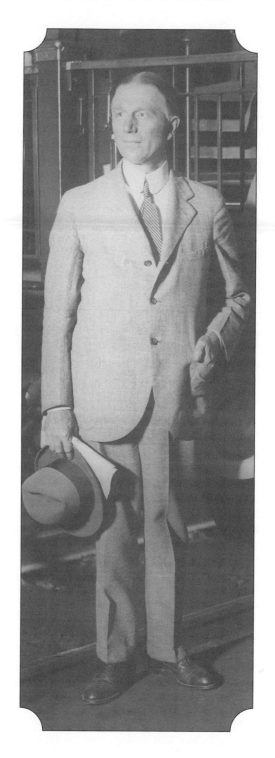

CHAPTER EIGHT

SOME CASES of PUBLIC NOTE and HUMAN INTEREST after 1930.

MY PLUNGE BACK INTO PRIVATE PRACTICE of the law had all the excitement of an uncertain leap from a high diving board. But the water became fun the moment I was immersed in it.

Whatever thorns my 1930 gubernatorial defeat had left in me were quickly washed out. I rejected the conventional vacation. What therapy could there be in fleeing the scene and moping on some distant beach? Life was like a proverbial "Irish fight." It was open to all, and something would be lost by not getting into it. I soon found myself running from one fight to another—Irish or otherwise.

Some of these fights were in the public arena, with plenty of the public sitting noisily on the bleachers. Some of them became part of the recorded history of the times, with prominent people in the leading roles. Some found their place among what lawyers call "leading cases." Perhaps some of them left an important moral as their legacies. The reader will judge.

With these considerations in mind, I have selected the following post-1930 cases and have deliberately not arranged them in chronological order. Rather, the sequence is with an eye toward drama—

the continuously exciting versatility of that strange being "Man," as he plays out his various roles of good and evil.

Einstein is reputed to have found a formula which solved the Universe, but he never claimed that it would include Man.

The Psalmist's question: "What is Man?" still waits for an answer. What now follows may accentuate the question, but certainly without presuming upon a solution.

———◆———

SECTION 1

The Remarkable Case of Richard Whitney, President of the New York Stock Exchange.

THIS IS TRULY A CLASSIC STORY of "a riddle wrapped in a mystery inside an enigma"—the insoluble enigma that is Man.

Early in the morning of Thursday, March 14, 1938, Edwin S. Sunderland, a partner in Davis, Polk, Wardwell, Sunderland & Kiendl, called on me. He said that Richard Whitney was under charges of embezzlements, and that the afternoon papers would break a story that the District Attorney of New York County, the United States Attorney, and the State Attorney General were racing for indictments and prosecutions. Would I at once undertake to represent Mr. Whitney? Mr. Sunderland made no suggestions.

After Mr. Sunderland left, Richard Whitney came. I had never met him. He was large, masterful and impressive—Napoleonic in type and manner. Probably no member of the Stock Exchange had in recent times enjoyed greater prominence and prestige than he. His membership dated back to 1912, and he had been its President from 1930 to 1935. He had held nearly all its offices of direction and trust. Since minutes might count, I questioned Mr. Whitney rapidly, racing the afternoon editions and district attorney actions.

What then occurred became matters of public report, principally by Mr. Whitney himself. I immediately recognized that here was a most extraordinary client. He announced emphatically that he would not plead either innocence or insanity. He was adamant that he had broken the law and the rules and was determined to face up to it at once and publicly. He expressed neither regret, remorse nor self-pity.

Courtesy of Bev Hanner / WRG

I vainly asked whether he had considered the consequences to his wife and two daughters. He assured me that he had told them of his intended course, and they were standing with him. In a moment of reflection, I happened to glance at the window. Immediately he said: "Nor will I take that way out."

I pointed out that prosecutions in three different jurisdictions seemed inevitable, perhaps by indictments this very day, and that the cumulative consequences could be appalling.

Nevertheless, he would leave no room for defense.

I said that this left open only one thought which occurred to me: he might consider possible advantages from surrendering and indicting himself in advance of the impending arrests or indictments by criminal authorities. I emphasized that I was not advising such a course. No lawyer could take that responsibility. I was only phrasing it for his consideration. The decision must be his solely, and, if he made it, it must be so presented.

He at once asked me to provide a stenographer and also to call an immediate press conference in my office.

In a steady voice he then dictated what he said was a full summary of his embezzlements. Only one sheet of paper, with carbon copies, and yet a statement which I believe to be without parallel. He signed them all. By that time the press was in the anteroom. There he personally handed out the signed copies, and said that there would be nothing further at that moment. I declined comment. There was a rush to telephones.

The statement read:

> *On January 26, 1938, I had an account in my firm, in which there were certain securities, a list of which is in the possession of the authorities. Some of these securities were the property of*

Mary S. Baird, the estate of Eila Haggin McKee, the New York Yacht Club, and the estate of George R. Sheldon. Since against these securities there were no debit balances, they were free and clear. Without the authority of these customers, I pledged their securities in a demand loan made to me on my personal note dated January 26, 1938, by the Public National Bank and Trust Company. The proceeds of this loan were deposited in my firm. At the time of the failure of my firm on March 8, 1938, the amount of this loan was $280,000.

On January 7, 1938, and previously, I had possession of certain other securities, a list of which is in the possession of the authorities. These securities were free and clear and were the property of the estate of George R. Sheldon. Without the authority of the estate, these securities were pledged by my authority in a demand loan made to my firm by the Corn Exchange Bank Trust Company, dated January 7, 1938. At the date of the failure of the firm the approximate loan value of these securities was $65,000.

In January 1938, Samuel S. Sands had an account in my firm in which there were certain securities, the value of which largely exceeded the debit balance in his account then appearing on the books. These securities were pledged by my authority in various loans to my firm without his authority and were sold during the latter part of January, or the early part of February 1938, with the result that these loans to my firm were reduced and the account thereupon showed and shows a credit balance of about $279,000 due to Samuel S. Sands.

I have in the past also authorized the unlawful pledge of the securities of other persons, including the Gratuity Fund of the New York Stock Exchange, all of which transactions are, I believe, fully shown on the records of the firm. In these latter instances there is no loss to anyone, since these securities were restored to their owners or are on hand for them with the firm's receiver. I am ready to make a detailed statement concerning these transactions.

> *I have very frequently been in touch with the receiver of my
> firm, voluntarily and at his request, in order to give him every
> assistance in the administration of the estate, and I shall continue
> to do so to the full extent of my power.*
>
> *I make this statement in accordance with my purpose to do
> all in my power to right the wrongs which have been done and to
> render every possible assistance to all concerned.*
>
> *I therefore place myself at the disposal of both the Attorney
> General and the District Attorney with a view to giving them,
> jointly or severally, whatever information I have, and to facili-
> tating them in the preparation of such formal charges against me
> as they deem necessary or proper.*
>
> *I fully realize the gravity of what I have done, and that a
> penalty must be paid. I also fully realize the nature and the con-
> sequence of the statement which I am now making, but I have
> nevertheless determined to make it.*
>
> — *RICHARD WHITNEY*

I called Thomas E. Dewey, the County District Attorney, and said
that Richard Whitney and I would like to see him at once.

When we entered, Mr. Dewey invited us to sit opposite him on the
other side of his desk. I noticed that he pulled open a lower drawer. I
smiled and said that, as a former District Attorney myself, I understood; but there was no need. Mr. Whitney was there to surrender and
indict himself. In fact, he had his indictment in hand. Mr. Dewey read
it, and said he would take it up to his grand jury then sitting on this
very matter.

He soon returned with an indictment. The three of us walked
across "the Bridge of Sighs" into Judge Owen W. Bohan's courtroom.
It was crowded to the doors and into the corridors. Mr. Dewey and I
asked for an immediate arraignment.

The Clerk read the indictment to Mr. Whitney and asked: "How
do you plead?" The indictment said in technical and in fuller words
what in summary Mr. Whitney had succinctly put in his paper. I told
the Court that, before Mr. Whitney pleaded, he asked leave to make a
statement. The Court said that only a plea of guilty or not guilty was

allowable. Mr. Dewey arose and said that he knew what Mr. Whitney had in mind to say and he felt that it would be in the public interest to let Mr. Whitney say it. The Court assented.

Then Mr. Whitney took out his paper. Holding it in a hand which never shook in the least, he read it aloud. The Court looked at him in astonishment. I doubt whether anything like it had ever been seen or heard before. A formal plea of guilty was entered. The Court directed that he go to the police station on the East Side for booking, finger-printing, and so forth. The sentencing was set for April 11. He was paroled in my custody (*The New York Times,* March 15, 1938).

Mr. Whitney turned to me. He said that the walk through the streets to the police station would be trying and humiliating, but he wished to do it *alone,* and I need not go. I replied that I was as much his lawyer on the streets as in the courtroom.

It was a tough walk. Word of it had spread. Mr. Whitney was not handcuffed. Crowds followed along. He made no effort to conceal his features. Flashbulbs were everywhere. A little girl, wriggling with excitement, ran up to me and said: "Oh, Mr. Whitney. Let me shake your hand." She wanted something to boast about ever after. I smiled and complied. As I recall, a flashbulb captured a picture of the little girl and myself.

When the formalities at the police station were completed, Mr. Whitney asked me to call upon his wife and himself that evening. He then took a cab home. His iron self-control and rigid poise had never wavered for a moment. I went back to my office and reported to Mr. Sunderland. I said that I would start drafting a plea for clemency and would show it to him when ready.

That night I called at the Whitney home. Mr. and Mrs. Whitney were sitting on the sofa holding hands. He told me that all the luxuri-ous furnishings and paintings would be auctioned off in a few days in order to raise funds toward his debt and his family's living expenses. He asked me to tell his wife in my own words what had occurred.

When I finished he kissed her; said it might be well for her to speak with me alone, and walked upstairs. She talked with me about visiting "my Richard" while he was in prison. She wanted to go to him whenever it was allowable. She talked tenderly of her daughters.

CHARLES H. TUTTLE, ADVOCATE

"I was as much his lawyer on the streets as in the courtroom."

I left with a lump in my throat. Words floated into my memory: "For better for worse, for richer for poorer."

The night before the sentencing I took to Mr. Sunderland's home the manuscript of what I was planning to say. He read it and said he would like to take it for consultation with Richard Whitney's wife and his brother and sister-in-law, Mr. and Mrs. George Whitney, who were all waiting nearby. I brought some sandwiches, coffee, and reading matter. When he returned, he said that no one wanted to change a word of it, nor did he.

On April 11, 1938, Richard Whitney and I were in court. He had expressly requested that no one of his family be present. Proceeding for sentence began. The maximum could be twenty years. I read my statement, portions of which were reported in *The New York Times* next morning as follows:

> *Mr. Whitney has neither avoided the law nor chosen the coward's course of flight from the country or from life.*
>
> *He still has courage. He still has character. Though his former prominence made confession inexpressibly hard and an unspeakable punishment in itself, nevertheless he has confessed. He has faced his friends, which perhaps is the hardest task of all. The strengthening and redemptive power of confession is a spiritual truth taught by every religion and all human experience.*
>
> *Fortunately the losses which his wrongdoing has caused have not fallen upon many persons and certainly upon none of slender means. Nor has there been claim that his acts were with any purpose of permanent spoliation. The spectacle of his fall constitutes in itself a deterrent which no one in like station will soon have the hardihood to defy; and the process of reconstitution and the material for it are already manifest.*
>
> *Save for his counsel, he stands here alone. He has chosen to drain this bitter cup by himself, without even the presence of those persons who sought the opportunity to intercede and who expressed the wish to be with him today.*
>
> *Even his own brother [George Whitney, partner of J.P. Morgan & Co.], who desired most earnestly to stand by him at this bar today, shoulder to shoulder, is at Mr. Whitney's own*

imperative wish now with the loyal wife and two daughters upon whom the shadow of grief and desolation today falls.

Mr. Whitney listened intently, standing erect and with no show of emotion.

The District Attorney had handed the Judge a prepared narrative enlarging in point of detail on what Mr. Whitney had himself said in his aforementioned public statement of March 14, 1938.

The psychiatric report which accompanied the probation report gave Mr. Whitney an "intelligence rating which could not be equaled by more than one percent of the American population."

The Judge then pronounced an indeterminate sentence of five to ten years to cover both indictments concurrently.

After the sentence, Mr. Whitney could have availed himself of the practice of motoring to Sing Sing in the sheriff's custody, upon payment of cost. He publicly declined this opportunity. Next morning he went through Grand Central on "the chain gang" with other prisoners, to the accompaniment of flashbulbs by the press.

Under the sentence, time off for good behavior could reduce the period of actual imprisonment to about three years. Actually, Mr. Whitney was released on July 8, 1941 — a total imprisonment of three years and three months. (*The New York Times,* July 9, 1941.)

After this sentence, further prosecutions of Mr. Whitney were dropped. Following his release he became employed as a foreman on a commercial farm in Massachusetts.

On returning to my home that evening after the sentencing, I found awaiting me a letter hand-delivered and written in longhand. It was from George Whitney. That letter is among my most precious professional possessions. I do not think I trespass by quoting this much:

> *While I realize there was nothing that I could say which is adequate, I did want to write you today to express my deep sense of gratitude for the intelligence, sympathy and loyalty with which you have advised my brother through the last trying weeks.*

On April 8, 1938, prior to the sentencing, the Securities and Exchange Commission opened its formal inquiry at 120 Broadway, New York City. I attended as attorney for Mr. Whitney. He was the first witness called by the Commission. Its Examiner warned him that he had a constitutional right to refuse to answer. The official transcript proceeds (p. 2):

> MR. TUTTLE: *Mr. Examiner, Mr. Whitney has had the occasion to be fully advised as to his constitutional rights, and from the very first, he has not sought to exercise them in any way and he does not seek to exercise them now.*
>
> THE EXAMINER: *Thank you, Mr. Tuttle. I want to be sure, however, that they appeared on the record.*
>
> MR. TUTTLE: *He has been before about five Government agencies for examination and at no time has he claimed his constitutional rights, and he is not claiming them now.*

The Examiner soon requested that there be received as Commission Exhibit 2 the foregoing public statement by Mr. Whitney and inquired whether I had objection. "No; I join in the request" (Vol. II, p. 47). Mr. Whitney then answered fully all questions put to him. His testimony ran for eighty pages.

The report of the Commission, dated November 1, 1938, stated that Mr. Whitney had begun his course of embezzling as far back as 1926. It also contained this statement (Vol. I, p. 9):

> *The collapse of Richard Whitney & Company may be traced directly to certain outside promotional and speculative ventures of Richard Whitney which had little or no connection with the brokerage business of the firm. These enterprises carried far afield of the brokerage business into the production and marketing of such unrelated products as applejack, peat humus, and mineral colloids. They were uniformly unsuccessful, and the resulting losses far exceeded the profits derived from the firm's brokerage transactions.*

The case of Richard Whitney ends where it began—as an enigma. To this day it has left me in complete bafflement. Here was a man who had reached the pinnacle of the financial structure and the respect and confidence of the economic world. He was a strict disciplinarian in enforcing the ethical rules of the Stock Exchange. Yet for twelve years

he had been engaging in accelerating embezzlements, apparently with
no thought of the criminality of his deeds or of vulnerability to the law.

And yet when the hour of retribution struck, he remained the same
imperious and unshaken figure, but with moments of tenderness, and
with iron fidelity to the code that, having dishonored all rules, he
would now honor them by accepting the penalties unflinchingly.

Perhaps there is a clue in two lines from Milton's *Paradise Lost:*

> *What though the field be lost?*
> *All is not lost—th' unconquerable will!*

EDITOR'S POSTSCRIPT: When the editors at *Time* magazine were considering
their top choices for "Man of the Year" in 1938, they observed: "Undoubted
Crook of the Year was the late Frank Donald Coster (ne Musica), with Richard
Whitney, now in Sing Sing Prison, as runner-up." The magazine's ultimate choice
was Adolf Hitler. "Lesser men of the year," explained *Time*, "seemed small indeed
beside the Führer." Three decades later, prolific author Louis Auchincloss wrote
a popular novel based on the case of Richard Whitney entitled *The Embezzler.*

SECTION 2

The Seizure of the Steel Mills in 1952 by the President of the United States.

ON APRIL 8, 1952, while Congress was in regular session,
Charles Sawyer, Secretary of Commerce, took possession of all
the principal steel companies and their plants, pursuant to Executive
Order issued by President Harry S. Truman.

The order recited a national emergency created by a prolonged
strike. It authorized the Secretary to prescribe the terms and conditions
of employment, and to continue operations through the current management except as he might otherwise prescribe. The Secretary could
continue the seizure as long as he might find it required in the interest
of national defense.

All the steel companies resisted and sued for injunctions. Their respective counsels assembled in Washington before Judge David A. Pine in the federal courthouse of the District of Columbia. I attended as senior counsel for my firm's clients, Armco Steel Corporation and Sheffield Steel Corporation.

I had misgivings. Was it likely that that little man sitting up there alone on the Bench would have "the guts" to enjoin the Secretary of Commerce from executing an order made by the President of the United States in the name of the national defense and of a very real national emergency — and backed by the entire Organized Labor of the country? Yet there he calmly sat with quiet dignity, embodying for the moment all that could preserve government by Constitution from being replaced by government by Executive Decree.

I observed his poise and weighed the searching questions which he put to all including myself. Deep down I felt that this lone man up there on the Bench was indeed "Pine" — stalwart and ready to withstand all storms. The eyes of the Nation were on him.

My main and rebuttal arguments before Judge Pine were specially printed and widely circulated by the steel companies. The following brief quotation therefrom presents what I conceived to be not only the issue of constitutional government but also the issue of freedom's survival:

> To say, as does the United States Attorney General, that the President in effect is "the steward of the nation" has implications that the people of the United States are wards of the steward.
>
> Hence, we have here a constitutional issue which rises far above the interests of any steel companies in this case or of labor unions. This is an issue which concerns the whole future of liberty in this country, because what can be done by a benevolent Executive imposing restrictions on himself, can later be done by one not so disposed when feeling the urge for unlimited power and a conviction that all is well as long as he is the steward of the American people and that the courts are not to be concerned with his idea of their welfare.

This concept that the powers of all branches of government were limited by the Constitution's specifications and that those not specified were not to be deemed a "residuum of power," was basic in Judge Pine's decision (103 F. Supp 562, 573★):

> *Neither singly nor in the aggregate do they grant the President, expressly or impliedly, as that term has heretofore been defined, the "residuum of power" or "inherent" power which authorizes him, as defendant claims, to take such action as he may deem to be necessary, including seizure of plaintiffs' properties, whenever in his opinion an emergency exists requiring him to do so in the public interest. Instead, in Congress is lodged, within Constitutional limitations, the power to "provide for the common defense and general welfare." Art. I, Sec. 8.*

The Secretary of Commerce then appealed to the United States Court of Appeals for the District of Columbia sitting *en banc*—nine judges. Unlike Judge Pine, it did not face up to the fundamental and preeminent constitutional issue. Instead, by a vote of five to four, the court stayed the preliminary injunctions issued by Judge Pine pending "a final determination" as to the evidence which the Secretary of Commerce claimed "fully proved" the emergency (197 F. 2d 582★★). With the aid of that loophole, the Executive Order and the seizure could stay in force almost indefinitely.

The steel companies rushed an appeal to the United States Supreme Court. All counsels met to consider strategy. The aim was to have *a single brief*.

But a brief by the equivalent of a bar association, where each member has pet views of his own for inclusion, loses force and consistency through its uncontrollable length. I finally withdrew and said that I would prepare a separate and short brief for our two clients, The Armco and Sheffield Steel Companies. In consequence, two briefs went to the Supreme Court—one long and one short. We built our short brief upon the text of the extraordinary admissions by Holmes

---

★ *Youngstown Sheet & Tube Co. v. Sawyer (US Dist. Ct. 1952).*

★★ *Sawyer v. Youngstown Sheet & Tube Co. (US Ct. App. DC 1952).*

Baldridge, the Assistant United States Attorney General, before Judge Pine and reproduced in the record on appeal:

> THE COURT (JUDGE PINE): *So you contend the Executive has unlimited power in time of an emergency?*
>
> MR. BALDRIDGE: *He has the power to take such action as is necessary to meet the emergency.*
>
> THE COURT (JUDGE PINE): *If the emergency is great, it is unlimited, is it?*
>
> MR. BALDRIDGE: *I suppose if you carry it to its logical conclusion, that is true. But I do want to point out that there are two limitations on the Executive power. One is the ballot box and the other impeachment.*
>
> THE COURT (JUDGE PINE): *Then, as I understand it, you claim that in time of emergency the Executive has this great power?*
>
> MR. BALDRIDGE: *That is correct.*
>
> THE COURT (JUDGE PINE): *And the executive determines the emergencies and the Courts cannot even review whether it is an emergency?*
>
> MR. BALDRIDGE: *That is correct.*

I was, however, in entire accord with the view that before the Supreme Court all steel companies should speak through a single counsel—John W. Davis, the foremost lawyer in the United States at the time. On May 12, 1952, the argument began. I was astonished to hear Mr. Davis open by saying that for the appellants there were two briefs before the Court, one long and one short, and that he recommended the Court read "Mr. Tuttle's short brief first."

By a vote of six to three, the Supreme Court reversed the decision of the Court of Appeals and affirmed and reinstated Judge Pine's injunction (343 U.S. 579★). Indeed, the Court went further and held that the fundamental constitutional issue was fully presented by the record and was "ripe for determination." The opinion closed with this sentence (p. 589):

> *The Founders of this Nation entrusted the lawmaking power to the Congress alone in both good and bad times. It*

★ *Youngstown Sheet & Tube Co. v. Sawyer (1952).*

would do no good to recall the historical events, the fears of power and the hopes for freedom that lay behind their choice. Such a review would but confirm our holding that this seizure order cannot stand.

On the other hand, the dissenting opinion (p. 708) described the President as "an officer on duty 365 days a year," and therefore possessed of "broad executive power...to avert disaster."

Thus ended (forever, I hope) the attempted precedent of seizing private property and governing by Executive Decree in time of peace and with Congress in session.

——————◆◆◆——————

SECTION 3

Indictment of James J. Davis, U.S. Senator and Secretary of Labor. The Drunken Juror.

IN THE LOOM OF LIFE, the flying shuttle of coincidence weaves the multicolored threads into unanticipated and unimaginable patterns. Such was the case of James J. Davis.

George Z. Medalie had succeeded me as United States Attorney. During his term, Pennsylvania Senator James J. Davis was indicted in the Southern District of New York for allegedly participating with others in illegally using the mails in furtherance of a lottery to raise funds for a charity. The lottery was conducted by the Fraternal Order of the Moose, of which James J. Davis was the General President; the charity was a large Illinois charitable institution for boys known as Mooseheart. Through Charles J. Margiotti, former Attorney General of Pennsylvania, I was retained to be trial counsel for Davis, to be assisted by Mr. Margiotti.

The case came to trial before Judge Frank Coleman and a jury. At first glance the defense seemed simple. No jury in New York would convict such a distinguished man for a part in a lottery to aid such a splendid charity. But in his opening, the prosecutor promised to show that some of the funds raised for Mooseheart had found their way into the Senator's personal bank account. Now that was a horse of another color!

Mr. Margiotti had brought on some witnesses from Mooseheart, including its Roman Catholic Chaplain. He called them to the stand, and elicited that there had been something of an understanding among the Moose to keep Senator Davis, the General President, out of acquaintance with the lottery.

That night I was sound asleep at home when the telephone rang at two in the morning. Margiotti was excitedly saying that "something terrible" had just happened, and he wanted my advice urgently.

The "something terrible" was that an Irish juror, in the back row, had just stormed drunkenly into his apartment and had demanded that the next morning Margiotti have thrown out of the jury box a certain Jewish juror, in the front row. Why? Because immediately after adjournment in the hall that juror had told others that he would not believe that Roman Catholic priest under oath.

Margiotti was concerned lest he himself be suspected or accused, however falsely, of planning to force a mistrial because of dissatisfaction with his witnesses. I replied that, now that he told me, he and I would not only be suspected but certainly accused of something far worse unless in the morning we informed both the prosecutor and the judge.

Before the trial resumed all counsel assembled in the judge's chambers. Margiotti told of the drunken visit at two in the morning. The judge marched us all back into the courtroom, ascended the bench, assembled the jury, declared the Davis trial in recess, and announced that he was "now sitting as a committing magistrate."

Margiotti was put under oath and repeated the story. The judge then called the offending juror from the back row. The poor fellow was frightened white. The judge told him of his constitutional rights and offered to adjourn for several days as a committing magistrate if the juror wanted to get a lawyer or have the judge assign one.

The juror stood still a while—with all eyes upon him and the pencils of the press poised. He then lifted his head, faced the judge and said that he did not want a lawyer; that what Mr. Margiotti had said was the truth; that the other juror's insult to the Catholic priest had made him so mad that he lost control, became drunk, and found himself in Mr. Margiotti's apartment demanding the other juror's removal.

There was again a long pause. Perhaps the juror's courageous honesty had saved him! The judge then interrogated all of the other jurors. They all denied uttering or hearing the alleged slur. The judge then marched all counsel back into his chambers. Of course it was a mistrial; but what to do with the announced role of the judge as "a committing magistrate?"

I ventured the thought that, if the sentence were to be imprisonment, the judge should insist on the juror first having or being assigned a lawyer. Perhaps, in the large crowd out in the hall, he had mistaken the source of the insult to the Catholic priest. No one could doubt that he had been blind drunk when he burst into Margiotti's apartment at two in the morning. On the other hand, he had made a courageous and honest confession. The prosecutor said he was not asking for blood.

The judge then marched us all back into the courtroom; resumed his role as "a committing magistrate"; gave the trembling juror a blistering lecture; and fined him $100! He then declared a mistrial of the Davis case.

I thought how true it was, as said of old:

> *The quality of mercy is not strain'd,*
> *It droppeth as the gentle rain from heaven*
> *Upon the place beneath. It is twice bless'd:*
> *It blesseth him that gives and him that takes.*

At the second trial of Senator Davis, I merely put on a flock of accountants who did their usual with figures and charts to explain how some of the lottery money mistakenly got into the Senator's personal bank account. I stressed the ancient rule of reasonable doubt and the Senator's spectacular life story from "puddler Jim" before blast furnaces in a steel mill to the Senate of the United States and the Cabinet of three Presidents.

Davis did not take the stand. He was acquitted.

SECTION 4

Spyridon Catapodis Sues Aristotle Onassis.
A Contract with the King of Saudi Arabia.

O N OCTOBER 17, 1955, Spyridon Catapodis sued Aristotle
Onassis in the New York Supreme Court for $14,210,000. The
amount represented an allegedly agreed compensation for alleged services in negotiating an agreement between Onassis and the King of
Saudi Arabia whereby Onassis would provide a fleet of tankers to carry
oil and in return would receive exclusive transportation rights.

Catapodis alleged that he successfully negotiated the thirty-year
agreement by paying, with the defendant's approval, substantial bribes
to important Saudi officials. In an affidavit executed in France,
Catapodis also alleged that when his compensation was refused, he was
"amazed" to discover that the defendant's signature on the written
agreement for his compensation had faded out. Worldwide publicity
was zealously given to these charges. In reply, Onassis publicly branded
them as malicious falsehoods. Thereupon Catapodis sued Onassis in
New York for $1,600,000 as damages for libel and in Washington,
D.C. for a like sum.

As counsel for Onassis, I moved and argued before Justice Samuel
M. Gold in our State Supreme Court to dismiss the Catapodis suit
for $14,210,000 on the grounds that the Court was *forum non conve-
niens*★ since the case was no concern of New York. Catapodis and
Onassis were residents of France, the alleged employment and breach
occurred in France, all the witnesses were in Europe or Asia, and the
alleged negotiations by Catapodis occurred in Saudi Arabia.

★ Not an appropriate site.

Judge Gold granted my motion with an extended opinion dated April 4, 1956, and officially reported in 2 Misc. 2d 234★. It has become a leading case settling the law as to the discretionary power of state courts to refuse jurisdiction over foreign controversies.

The core of the battle centered around the fact that in the name of Onassis' first wife, there were residential houses in Sutton Place, New York City, and in Oyster Bay, Long Island; that Onassis' marriage had been in this state; that she was listed in the telephone book at those addresses; that his two children had been born here; that he had at the time been present in these houses; and that in fact he was a domiciliary of New York.

Catapodis also charged that because of the wealth and influence of Onassis, he could not receive equal and impartial justice in the French courts. Judge Gold replied that he was "in no position to hold that a fair trial might not be held in the courts of France," and that, as to the attempt of Catapodis to besmirch Onassis for bribery (p. 244):

> ...*plaintiff himself, by his own admissions, sought to procure the contract for defendant and participated in the alleged briberies which he now criticizes.*

Later Catapodis formally abandoned his appeal from the dismissal.

As to the libel suit, I obtained court orders for the examination of Catapodis and others before trial and for the production of records relevant to the issues. As stated in one of my motions, my object was to obtain proof that the purpose of the Catapodis charges and the world-wide publicity given to them was "to seek to cause the King of Saudi Arabia to cancel or modify the aforesaid contract with the defendant (Onassis) and to injure the defendant in business and reputation."

Pursuant to these orders I conducted many sessions of examination before trial, and obtained the judicial overruling of objections to my questions. The trial became hot. Suddenly Catapodis rang down the curtain by discontinuing both libel suits (2 Misc. 2d 234, 236), and I so notified Onassis by letter of May 10, 1956.

★ *Catapodis v. Onassis (Sup. Ct. 1956).*

Thus, within the space of a year, all three of the fantastic Catapodis suits were knocked out.

In his 1968 book *Onassis,* author Willi Frischauer offered the following commentary on the foregoing:

> *True or false, the public airing of this dirty washing might have harmed Onassis' reputation irretrievably had the whole affair not suddenly taken a fantastic twist. In the United States, Onassis' lawyers fought the suit on the ground that neither he nor Catapodis was a citizen, and the case was duly thrown out of the court as beyond American jurisdiction.* *

SECTION 5

Gene McCann Sues Wall Street for Millions.

I N 1935 ONE GENE MCCANN, an ex-prizefighter, began an action in Federal Court in the Southern District of New York against most of Wall Street, including the New York Stock Exchange, the Curb Exchange, many of the biggest banks, investment houses, prominent financial individuals, and the National and City Better Business Bureaus—89 defendants, aggregating through their partnerships some 600 persons.

He charged that, in violation of the anti-trust laws, they all conspired to destroy his business as a stock broker in order to rid themselves of his competition. He asked treble damages totaling $30,000,000.

I was retained by the defendants as their trial counsel.

On March 3, 1936, the case came to trial before Judge Frederick H. Bryant of the Northern District, then on assignment in the Southern District. The trial took three weeks. The type-written narrative covered more than 800 pages. The documents introduced filled eighteen

---

* Willi Frischauer, *Onassis* (New York: Meredith, 1968), 163.

THE UNITED STATES ATTORNEY AT HIS DESK
IN THE FEDERAL BUILDING, *New York City*

volumes. The plaintiff's principal witness was himself, and much of the testimony consisted of my cross-examination of him. His trial counsel was Mr. Richardson.

At the close of the trial the jury rendered a verdict for all the defendants, and McCann's complaint was thereupon dismissed on the merits.

McCann then appealed to the United States Court of Appeals which, on November 13, 1939, unanimously affirmed with an opinion by Circuit Judge Learned Hand (107 F. 2d 908*). McCann then unsuccessfully petitioned the Supreme Court of the United States for a writ of certiorari (i.e., for leave to appeal) (309 U.S.684; April 8, 1940). In both these appellate courts he acted as his own attorney.

Shortly after he served his petition to the Supreme Court, he circulated to the defendants the following threatening notice, principally about myself, and expressed intention to move for my disbarment:

> *PLEASE TAKE FURTHER NOTICE that in his summation, and brief on your behalf before the Circuit Court of Appeals, your trial counsel, Charles H. Tuttle, Esq., referred to matters not included in the Record in the case at bar and violated divers other canons of legal ethics, that the undersigned will move the Supreme Court to strike from any brief that may be admitted to that Court on behalf of respondents in opposition to the aforementioned petition any matter not included in the Record, and that the undersigned will also move the said Supreme Court to punish for contempt, and to disbar from practice of law before that Court, all attorneys for respondents who acquiesce in such unethical conduct by failing to file their protest with the said Supreme Court and the undersigned.*

On his appeals McCann's prominent grievance was that I had unconscionably inflamed the jury against him by too passionate denunciations in my summation. In his brief of 156 pages before the Supreme Court, he reproduced many selections from what I had told the jury.

---

* McCann v. New York Stock Exchange (CA 2d 1939).

A month after the Supreme Court had denied him leave to appeal, McCann moved in that Court for a "rehearing" of his application.

The principal ground of his motion was that, three days after the Supreme Court's decision, there appeared in *The New York Times* an announcement that Judge Bryant's son (Robert Boyce Bryant) had become engaged to my daughter Jasmine Tuttle. His brief went on to say (pp. 2, 3):

> *The contemplated intermarriage between the families of the trial Judge and the defendants' trial counsel in the case at bar so shocked your petitioner that he investigated this relationship and learned the following facts:*
>
> a. *A lady who appeared on numerous occasions during the lengthy trial of this cause and who maintained a friendly attitude toward defendants' trial counsel, Mr. Tuttle, and who was known to petitioner only as a lawyer (which she is) and who frequently visited the trial Judge in his chambers and on occasion immediately thereafter conferred with Mr. Tuttle, and who was not suspected as a liaison between such trial counsel and the Judge, is now revealed as Mrs. Bryant, the wife of the Judge.*
>
> b. *During the course of the trial, Mrs. Bryant on several occasions was entertained at the home of Mr. Tuttle.*
>
> c. *The Tuttle and Bryant families have had intimate social relationships for a number of years prior to the trial of this cause.*
>
> d. *Judge Bryant and Mrs. Bryant have on a number of occasions prior to the trial, been house guests of Mr. and Mrs. Tuttle in the latter's Lake George home, remaining over weekends.*
>
> e. *The affianced son and daughter of the respective families were fellow students in Cornell University during the time of the trial and "going together."*

...Had petitioner known who the woman attorney was who acted as liaison in the courtroom between Tuttle and the trial Judge, he would have moved for a mistrial.

On the basis of these so-called "facts," McCann asked the Supreme Court to declare that Judge Bryant had been disqualified, that I had been and was in contempt of court, and that a new trial was necessary.

I replied with a brief affidavit that before the trial I had met Judge and Mrs. Bryant socially only once; that the engagement between his son and my daughter had not occurred until four years after the trial; and that Mrs. Bryant had been in the courtroom during the trial because she was the Judge's law clerk and herself a lawyer.

On May 6 1940, the Supreme Court denied without comment McCann's motion for "a rehearing" (310 U.S. 656).

Years passed. One day I was walking from Grand Central subway station to the Bar Association Building at 42 West 44th Street. As I passed the Roosevelt Hotel someone came up behind me and hissed in my ear: "Louse." I turned. It was Gene McCann.

Since I was not sure whether he was referring to me or to himself, I shall end this narrative with that word hanging in the air.

SECTION 6

The Bank of United States Closes. Legal Titans Battle.

DURING THE ECONOMIC DEPRESSION of the early 1930's, the doors of the Bank of United States closed. Its president was Bernard K. Marcus; its vice-president was Saul Singer; its general counsel was Isidor J. Kresel; and Herbert Singer, Saul Singer's son, was a law clerk in Mr. Kresel's office.

Immediately the public outcry rose like a tidal wave. Max Steuer, the Bar's most redoubtable cross-examiner, volunteered to act as special prosecutor without compensation. Marcus, the two Singers and Mr. Kresel, were indicted under Section 305 of the Penal Law, which declared that "any officer, director, agent or employee of a corporation subject to the Banking Law who abstracts or willfully misapplies any of the moneys, funds or property of such corporation, or willfully misapplies its credit, is guilty of felony."

The specific charge was that they procured the Municipal Safe Deposit Company, the Bank's wholly owned subsidiary and itself subject to the Banking Law, to pay to the Bolivar Development Corporation $2,009,518.45 to buy twenty-five shares of the Premier Development, which thereupon used the money to reduce its excessive indebtedness to the Bank. Marcus and Saul Singer were directors of the Municipal Safe Deposit Company.

The trial was in the Court of General Sessions. It lasted ten weeks. Emory Buckner, my predecessor as United States Attorney, was counsel for Saul Singer, Harold Medina for Herbert Singer, and I for Marcus. Mr. Kresel was ill and was severed from the trial. Mr. Steuer was the prosecutor and in his best form throughout. The courtroom was continuously packed to the walls with depositors. The press was ravening.

The central issue of law was the meaning of the statutory words "willfully misapplies." The trial court ruled that they were equivalent to voluntarily doing the act charged. It therefore permitted no defense to the effect that the act charged was done in good faith, and in reliance on the advice of distinguished counsel, and without any personal profit.

In effect, the defendants were guilty if they knowingly used the funds of the Municipal Safe Deposit Company in a way which in law was not within its corporate purposes. The trial court specifically charged the jury that the defendants were not on trial as officers of the Bank of United States. They were not charged with larceny. The jury need not find that they individually benefited. Self-enrichment or personal profit was not an element of the crime. Actually, it was conceded that no one had profited or lost and that what was done had no effect on the closing of the Bank.

Preparation for the trial covered weeks. Mr. Buckner and I had many conferences together and at times with Mr. Medina. All of us recognized that the public atmosphere could not be worse, and that the case was ready-made for Mr. Steuer's extraordinary talents.

My view was that Mr. Steuer would seek to try the case on defendants' management of the Bank and not on the indictment's narrow issue of the Municipal Safe Deposit Company, and that to put Marcus or Saul Singer on the stand would deliver to Mr. Steuer just such a wide-open opportunity on cross-examination. I felt that as to the prosecution's direct case we could prevent any effort to color the case with personal dereliction; that any contrary rulings would furnish valuable exceptions; and that the trial court's interpretation of the statute was reducing the case to a question of law which could be reviewed on appeal. Mr. Buckner, on the other hand, felt that by putting the defendants on the stand and thus subjecting them to Mr. Steuer's "full treatment," there was a fair chance that, if they stood up manfully, the jury might accord them a verdict.

Finally the prosecution rested and our motions to dismiss were denied. Early next morning, Mr. Buckner called me on the telephone to say that he had carefully reviewed all our conferences and had finally determined to call Saul Singer as a witness. I said that this would force me to call Marcus as a witness, but that in fairness Saul Singer should be the first to confront Mr. Steuer's fire. He agreed.

The cross-examination of Singer lasted for days and was a slaughter. Poor Singer was no match for the sword-play of Mr. Steuer who made the case seem a trial of whether mismanagement by the defendants was the cause of the shutting down the Bank. Mr. Kresel, having partly recovered from his illness, was called. The clashes between him and Mr. Steuer were so thrilling that they became daily diet fed to the eager public by the press.

But this autobiography is no place to retry the case. The jury convicted the three defendants, and the conviction was affirmed by the

Appellate Division and the Court of Appeals, with dissents in both courts (235 App. Div. 397; 261 N.Y. 268★). The Court of Appeals, however, dismissed the indictment of Herbert Singer. Harold Medina's argument in that Court was a moving masterpiece of the forensic art. Young Singer had aided as a clerk but not as a participant. The Court of Appeals unanimously so agreed.

After the decision of the Court of Appeals, Mr. Kresel was brought to trial on the same indictment and was convicted. His appeal was removed to the Appellate Division, Third Department, which in January, 1935, reversed and dismissed the indictment (243 App. Div. 137). The prevailing opinion declared (p. 144):

> *The evidence is insufficient to warrant his [Mr. Kresel's] conviction. The judgment in this case is grossly wrong and a wicked perversion of justice.*

From that dismissal the prosecution never appealed to the Court of Appeals.

Thus the story of this indictment closes with what to some is an extraordinary anomaly. As to Mr. Kresel, the Appellate Division said (243 App. Div. 137, 142):

> *He [Kresel] swore that he believed the plan to be within the law. . . . When the appellant gave the advice the question was unsettled. . . . A lawyer is not to be held criminally responsible because he honestly gives mistaken advice upon a doubtful question of law. . . . Infallibility is an attribute of neither lawyer nor judge.*

Nor, I comment, is "infallibility an attribute" of the client who in good faith relies upon his lawyer's advice upon such "a doubtful question of law."

Since the conviction of their lawyer was "a wicked perversion of justice," why otherwise as to the conviction of his clients, Marcus and Singer, who relied on his advice?

★ *People v. Marcus (1933).*

Jules Fink and the Jockey Club.
A Talk with Bernard M. Baruch.

O N FEBRUARY 28, 1950, I was told by the receptionist that a Mr. Jules Fink wished to see me. I knew nothing of him.

Fink told me that he was the owner of six thoroughbred race horses; that the Jockey Club, which had annually given him a racing license for some five years, had refused a renewal; and that the Club would not tell him why. He said the refusal could destroy the value of his horses.

I was skeptical about him, and asked for references. He told me that if I were in next day at 11:00 o'clock, Bernard M. Baruch would telephone me, vouch for him, and urge that I act. I laughed to myself.

I had been for years a colleague of Mr. Baruch on the City's Board of Higher Education. I recognized his voice on the telephone next day at 11:00 a.m. He said that Fink was his consultant at the racetrack; that he would vouch for his character; that he himself had been refused the reasons; that he regarded the Jockey Club's action as offensively arbitrary; and he hoped I would do what I could.

Fink returned. I told him that several decades previously, when I was with Davies, Stone & Auerbach, I had had a partner whom I believed had since become the counsel for the Jockey Club. I would call him from another room.

I told my former partner that I did not wish to become involved in a possible case of doping a horse or bribing a jockey or the like, and that if such were the fact I would keep his statement in confidence and simply decline to undertake Fink's case. His reply was "I cannot tell you." I asked whether he meant that he did not know or that he would not. He repeated: "I cannot tell you." I confess I became mad. "That answer," I said, "has put me in Fink's case as of right now."

Accordingly, I began suit against the Jockey Club. The Club was a private and very exclusive body run by a board of directors privately selected. By act of the Legislature in 1934 (Ch. 310, sec. 5) the Club had been authorized to license owners, trainers and jockeys. I charged that the power to license was exclusively a function of the State itself and could not be constitutionally delegated to a private individual or a private body.

The Appellate Division, First Department, unanimously held against me without even writing an opinion (277 App. Div. 861*). I appealed to the Court of Appeals. After full argument, that Court unanimously reversed (302 N.Y. 216 [1951]) and held unconstitutional the Legislature's Act of 1934.

In its opinion the Court of Appeals said (p. 225):

> *In our view the delegation by the Legislature of its licensing power to The Jockey Club, a private corporation, is such an abdication as to be patently an unconstitutional relinquishment of legislative power in violation of section 1 of article III of the Constitution of this State which provides: "The legislative power of this State shall be vested in the Senate and Assembly."*
> *... Even if the legislature's power to license had been delegated to a governmental agency, the statute now challenged would have to be stricken down for lack of guides and proper standards.*

The salutary teaching of that decision is that in our constitutional system of government, under law there is no room at all for the delegation of the power and sovereignty of the State to a private individual or private body. Nor is there room for private officialdom depriving a man of his property and rights without telling him why.

Mr. Baruch called and thanked me.

---

* *Fink v. Cole (1950).*

SECTION 8

The Audacity and Fall of Martin T. Manton, Senior Judge, U.S. Court of Appeals.

WHEN I BECAME United States Attorney, Martin T. Manton was Senior Judge of the United States Circuit Court of Appeals for the Second Circuit. As such, he ranked next to the Justices of the Supreme Court of the United States.

During my preoccupation with the Judge Winslow matter in 1929 and accompanying bankruptcy investigation★, Judge Manton invited me to his chambers and said that he would like to recommend me to the President for appointment to his Court. He spoke as if his recommendation could have decisive weight. I warmly thanked him and asked for several days to consider. Here was what could be a wholly new direction for my life; but I never had had ambition for a judgeship, and felt no talent or taste for its obligations and confinements. I respectfully declined.

Years passed. In August 1932 I was sitting on the porch of my summer home at Lake George with my feet on the railing and my mind on the glittering water. Someone brought me the day's *New York Times*. My eyes popped, and my feet came down with a bang.

There, on the first page, was a big headline that the American Brake Shoe and Foundry Company, a client of Breed, Abbott & Morgan, had filed in the Federal District Court a creditor's bill in equity for the appointment of a temporary receiver for the Interborough Rapid Transit Company. The article said that Circuit Judge Manton had ex parte: transferred the case to himself and out of the hands of District Judges; appointed Victor J. Dowling and Thomas E. Murray temporary receivers; appointed Chadbourne, Stanchfield & Levy (of which firm Dowling was a member) as attorneys for the receivers; and designated himself as the judge in charge of the receivership.

★ See Chapter 6, Section 5, "*The Conduct of Federal Judge Winslow...*"

I rushed to the telephone and talked to my partner who had charge of starting the action. Of course, a creditor's class suit in equity was proper and normal because the Interborough was admittedly insolvent, its creditors were entitled to the protection of a receivership, and our client was a very large and representative creditor. But, I said, the ensuing actions of Judge Manton in grabbing the case would cause "all hell" to break loose, and make it vital to see that neither our client nor ourselves were burnt in the judicial holocaust. I left for New York at once.

Almost immediately, stockholder suits were begun and motions made in the District Court to vacate everything that Judge Manton had done because of lack of jurisdiction. Our client was included as a defendant. The unheard of and unseemly spectacle thus presented was a line-up of the District Court Judges against the Senior Circuit Judge. Nearly every law firm of prominence "got in the act." The press and civic bodies began to demand investigations.

On October 13, 1932, and after extended argument in which I took part, District Judge Woolsey rendered an extended decision (1 F. Supp. 809*). He characterized Judge Manton as a "usurping or intruding judge" and held that Judge Manton's orders were without jurisdiction and void. But he in no way questioned the sufficiency and propriety of our client's complaint or of its capacity to sue representatively on behalf of creditors.

On appeal Judge Woolsey's orders were unanimously reversed by the United States Court of Appeals (Judge Manton not sitting) (61 F. 2d 934). The reversal was unanimously affirmed by the United States Supreme Court (289 U.S. 479; May 29, 1933).

But the opinion of the Supreme Court closed with the rebuke to Judge Manton that "the possession of power is one thing; the propriety of its exercise is another"; and that he should consider withdrawing from further participation in the receivership proceedings and thus "open the way for another judge with appropriate authority to conduct the further proceedings."

Throughout all these proceedings the legitimate interest of our client (the American Brake Shoe & Foundry Company) and of the creditor class that it represented, was kept free from challenge in any of

---

* *Johnson v. Manhattan Railway Co. (DC NY 1932).*

the judicial cross-fire. Judge Manton decided to disregard this recommendation by the Supreme Court, saying: "I must continue the performance of my duties to judicially supervise these receivership proceedings" (4 F. Supp. 68; June 28, 1933★).

In 1938 Judge Manton was indicted for conspiracy with others to obtain bribes for favorable decisions. He was convicted; and the conviction was affirmed on appeal (107 F. 2d 834★★). The Supreme Court denied him leave to appeal (309 U.S. 664). Neither the American Brake Shoe Company nor its creditor's equity suit, nor the foregoing Interborough Rapid Transit Company receivership were part of the subject matter of the indictment.

Before his trial, Judge Manton sought trial counsel. Among others, he consulted me. But I pointed out that if he took the witness stand in his own defense (as he said he intended to do), the prosecution might seek to cross-examine him as to his course in the Interborough receivership; if so, my presence as his trial counsel would, in that event, embarrass him and myself, and, in view of Canon 19 of the Canons of Professional Ethics, might compel me to ask leave to withdraw.

If one were a complete pessimist one might well argue that the human scene shows that Death is the only officiator not amenable to bribery.

SECTION 9

Putting Saints on the Façade of St. Thomas Church, New York City

GEORGE S. SCOTT DIED in 1912. He had been a prominent communicant and generous supporter of St. Thomas Episcopal Church, Fifth Avenue and Fifty-third Street, New York City.

Sensing that his four children might not have descendants of their own, he directed by his will that, if they all died childless, the remainder would go to St. Thomas Church:

★ *American Brake Shoe & Foundry Co. v. Interborough Rapid Transit Co. (DC NY 1933).*
★★ *United States v. Manton (CA 2d 1939).*

...for the purpose of erecting and maintaining, in such place as they (the church vestry) may select a building or buildings for the care of persons suffering from tuberculosis, to be called the Scott Memorial Home.

As it so happened, all Scott's children died childless—the last one on December 18, 1957. The remainder of Scott's estate thereupon vested in St. Thomas Church for the purpose stated. Its value was $1,600,000.

Everyone agreed that, although tuberculosis had been a prime killer when Scott's will was drawn, medical science had so advanced that by the end of 1957 a home for sufferers from tuberculosis was outdated. In consequence, St. Thomas claimed the remainder outright for its own charitable uses.

On the other hand, the State Attorney General claimed that, if the Church took the remainder at all, it would be obliged to hold and use it as a trust for whatever charitable purpose the court should determine to be *cy pres* (old French for "next nearest") to the testator's intent.

Thereupon the Surrogate determined that the *cy pres* was "the care of persons suffering from respiratory or thoracic diseases," and that, since St. Thomas Church felt itself unable to make such use of the fund, the Surrogate would designate an agency to take over the fund and use it for "the required result" (19 Misc. 2d 18★). The Church appealed to the Appellate Division which unanimously affirmed the Surrogate (10 A.D. 2d 556).

The Court of Appeals granted leave to appeal; but, since that court had no power to review questions of fact, and the question of "next nearest" was eminently one of fact, the prospect was dark indeed.

I advised the vestry of the Church to adopt and authorize me to include in my brief for the Court of Appeals a resolution greatly softening its outright claim to the fund. The terms of that resolution and what came of it will soon be stated.

With this background, I found myself on my feet at the bar of the Court of Appeals. Immediately, several judges asked why the issue was not one of fact and hence concluded by the unanimous affirmance

---

★ *In re Scott's Estate (Sur. Ct. 1959).*

below. I argued that the substitution of "respiratory and thoracic diseases" was so arbitrarily far from any conceivable intent on the part of
the testator as to be an *error of law,* and that some consideration should
be given to Scott's long connection with St. Thomas and his obvious
solicitude for it. But I sensed that I was not getting anywhere.

Suddenly Judge Van Voorhis leaned forward and asked: "Is there
not a middle ground?" I pointed to the belated resolution of the vestry
appearing in my brief, and suggested that the ideal *cy pres* would be to
recognize Scott's devotion to the Church by: a) providing from the
fund the comparatively small sum of $350,000 to complete the façade,
together with a bronze Scott memorial tablet; and, b) by giving the
balance as a Scott Memorial Fund to a great Episcopal institution, St.
Luke's Hospital, which had a large convalescent clinic in delightful
surroundings in Connecticut. The Attorney General's spokesman
vigorously protested, and denounced the vestry's resolution as a
belated afterthought invented after the decision below. I went back to
the City with "my fingers crossed" all the way.

After two months' deliberation the Court of Appeals reversed both
lower courts by a vote of 4 to 3 on December 1, 1960 (8 N.Y. 2d 419).
The Court's opinion, written by Judge Van Voorhis, held that their
cy pres pitch for "respiratory and thoracic diseases" was so remote as to
be error of law, and that (p. 428):

> *Nevertheless it does not follow that none (of the fund) should
> be expended on this edifice, since we are persuaded that the
> testator was concerned among other matters with attaching his
> family name, if possible, to a building or buildings maintained
> by St. Thomas Church. Appellant's brief states that the church
> vestry has modified its original position by adopting a resolution
> "that $350,000 be used to provide an appropriate outward and
> visible memorial on the Fifth Avenue façade of the Church,
> and that the income from the balance be devoted to the establish-
> ment and maintenance of a clinical program in conjunction with
> St. Luke's Hospital or some other Episcopal hospital willing to
> provide and designate such a program as a memorial to George
> S. Scott and his family."*

A judgment accordingly was entered, and the fund was so used. The $350,000 completed the façade as originally planned, plus a bronze memorial tablet to George S. Scott. St. Luke's Hospital got the balance for its clinic, also to be in memory of George S. Scott.

A main feature in completing the façade was the addition of rows of statued saints in the high-arched entry. When Dr. Morris, the rector, came down to a victory celebration at the Wall Street Club, I gently intimated that the Roman Catholic Church had a St. **Charles** Borromeo; that it was not too late for the Anglican Branch to have a St. **Charles** also; and that the rows of statued saints facing Fifth Avenue

would be a nice place for his inclusion. Unhappily, I made less progress with the rector than I had made with the Court of Appeals.

On occasional meetings with Judge Van Voorhis, he has confided that doubtless there was on the façade a carved saint with his name on it; but, if so, the statue was so lost in its lofty Gothic tangle that he had not been able to discern it from the street.

Alas, I am afraid one has to be dead a long time to be marbled as a saint!

ST. THOMAS CHURCH, *Fifth Avenue*

The statues of the Scott Memorial are featured prominently in this classic Norman Rockwell painting, *"LIFT UP THINE EYES,"* created in 1969, the same year Charles Tuttle wrote the story of the St. Thomas façade for his memoirs.

The Rhode Island U.S. District Court Is Plumbed for Women Jurors.

O N NOVEMBER 18, 1946, the Federal Grand Jury in Providence, Rhode Island, returned an indictment charging eighteen defendants with having violated anti-trust laws by combining to restrain interstate trade in the sales of chlorinating equipment for use in the sanitary field. Charged as principal offender was the Wallace & Tiernan Company, a large corporation in Belleville, New Jersey, with annual sales for 1948 cited to be in excess of $14,000,000.

The only federal courthouse in Rhode Island was in Providence. The building dated back to the Civil War; its ancient plumbing facilities reflected the fact that women had never been allowed on the court's grand and petit juries. The courthouse had always been exclusively a masculine enclave in Rhode Island, notwithstanding that the female population of the State outnumbered the male and notwithstanding that the League of Women Voters in Providence had for years encircled the court with protest.

Shortly before the indictment was filed, the Supreme Court of the United States held in *Ballard v. United States* (329 U.S. 187 [1944]) — a case coming up from California — that where a state law made women eligible for state grand and petit juries, they became equally eligible for the federal jury service, and any systematic exclusion of them invalidated the proceeding.

The State of Rhode Island had an amazing statute which made women eligible for state jury service in the populous counties of Providence and Newport but excluded them in the three less populous counties. No such statutory curiosity had been before the Supreme Court in the *Ballard* case.

Nevertheless, as counsel for Wallace & Tiernan (and to the accompaniment of cheers by Rhode Island's League of Women Voters), I moved to dismiss the indictment as a nullity because of the Federal Court's unconstitutional systematic exclusion of women from jury service.

Federal Judge Hartigan seemed dismayed. He said that he was merely a judge and not a plumbing expert, and he doubted that the old building had been designed for other than men. Besides, the state law made women ineligible in a majority of the counties—three out of five. I assembled affidavits from eager plumbing concerns in Providence that, for a comparatively modest sum, they could provide the required additional facilities. I also submitted statistics that where by state law women were eligible, less than five percent sought exemption—a record men did not attain.

The result was that counsel for the government and my associates and I went over the building inch by inch, drawing up floor diagrams, exploring locations, assessing costs, and procuring expert opinions from plumbers and architects. The newspapers of Rhode Island also took up the hue and cry. They were unanimous for women jurors everywhere.

Finally, Judge Hartigan rendered an extended opinion which went minutely into the washroom problems and (I thought) sadly concluded:

> *The question raises sufficient doubt in the mind of the Court to resolve that doubt in favor of the defendants. ... The defendants' motions to dismiss (the indictment) are granted.*

(*In re Wallace & Tiernan Co.*, 76 F. Supp. 215, 216*).

Immediately the League of Women Voters marched triumphantly into the old Federal Building. By the time I left Providence, women were beaming from all the jury boxes, and the politicians were rushing to change the state law so as to make them eligible in the other three counties. The masculine rout was complete.

I recall that there was a movement to make me an honorary member of the League of Women Voters; but that was over twenty years ago. I have been in Providence only once since.

The moral seems to be that ingenious discrimination in plumbing should not be deemed to create discrimination in matters of capacity to administer justice.

---

* *(USDC, Dist. R.I. 1948).*

SECTION 11

Legalizing "The United Church of Christ." The Legacy of Dr. S. Parkes Cadman.

A S I LOOK BACK OVER MY PROFESSIONAL LIFE, the memories of this particular case and its outcome are among the happiest of all.

For me the story starts with an outstanding minister of the Gospel and civic leader, the Rev. Dr. S. Parkes Cadman, pastor of the Congregational Church in Brooklyn. After his death on July 12, 1936, the Church was appropriately named "Cadman Memorial Church."

Dr. Cadman was the first Protestant clergyman to establish a radio pulpit with a regular coast to coast program. He was eagerly listened to by millions. For many years until his death I had the honor of being the treasurer of what was called "The Cadman Radio Pulpit." Dr. Cadman was a man of the broadest theological and liturgical views, and an early proponent of what has now come to be known as the ecumenical movement.

Once a month he presided at a large dinner at the Hamilton Club in Brooklyn for outstanding men in the public life of the borough regardless of creed or color. The privilege of being a guest was eagerly sought by Brooklyn's chief officials, educators and professional men. Notwithstanding that I was a Manhattanite, I was included because of my office with the Cadman Radio Pulpit.

In order that all the diners could talk freely without concern for publicity, the rule was strict that everything said was in the utmost confidence and off the record. A violator was not invited again.

The table talk was scintillating and far-ranging. After dinner we all gathered around Dr. Cadman in his library and listened to his marvelous discoursing on some vital topic of the moment — municipal, national or international. One and all left with a clearer vision and a better insight into the moral aspect which underlay the particular human problem which Dr. Cadman had analyzed.

The Congregational churches traced their origin to the Reformation in England dating to 1581, and in this country to the Pilgrims in 1620. By tradition and usage, the approximately 5800 churches in America in 1950 were independent, self-governing fellowships without any central ecclesiastical control, but organized into district associations, state conferences and conventions and a General Council, national in scope.

In 1931 — during Dr. Cadman's lifetime and under his leadership — the "Congregational Christian Church" came into being pursuant to a "Plan of Union of the Congregational and Christian Churches." The Plan contained the following:

> *Invitation is extended to other bodies to join this union. In the event of favorable action by one or more national bodies, it is agreed that a new and more inclusive name shall be chosen for the General Council. . . . If a desire for that unity for which the Master once prayed be the actuating motive of all plans and all acts, the way will become clear, as we proceed, where now it may appear filled with uncertainties, hesitation and hindrance. We may be sure that no legal entanglements will be too difficult, no ecclesiastical customs too deeply fixed, no sentiments seem too precious to yield, no ambition or personal commitments too intense, if the will to achieve be ours and the Spirit of God lead us. Going forward, thus led, we may ourselves secure, and may make plain to others, the road to joyous fellowship and enlarged usefulness.*

No other religious body in America had made as many gestures toward union with other religious bodies as had the Congregational Christian denominations.

After Dr. Cadman's death, a further proposed merger, to be known as "The United Church of Christ," took form in 1947 in accordance with a "basis of Union" between the Congregational

Christian Churches and the Evangelical and Reformed Church. The
Plan was similar to that which was successful in 1931. It was approved
overwhelmingly in a referendum to all voting levels of the Congregational Christian Churches. Nevertheless there was a small but potent
minority which opposed with determination, even to the point of a
threatened schism. The ground of opposition was that the Evangelical
and Reformed Church was Presbyterian rather than Congregational
in its polity.

Amazingly, the Cadman Memorial Church, which had fallen under
different influences after Dr. Cadman's death, was a leader in the opposition.

In 1949 this Church, suing under the name of the "Cadman
Memorial Congregational Society of Brooklyn," began a class suit in
the New York Supreme Court in Brooklyn to enjoin the Basis of
Union and any action under it. It moved for a declaratory judgment of
illegality. The motion came on for trial and argument before Mr. Jus-
tice Steinbrink, and was opposed by the attorneys for the General
Council of the Congregational Christian Churches of the United
States.

Judge Steinbrink granted the motion and entered a judgment
enjoining as illegal any union with the Evangelical and Reformed
Church (197 Misc. 124*). In his opinion, Judge Steinbrink used strong
words of condemnation. To quote one passage:

> The Basis of Union is a conglomeration of confusion and
> conflicting statements with a cacophony of ideas. There are so
> many vague provisions in the Basis of Union; there are so many
> differing viewpoints as illustrated by the testimony of both clerics
> and laymen who have testified, and more especially empha-
> sized in the defendant's trial brief, where in supplement No.1,
> there are numerous quotations from the Basis of Union followed
> by the statement, "this requires explanation." If defendant's
> counsel believes that so much of the Basis of Union requires

---

* Cadman Memorial Congregational Society of Brooklyn v. Kenyon (Sup. Ct.
1950)

explanation, then it is small wonder that the nonlegal mind, and especially the ministers, sense danger to themselves and to their churches in this document.

After Judge Steinbrink's decision, the General Council of the Congregational Christian Churches of the United States retained me as its counsel to brief and argue its appeal to the Appellate Division.

On studying the record, I found that the judgment entered by Judge Steinbrink was the complete antithesis of what Dr. Cadman had been known by me to believe and represent.

The judgment did not merely enjoin the Basis of Union; it perpetually *excommunicated* any church or member thereof who joined the proposed Union. It adjudged in advance forfeiture thereby of all right to, benefit from and voice in, the temporalities and spirituality of the denomination. It further perpetually enjoined the General Council "present and future" from "uniting with any other body or organization whatsoever" "by or through any method or means whatsoever." Any churches which joined the proposed union thereby "removed themselves from the Congregational Christian fellowship."

The judgment effectively locked up the Congregational Christian Church in solitary confinement and appointed the courts as its jailers. It could go further and obstruct and even defeat the growing movement for federated unity among the scattered Protestant denominations. Was it from Dr. Cadman that I felt a call to break open the jail and free the prisoners?

In utter disregard of my own strict rule against such monstrous imposition on an Appellate Court, my brief ran over 180 pages.

The appeal was argued by me in March 1952, in the Appellate Division, Second Department, before Presiding Justice Nolan and Justices Adel, MacCrate, Schmidt and Wenzel. The decision was not only a reversal but a dismissal of the complaint with costs, Judge Wenzel alone dissenting. The court's opinion was (279 App. Div. 1015-6):

> *In controversies such as this, ecclesiastical or doctrinal questions may be inquired into only insofar as it may be necessary to do so to determine the civil or property rights of the parties.*

The civil courts do not interfere with ecclesiastical matters in which temporal rights are not involved. Plaintiffs have failed to establish any right or interest in or to the funds or other assets which plaintiffs asserted were held in trust, which requires or permits a determination of the ecclesiastical issues presented.

Plaintiffs then appealed to the Court of Appeals where (on my seventy-fourth birthday, April 21, 1953) extended argument on even more extended briefs took place before Chief Judge Lewis and Judges Desmond, Fuld, Dye, Froessell and Conway. On January 7, 1954, the decision of the Appellate Division was affirmed, Judges Froessell and Conway dissenting (306 N.Y. 151). The plaintiffs' motion for re-argument was denied on March 11, 1954 (306 N.Y. 851).

In its opinion, the Court of Appeals said:

On this record, the proof having established that the Basis of Union is voluntary and in no way interferes with Congregational faith or manner of worship, and the plaintiffs having failed to establish any direct or beneficial interest in and to the unrestricted funds of the General Council, its various boards, agencies and instrumentalities, and having failed to show that such general funds are to be used for other than authorized charter purposes, the complaint was properly dismissed on the merits.

Concerning Dr. Cadman, the Court of Appeals noted:

According to the record, the Cadman Church occupies a unique place among Congregational Christian Churches, being not only one of the oldest in America, but one of the largest. ...Its name honors the memory of a distinguished former preacher, the Reverend S. Parkes Cadman.

I felt honored to have the privilege of laying this decision at his feet, where his memory will ever stand among the other immortal servants of Christ in this our America.

The United Church Of Christ was legitimately born!

SECTION 12

Combat with Louis Nizer in the Case of Victor Ridder, the Refugee Professor.

For many years I had the privilege of close friendship with Victor Ridder, a prominent civic and philanthropic leader in New York City. During his career, Victor was frequently entrusted by governors and mayors with governmental roles. His father had come to America to liberate himself from Kaiser Wilhelm's regime, and had founded a nationwide chain of German-American newspapers. The New York City *Staats-Zeitung* was one. When his father died, Victor and his brother Joseph inherited the chain.

For years three men came on Saturday afternoons to Victor's apartment to play contract bridge with him. One was Nathan D. Perlman, a Justice of the Court of Special Sessions, and President of B'nai Brith; the second was Hubert T. Delany, a Justice of the Court of Domestic Relations; and the third was myself. Victor was a dedicated Roman Catholic. A fraternal gathering of such a foursome—bringing together a Jew, a Negro, a Protestant and a Catholic—would have been inconceivable many years previously.

During World War II, Friedrich Wilhelm Foerster, a refugee professor, was given a lectureship at Columbia University. In a public statement he called Victor Ridder "a concealed Nazi." Victor responded by publicly denouncing the Professor as "a malicious liar." Whereupon Foerster retained the redoubtable lawyer Louis Nizer and sued Victor for libel and $100,000 in damages. Obviously, the issue was of the simplest: Was Victor a concealed Nazi, or was Foerster a malicious liar?

Victor's defense was conducted by the staff lawyers of the *Staats-Zeitung*. The case was tried before Justice Pecora and went to the jury for a verdict in the midst of the greatest ticker tape parade

Broadway had ever known. The Conqueror of the Nazis, General Dwight D. Eisenhower, was riding in laurelled triumph to City Hall. Everyone, including the jury, was hanging out of windows, singing and shouting adulation. All the country's great were assembled on the City Hall's steps, with a full battery of supporting orators. Victor's chance was less than the proverbial snowball in you know where.

When things quieted down, the jury filed in and asked the Judge what was the maximum they could award the plaintiff. The Judge said not more that the $100,000 asked in the complaint. The jury room's door revolved. The verdict was $100,000.

Several weeks later, when the four bridge cronies were assembled in Victor's living room, he asked me to come into the case and conduct his appeal.

On studying the record I saw what chiefly had gone wrong. Louis Nizer was a master of provocation and insinuating cross-examination — second only to Max Steuer, in my experience. Victor's temper was proverbially volatile, and Nizer's cross-examination had blown it sky-high. Anyone interested in reading that cross-examination will find it verbatim in Nizer's bestseller, *My Life in Court.*

My brief in the Appellate Division largely focused on that cross-examination and on what I claimed to be its inflammatory appeals to prejudice (with General Eisenhower coming from the horizon), and what I also claimed were highly prejudicial rulings in the course of the trial.

Louis and I then waged battle at the podium of the Appellate Division. Ultimately, that Court rendered the following decision (275 App. Div. 665★):

> FRIEDRICH W. FOERSTER, Respondent, v. VICTOR F. RIDDER, Appellant. Judgment unanimously reversed and a new trial ordered, with cost to the appellant to abide the event, unless plaintiff stipulates to reduce the judgment to $15,000 in which event the judgment, as so modified, is affirmed, without cost. No opinion. Settle order on notice. Present — Dore, J.P., Cohn, Callahan, Van Voorhis, and Shientag, J.J.

★ *Foerster v. Ridder (1949).*

I felt a little brotherly sorrow for my professional friend, Louis Nizer, who must have had the case on a very pleasing contingency in the event that the verdict for $100,000 stood.

Victor's payment of $15,000 ended the case. When he died some years later, the great of the City came to his funeral to do him honor.

There should be a "Handbook for Witnesses," with its first chapter devoted to how to keep cool when faced with hot cross-examination.

> *When a man points a finger at someone else,*
> *he should remember that four of his fingers*
> *are pointing at himself.*
> — LOUIS NIZER

SECTION 13

Combat with Louis Nizer in "The War of the Roses."

IN HIS POPULAR AUTOBIOGRAPHY, *My Life in Court,* Louis Nizer writes at length about "The War of the Roses," and narrates his "victory" for Eleanor Holm Rose on her divorce action against the famous theatrical producer, Billy Rose, who was represented by the eminent attorney, Arthur Garfield Hays.

While ruminating on the Rose case in his 1961 book, Mr. Nizer made this statement:

> *The Rose case, like many others involving more prominent participants, need never have become a public, knockdown and drag-out fight. Since only money stood in the way, it is not inappropriate to point out that ultimately Rose paid far more (including a substantial property settlement) than he could have settled for, and in addition, he had to pay accumulated counsel fees to distinguished counsel, a former gubernatorial candidate, Charles H. Tuttle, whom he brought into the case, and to me as Eleanor's counsel.**

★ Louis Nizer, *My Life in Court* (New York: Doubleday, 1961), 181.

Lest this statement leave the impression that I was a captive adornment in the triumphal procession, I adopt Al Smith's famous slogan *"Let's look at the record."*

My sole connection with "The War of the Roses" was to act as counsel in opposing **two** motions by Mr. Nizer.

The first motion, dated October 2, 1952, was for the discovery and inspection of all books, records, documents, papers, memoranda, income tax returns, etc., relating, directly or indirectly, to the affairs of Billy Rose, of every person or corporation acting as his agent or trustee, and every corporation or partnership which he controlled "for the years 1940 to date" — a period of twelve years.

The motion was granted at Special Term, but with limitation to the period "from January 1, 1945 to date," and without prejudice to an application to extend the period back to November 1939.

Billy Rose appealed; and I was retained by his attorney to brief and argue his appeal. My contention in the Appellate Division was that the order for discovery was "unreasonable, oppressive and far beyond any legitimate requirement of justice herein"; that Mr. Nizer's motion was designed to be "as oppressive and arbitrary as ingenuity could devise"; and that it should have been denied.

The decision of the Appellate Division was unanimous reversal and a denial of Mr. Nizer's motion. The Court said (282 App. Div. 682★):

> *Order unanimously reversed and the motion for discovery and inspection denied. We think the extraordinary remedy of discovery and inspection is unnecessary in the circumstances in this case. Application may be made for modification of the order for examination before trial so as to enable plaintiff to compel production of books and records before the referee named by Special Term, who will supervise the use of same for the limited purposes provided in section 296 of the Civil Practice Act. Settle order on notice.*

Some months later the Appellate Division heard Billy Rose's appeal from an order for his examination before trial. I contended, among other things, that the procrastinating tactics of Mrs. Rose's

---

★ *Rose v. Rose (1953).*

attorneys were designed to compel Billy Rose "to continue to pay this enormous temporary alimony, and to suffer dispossession of his home, and to suffer further postponement of the final trial."

In response, the Appellate Division unanimously ruled on December 10, 1953 (282 App. Div. 1028):

> *We are unwilling that additional and circuitous collateral proceedings delay a final judgment in this case. The further examination now directed shall proceed promptly and continuously before the Referee. It shall be completed on or before January 15, 1954, and the trial of the action promptly resumed and continuously prosecuted to judgment. Settle order on notice.*

I am treasuring the ensuing letter from Billy Rose:

> *Thanks, dear Charles—and for the rest of my fool life, call on me for anything.*
>
> – BILLY ROSE

SECTION 14

Archbishop, Later Ecumenical Patriarch, Athenagoras. "The Grand Cross of the Order of the Holy Sepulchre."

SHORTLY AFTER THIS GREAT Christian leader and statesman came to the United States to be Archbishop of the Greek Orthodox Church for the Diocese of North and South America, my posts with the National Council of Churches and with the Protestant Council of the City brought me the privilege of contacts with him.

From the first I sensed his vision of Christianity as a united brotherhood of man. In the power of his vision, he steadily marched forward, receiving worldwide honors as he went about exchanging the kiss of peace with the leaders of all branches of Christendom, helping to heal the fratricidal wounds that have festered for over a thousand years.

He loomed as large and impressive physically as he did spiritually—about seven feet
tall, with the raiment, staff, medallion and
beard of office, and with kindly eyes deeply set
in a patriarchal face.

In the legal field I had the honor of advising him from time to time on matters of
American law. Finally, came a serious law suit.

Archbishop Athenagoras had been duly
appointed and consecrated to head this great
American See by the Primate and Holy Synod
of the Greek Orthodox Church. Nevertheless,
in September 1942, a dissident priest claimed to
have become in this country a "Bishop of the
Eastern Orthodox Church" and head of a rival
diocese of that name. He was proposing to consecrate an "Archbishop" for it.

PATRIARCH
ATHENAGORAS

In an encyclical and from the pulpit of the Greek Cathedral in New
York City, Athenagoras denounced him as an imposter and ecclesiasti-
cally a layman, and warned the faithful against deception. Thereupon the
"Bishop" sued the Archbishop and his Diocese in federal court, charging conspiracy and libel, and asking damages in the sum of $100,000.

As counsel for the defense, I moved to strike out the complaint or
major portions of it as impertinent and scandalous. The judge denied
my motion (7 F.R.D. 223*).

Thus there seemed to be transferred from the Primate and Holy
Synod of the Greek Orthodox Church to a jury in New York the determination of who was Archbishop of North and South America.

The trial opened before Judge William Bondy and a jury. The *mise
en scene* was typical of our American pluralistic society and system of
government. The Judge was a Jew. The jury, the composition of which
was fought over for hours, contained Catholics, Jews, Protestants and
doubtless some of no religious adherence. Not one of them knew anything about the Greek Orthodox Church.

I advised Archbishop Athenagoras to stay at home. I did not wish
this grand man, episcopally arrayed as he would be, to be subject to the

---

* *Contogeorge v. Spyrou (US Dist. Ct. SDNY 1946)*

humiliation of courtroom curiosity and the flashbulbs of the press. I would try to win on the cross-examination of the plaintiff himself.

The plaintiff's counsel directed much of his case to the Canons of the Council of Nicaea held in Asia Minor in 325 A.D. — the first Council of the Christian Church. My opponent's real purpose, it seemed to me, was to get these Canons before the jury, for they were filled with the Fourth Century anathemas and vengeance calls against the Jews as deicides. Here in the courtroom was a Jew on the Bench and three or four more in the Jury Box. The plaintiff would pose as a reformer dedicated to purging such bigotries and bigots from the Greek Orthodox Church. There was danger in the air.

On cross-examination I sought to shift attention back to the true issue: Was the plaintiff an imposter and did the defendant have a right in law to defend his own title and his Church by warning his people?

Much material had been assembled. Detail by detail, I dragged out the history of the plaintiff's real life and the methods by which he had created himself a "priest" and then a "bishop" with power to consecrate an "archbishop." Gradually those bitter Canons of the Council of Nicaea faded from the focus of the case.

When the plaintiff's counsel "rested," I did likewise. Summations and the Judge's charge followed. At 10:00 p.m. the jury retired. Judge William Bondy invited counsel into his chambers to await the verdict. As soon as the door closed, he turned to me and said with a half-smile: "Charlie, I was laying for you. If you had asked me, a Jew, to charge that jury about those Canons of the Council of Nicaea, I would have pinned your ears right back against your head, Fortunately for you, you did not." I smiled in turn and said: "Will, you yourself know you let in those Canons over my objections that they had nothing to do with this case."

Scarcely had this exchange ended when the bailiff knocked on the door and said that the jury was coming in for more instructions.

We all filed back into the courtroom. The foreman arose and said: "Your Honor, we would like instructions about those Canons of the Council of Nicaea. What do they mean? What bearing have they?"

The Judge reddened as he caught my dancing eye. He knew I was saying to myself: "Now, Will, go to it. Pin *their* ears back!"

GRAND CROSS RECIPIENT CHARLES H. TUTTLE, *1945*

In honor of his distinguished career of service, Charles Tuttle was awarded "The Grand Cross of the Order of the Holy Sepulchre" by the Greek Orthodox Patriarch of Jerusalem. Charles Tuttle became one of only four Americans to receive this unique award. The other three were all U.S. presidents: Warren G. Harding, Franklin D. Roosevelt, and Harry S. Truman.

His reply to the foreman was a gem of good sense, if not good law. He simply said: "Gentlemen, I am merely a civil judge here in new York. I know nothing about the Canons adopted in Asia Minor in 325 A.D. You must do the best you can with them." They turned away crestfallen. They had looked forward to reconvening that Council of 325 A.D. right in the courtroom.

After an hour the jury returned with a verdict for Archbishop Athenagoras.

I never learned what the jury made of those ancient Canons, if they made anything of them.

There followed a banquet at the Archbishop's residence. Bishops and prominent laymen sat around the heavily-laden table. Mrs. Tuttle always recalled happily the solicitude of the Archbishop for her comfort and pleasure. Certainly I myself soon found reason to be grateful to him for his kindly warning as to the strength of the Greek wines. I have since wondered how old Homer kept his Epic going in the banquet halls of ancient Attica.

Thereafter I had the happiness of a continued relationship. One night I was rushed off to St.Vincent's Hospital for an emergency operation on my gall bladder. I was beginning to recover when word came that Archbishop Athenagoras would visit me the next day.

My mental faculties were still quite misty. I knew I was in a Roman Catholic Hospital cared for by kindly nuns. Had not the Roman and the Greek Church exchanged anathemas once upon a time? I slipped word to my wife to try to have some Protestant friends on hand as intermediaries when the Archbishop came. After a while the door of my sick room opened and the Mother Superior was smilingly escorting the Archbishop. She stood respectfully while he gave me his greeting and his blessing. *Why do Christians have to act otherwise?*

Some time later word came that the Patriarch of Jerusalem had awarded to me "The Grand Cross of the Order of the Holy Sepulchre"— the highest lay honor of the Churches of the Eastern Confession, and that it would be presented by Archbishop Athenagoras in a public ceremony in the Hellenic Cathedral in New York City on June 3, 1945. I need not attempt to describe my turbulent emotions when, in the presence of over a thousand persons, I came to stand before the

Archbishop seated on his throne; and while he placed the ribbon of the Order about my shoulders. The cross itself is a beautiful composition of precious stones and metals. *"Jesus Hominum Salvator."*

I keep the ribbon and the cross in my safe deposit vault. I hope it will be an heirloom very precious in the hearts of my descendants.

I also received from the Archbishop an engrossed copy of his address at the time of the presentation. It reads:

> *One of my official acts, during my fourteen years as head of my Archdiocese, that has given to me more than genuine pleasure is this happy occasion today.*
>
> *I am pleased because an adequate opportunity has been finally given to me to pay tribute to a man for whom I hold the highest personal affection and admiration. I admire him not only for his brilliant legal talent as one of America's outstanding trial lawyers but for his social and religious consciousness as well.*
>
> *Despite the pressure of a busy legal career, he has always found time to serve with distinction not only his own church, but ours as well. He has answered my every call with valued advice and sound judgment. I publicly acclaim at this time my personal dept of gratitude to him.*
>
> *In recognition for these many services, His Beatitude, Timotheos, the Patriarch of Jerusalem, has bestowed upon him the Grand Cross of the Order of the Holy Sepulchre. His Beatitude has delegated to me the happy privilege of presenting the award with this citation:*

HONORABLE CHARLES H. TUTTLE, DISTINGUISHED AMERICAN, BRILLIANT TRIAL LAWYER, LEADER IN THE RANKS OF THE PROTESTANT CHURCH, SPONSOR AND ADVOCATE OF LAWS FOR THE ELIMINATION OF RACIAL AND RELIGIOUS DISCRIMINATION, DEVOTED PUBLIC SERVANT,

CHAMPION OF RELIGIOUS FREEDOM, LOYAL AND DEVOTED
FRIEND OF THE GREEK ORTHODOX CHURCH, I HAVE THE
HONOR TO BESTOW UPON YOU THE HIGHEST AWARD OF
THE EASTERN ORTHODOX CHURCH, THE GRAND CROSS
OF THE ORDER OF THE HOLY SEPULCHRE, AS OUR TOKEN
OF DEEP GRATITUDE FOR YOUR MANY VALUED SERVICES
TO THE CAUSE OF THE ORTHODOXY IN AMERICA.

Later, after he had become the Ecumenical Patriarch and was installed in Constantinople (Istanbul), I received from him a letter, dated February 14, 1957, which ended with these gracious words:

All my best wishes and blessings to Mrs. Tuttle, to all your family and to your skilled staff.

With esteem and affection,

THE ECUMENICAL PATRIARCH, ATHENAGORAS

The final sequel was at the White House. In 1950 the Federal Council of the Churches of Christ in the United States had delegated a committee of three to visit President Truman and acquaint him with its plan to enlarge and become the National Council of Churches of Christ. As we were leaving, after an hour's cordial discussion, I said: "Mr. President, I was delighted to see that Archbishop Athenagoras, on leaving to become the Ecumenical Patriarch in Constantinople, had the honor of bestowing on you the Grand Cross of the Order of the Holy Sepulchre."

"Yes" he said, "it was a moving ceremony. I have heard that there were only three others in the country. Do you happen to know who had received them?" I replied: "President Harding and President Franklin D. Roosevelt." When I paused, he said: "Who was the third?" I trust I answered with a proper mien of modesty.

I hope, probably against heavy odds, that no one will be so unkind as to believe that I purposely led along the President of the United States to such a climax.

PRESIDENT HARRY TRUMAN
Grand Cross Recipient

Courtesy of FDR Library

SECTION 15

The Authority of the Russian Orthodox Church of North America over Church Property

THIS CASE IS THE STORY of a long struggle of the Russian Orthodox Church in America to free itself from the captivity and near extinction imposed by Josef Stalin and the Communist dictatorship upon the Mother Church in Russia.

The Communist–Atheist dictatorship in Moscow regarded as archenemies religion and its principal embodiment in the Russian Orthodox Church. Religion was the "opiate of the masses" (Karl Marx, 1844). The Church was an ally of Czarism. It would be allowed a shadow existence, principally because its organization could be used as a lackey for projecting the Kremlin's influence and propaganda into and over foreign lands.

During the period before immigration from the Eastern world had come to our West coast, Russian Orthodox missionaries, traveling south by way of the Bering Straits had reached what is now San Francisco, at about the same time the Spanish Catholic missionaries were arriving there by way of Mexico. The Russian missionaries gradually moved east. Long before the Russian Revolution, they had established "the St. Nicholas Cathedral of the Russian Orthodox Church" in New York City.

With the Russian Revolution, the Russian Church in the motherland fell under the power of Communism. Many of the priests and bishops were slain or exiled to Siberia. The Patriarch in Moscow survived as a useful tool to the Communist State. Through him, Stalin engineered the appointment of a renegade priest as a sort of Apostolic Delegate who came to America and established himself and his sons in the St. Nicholas Cathedral.

The unfortunate Moscow Patriarch had been so completely reduced to licking the boots of Stalin that he officially addressed him as "the God-appointed leader"; the Patriarch's official publications castigated the United States as the "fornicatrix of the resurrected Babylon," "the Washington Cain," "the beast of the Apocalypse," "the contemporary blood-thirsty Baal," and "the great blasphemy from the Christian point of view that these [American] people call themselves Christians."

The Russian Orthodox Church in America refused to recognize such a forced appointment. In a succession of American *sobors* [conventions], it established its own organization which, while loyal to the "Mother Church" in Russia, could not accept orders and appointments emanating from Moscow as long as the Patriarch was a captive. The New York legislature enacted a statute in 1945, amended in 1948, in effect requiring the churches formerly subject to the Mother Church in Russia to be governed by the American ecclesiastical body.

The American Church thereupon sought to eject the "usurper" from the Cathedral. I was retained as its counsel. Years of bitter litigation ensued, which went up and down the ladder to the Supreme Court of the United States. There were at stake not only the New York Cathedral but also the many parishes throughout North America.

JOSEF STALIN

Stalin was causing the Moscow Patriarchate to appoint pliant priests to come to America and attempt to oust the local priests and bishops from their churches, sees and institutions.

The New York Court of Appeals steadily upheld our suit and repeatedly ordered "the usurper" out of the Cathedral (302 N.Y. 1★; 306 N.Y. 38★★; 7 N.Y. 2d 191). Just as steadily, the Supreme Court of the United States reversed (344 U.S. 94 [1952]; 363 U.S. 190 [1960]).

★ *Kedroff v. St. Nicholas Cathedral of the Russian Orthodox Church in North America (1951).*

★★ *Kreshik v. St. Nicholas Cathedral of the Russian Orthodox Church of North America (1953).*

That Court held that since the actual occupant of the Cathedral was in form and letter "the appointee of the Patriarch of Moscow" to occupy the Cathedral, neither the New York legislature nor the New York courts had constitutional power to determine whether the appointment was the free act of the Patriarch. That, said the Supreme Court, was by Canon Law "strictly a matter of ecclesiastical government" (363 U.S. 190).

I argued that such reasoning gave the atheist Stalin by *"canon law"* an extraterritorial jurisdiction over property, persons and religion in the United States which he could not for a moment have by *"civil law."*

But the battle was by no means lost. The greater prize was the local parishes, institutions and bishoprics; and in that field I continued with the fight. Here the legal situation was reversed.

The appointees of the American Church were in possession, and the appointees of Moscow were trying to oust them. The Americans were *in* by "canon law," and could not be put *out* by "civil law."

The Supreme Court and the lower courts unanimously sustained the lower courts in repelling the invaders. *(Russian Orthodox Greek Catholic St. Peter and St. Paul Church of Lorain, Ohio v. Burdikoff* (189 N.E. 2d 451) decided July 25, 1962; certiorari denied (374 U.S. 808); *Romanian Orthodox Missionary Episcopate v. Trutza,* (120 F. Supp 183; aff'd 205 F. 2d 107; certiorari denied (346 U.S. 915).)

In the first of these two cases, the Court of Appeals of Ohio posited the nub of its decision thus (pp. 454-5):

> *Here the patriarchal church (in Moscow) seeks, in effect, by means of the subterfuge of the Reverend George Burdikoff, to eject those who have occupied the church herein for a period of thirty-five years.*

While these court battles raged, the American Russian Church established its own Cathedral in New York City and made it the seat of Leonty, its own Archbishop and Metropolitan.

In the summer of 1962, after the pro-
tective decisions last mentioned, the
Archbishop invited Mrs. Tuttle and
me to a Sunday morning service at
his Cathedral, and to be his guest
later at his summer residence on
Long Island.

When we arrived at the Cathedral, we found neither chairs nor
pews, and were told that the congregation and the clergy stood throughout
the service. I was prepared to be appalled,
when a welcoming committee came forward
and escorted Mrs. Tuttle and me to a
small balcony which had been provided with several comfortable

HÉLÈNE WHEELER
TUTTLE

chairs. The devotional spirit of the service, the organ music, and the
singing of Russian anthems and hymns were deeply moving.

After the service, the Archbishop escorted us in his car to his country place, where a lavish banquet was provided for us, attended by
numerous bishops, priests, and prominent laymen. Strange Russian
foods moved in succession before me, until I was reduced to politely
nibbling. Wine cups of the familiar type abounded, but I became fasci-
nated with the presence among them of a small glass about an inch high
and without a pedestal.

Ultimately someone filled it with a colorless liquid. As I raised it
for a sip, the Archbishop whispered that vodka was to be poured down
in one gulp, otherwise it would burn the lips. I have never understood
how Hélène got it down; but the effect was soon electric. She became
the center of a number of bishops and there were bursts of laughter far
from Episcopal.

We left with a feeling of reverence and gratitude for the Founding
Fathers who had given us a land where religion could flourish in
freedom—and, under shelter of the First Amendment, have a sanctuary which neither the State nor the Masters of the State could
invade.

---><♦><---

SECTION 16

The Removal of the Federal Judge from the Occidental Petroleum Corporation Suit

THE OCCIDENTAL PETROLEUM Corporation held 40,000 of the 140,000 preferred shares of the Parker Petroleum Corporation, which in 1962 was in bankruptcy liquidation in the United States District Court for the Western District of Oklahoma.

The following remarkable narrative is on record (303 F. 2d 55★; 372 U.S. 915; 373 U.S. 906★★); but I have never encountered the like of it.

For some months, the federal judge in charge had been conducting hearings in chambers affecting and directing the procedure and merits of the reorganization proceedings. In those in-chamber proceedings he had, according to the transcript:

> *repeatedly expressed violent and abusive prejudgment and antipathy as to the rights and actions of Occidental, a highly interested party;*
>
> *constantly denounced a principal officer in extremely indecent and slanderous language;*
>
> *personally ordered that Occidental and its attorneys be given no notice of the hearings in chambers and that they be excluded therefrom; and,*
>
> *personally directed that they not be allowed to procure copies of the official transcripts recorded by the official court stenographer.*

★ *Occidental Petroleum Corporation v. Chandler (CA 10 Okla. 1962).*

★★ *Chandler v. Occidental Petroleum Corporation (1963).*

For example, in these private hearings and without any judicial substantiation or process of law, the Judge referred to the principal officer and his associates in Occidental as "thief," "son of a bitch," "these vultures," "shady characters," and so forth—and threatened to bring the Occidental officer "in chains."

Even after the statutory affidavit of disqualification was filed, the Judge continued to act. He evaded the requirements of the statute by referring to a conversation which he said he had with a third person stating that he intended to disqualify himself as to *"any questions of fact"* involving Occidental.

We secured immediate intervention by the United States Court of Appeals, Tenth Circuit. It issued a subpoena to the official stenographer who recorded and made transcripts of the proceedings in chambers. Thereupon the Judge seized the transcripts, and endeavored to have the frightened stenographer testify that he had not officially had the transcripts, but had acted as "secretary" to the Judge, and that the proceedings in chambers had not been judicial.

The stenographer refused to comply and told the story to the Court of Appeals. That Court called for the attendance of the Judge and procured the transcripts from him in advance. The Judge did not appear.

Several days later the Judge requested by telegram a "hearing *en banc,*" he himself to be one of the Court. A court *en banc* (excluding the Judge) was immediately convened; but instead of appearing, the Judge sent an attorney who stated that the Judge had become occupied with another matter, the nature of which he (the attorney) had not been informed.

By unanimous decision on April 20, 1962, reaffirmed on June 1, 1962, the Court of Appeals ordered that the Judge "shall proceed no further" and that "all further proceedings be heard and determined" by another judge.

The opinion declared that the Judge's conduct in chambers had been improper; that he had "tried to prevent a court officer from the performance of his official duties and responsibilities"; and that he had shown "personal enmity, hostility, bias and prejudice against

242   L I F E   S T O R I E S

Occidental." The United States Supreme Court twice refused leave to appeal (372 U.S. 915; 373 U.S. 906).

The bankruptcy proceeding thereupon continued before another judge and the rights of Occidental were properly adjudicated.

SECTION 17

The United Brotherhood of Carpenters & Joiners of America and the Anti-Trust Law

ON A DAY IN 1932 two men called. They introduced themselves as William L. Hutcheson, President of the United Brotherhood of Carpenters and Joiners of America (the International), and Charles W. Hanson, President of the New York State Brotherhood. Both men were impressively large in stature — and, in status, manner and word, top-ranking labor leaders. I had never before had contact with them or the Brotherhood.

They explained that the Brotherhood's counsel for its eastern United States affairs had retired. Would I take his place? They offered very agreeable terms. Then and there began not merely a professional but also a personal relationship which resulted in my becoming general counsel to the International Brotherhood, lasting until the death of both men.

In this relationship, I conducted many litigations around the country on behalf of both the International and State Brotherhoods. I shall write about only one — because that one became a noted leading case in labor law under the Sherman Act, the Clayton Act, and the Norris–La Guardia Act.

After his election as President of the United States in 1932, Franklin Roosevelt appointed Professor Thurman Arnold as head of the Anti-Trust Division of the Department of Justice.

Since FDR's administration was commonly regarded as "pro-labor," every one was surprised when Mr. Arnold embarked on a nationwide campaign to end, by using the Sherman Anti-Trust Act as a blunderbuss, what he regarded as "abuses" on the part of Organized Labor. These abuses, according to Mr. Arnold, included jurisdictional strikes, sympathetic strikes, strikes to compel purchasing union labeled goods, and strikes in derogation of the National Labor Relations Board's certificates of election as bargaining agents. In his view, these familiar union practices were illegal restraints of trade.

In pursuit of this campaign, Mr. Arnold obtained indictments across the country, each separately based on the Sherman Act and running to one of these "abuses." Principal defendants were the United Brotherhood, "Big Bill" Hutcheson, and some associates. Peradventure it was only a coincidence that the United Brotherhood was then the only *big Republican* labor union in the country.

I moved on demurrer★ to dismiss each of these indictments on the grounds that it stated no criminal offence.

Mr. Arnold telephoned me an invitation for Mr. Hutcheson and myself to a private luncheon in the Department of Justice. After the amenities, Mr. Arnold said he thought it might be constructive to discuss possible disposition of the indictments by substituting civil procedure by way of consent decrees enjoining the respective "abuses."

Mr. Hutcheson's face clouded. He said that he had always been a union man and he would not buy himself out of any indictments by consenting to any injunction against what union labor had traditionally found necessary to its defense. He would fight the indictments in the courts, win or lose.

The test case, which thereupon came to the United States Supreme Court, was the indictment in *United States v. William L. Hutcheson et al.* (312 U.S. 219), decided February 3, 1941. It involved the rights not

---

★ Demurrer: a challenge to the legal sufficiency of the opponent's pleading.

only of the United Brotherhood of Carpenters but of all organized labor as well. Mr. Arnold argued it on one side and I on the other.

Factually it was a struggle between two unions seeking exclusive employment by a manufacturer for the installation of certain machinery. The Carpenters had recommended to their members and friends not to buy the employer's products unless the Carpenters were given exclusive employment. The Supreme Court held by a vote of 6 to 2 that, in view of the Norris-La Guardia Act, the indictment charged no criminal offence against the Sherman Act. The Court said (p. 236):

> *It was precisely in order to minimize the difficulties to which the general language of the Sherman Law in its application to workers had given rise, that Congress cut through all the tangled verbalisms and enumerated concretely the types of activities which had become familiar incidents of union procedure.*

On the authority of this decision, there followed a series of *per curiam* decisions by the Supreme Court dismissing indictments directed by Mr. Arnold against other so-called "abuses" by organized labor (See 313 U.S. 539).

This decision remained the controlling law until the Taft-Hartley Act of June 23, 1947.

In my book, "Big Bill" remains the portrait of a man prepared to die with his boots on.

SECTION 18

Foreign Commerce in Liquor by Air and Sea. The Supreme Court Cuts the Gordian Knot.

T HE IDLEWILD BON VOYAGE CORPORATION sold tax-free liquor to travelers by air to foreign countries. The sales were made at its office on the second floor of the Customs House at New York's Idlewild (now Kennedy) Airport. On presenting his travel ticket, the traveler could select and pay for (without tax) not more than three bottles. These were then put in a sealed container and delivered to the plane's purser for delivery to the purchaser when the plane landed on foreign soil.

The Idlewild Corporation had purchased the liquor from federally licensed warehouses throughout the State of New York, and had brought it to Idlewild in federally licensed trucks. All these operations were specifically licensed by the United States Treasury Department pursuant to federal law.

Suddenly the New York State Liquor Authority and the State Attorney General ruled that since these operations were on New York land, they were illegal because they were not licensed and were incapable of license under New York law. Civil and criminal prosecutions were threatened.

Thereupon there ensued in lower federal courts a fantastic tangle of contradictory decisions, no less serious for being so comic.

The first federal judge denied my motion for an injunction on grounds that the question of law should first be presented to the state courts (188 F. Supp. 434★). On my appeal to the United States Court of Appeals, that Court said that the lower court was wrong and that it

★ *Idlewild Bon Voyage Liquor Corp. v. Rohan (Dist. Ct. N.Y. 1960).*

should have decided the merits, but the Court of Appeals had no jurisdiction to reverse and order the lower court to go to the merits. My appeal was dismissed (289 F. 2d 426).

I then renewed in lower court my motion for an injunction. The federal judge there presiding denied my motion on the ground that, although the Court of Appeals had said that the first federal judge was wrong, nevertheless it had not reversed the erroneous decision which in consequence remained "the law of the case" (194 F. Supp. 3).

Tired of being the buck in this expensive judicial battledore and shuttlecock, I applied to the Supreme Court of the United States for and obtained a writ of peremptory mandamus ordering the lower federal courts to take jurisdiction and proceed to decide the merits (370 U.S. 713★).

In compliance, a three-judge District Court was convened. After extended argument and briefing, it held that the State Liquor Authority could not forbid what, under federal law, the United States Treasury Department had licensed as legitimate tax-free foreign commerce (212 F. Supp. 376). This decision was affirmed by the United States Supreme Court, two Justices dissenting (377 U.S. 324★★). The Court held (to quote its headnote):

> *Though the State has power under the Twenty-first Amendment to regulate transportation through its territory of intoxicants to avoid their diversion into domestic channels, the Commerce Clause deprives the State of power to prevent transactions supervised by the Bureau of Customs involving intoxicants for delivery to consumers in foreign countries.*

Thereupon, New York's sister state of New Jersey sympathetically picked up the fallen torch. Its contention was that federally licensed sales in New Jersey of tax-free liquor to foreign-bound vessels and planes for consumption outside New Jersey's territorial waters could not be made without a general license from and payment of a fee to that state. New Jersey's claim was thereupon rushed to the Supreme

---

★ *Idlewild Bon Voyage Liquor Corp. v. Epstein (1962).*

★★ *Hostetter v. Idlewild Bon Voyage Liquor Corp. (1964).*

Court of the United States, which without argument granted my motion for a summary judgment overruling New Jersey on the authority of its own foregoing decision in the *Idlewild* case (389 U.S. 29★).

How comforting to the traveler the knowledge that three friendly bottles of his favorite brand, bought tax-free in the United States, would be welcoming him as he stepped down on foreign soil!

◆

SECTION 19

A Trust Company's Strange Façade Leads to the New York Dock Company Case.

S EVERAL YEARS AFTER LEAVING OFFICE as United States Attorney, I received a call from a gentleman introducing himself as William J. Wason, president of the Kings County Trust Company. Would I come over since there was a matter involving many papers? Thereupon began both a personal and professional relationship which lasted for years.

I had become accustomed to the imposing palaces of finance which loomed about Wall Street. But the somewhat weather-beaten sign "Kings County Trust Company," the well-worn brownstone stoop, and the railing with little of its ancient lacquer, gave me surprise. Inside there were several old cashier cages with elderly attendants. The guard showed me into a small rear room—little more than a cubbyhole. There sat President Wason.

He produced a sheaf of papers and outlined the problem. He wanted me to act as special counsel. I made some tentative suggestions, subject to further study. At the end, he smilingly suggested that, in view of the building's appearance, I might be concerned about my

---

★ *Lordi v. Epstein (1967).*

compensation. He then showed me the Trust Company's financial statement for the year. My eyes popped. Evidently conservatism in appearance was magic for trustworthiness in Brooklyn.

One legal matter led to another until in May 1933 I was retained for the New York Dock Company in a suit by one Mr. Gallagher (a stockholder with 6,500 shares) against the company, Mr. Wason and other officers and directors. The plaintiff charged conspiracy to divert $1,250,000 in illegal dividends declared in 1929.

The trial before Justice Hallinan was lengthy. His opinion ran nineteen pages with twenty-two subheadings. His judgment dismissed the complaint "on the merits" (19 N.Y. Supp. 2d 789★). The dismissal was unanimously affirmed by the Appellate Division (263 App. Div. 878). The Court of Appeals denied the plaintiff leave to appeal (288 N.Y. 737).

A principal point established was that directors, in declaring a dividend on preferred stock, "were entitled to accept in good faith the judgment and advice of their accountants" that the surplus for the year was adequate.

When I recall that old weather-beaten façade as I first saw it—and the financial report of what was behind it—I can see clearly that ostentation is not necessarily the best advertising.

SECTION 20

Eradicating the Poisonous Weed of Apartheid

THE ALFRED H. MAYER COMPANY, a Missouri corporation, was developing in the suburbs of St. Louis a community of 2,700 families, the equivalent of a municipality of over 10,000 persons. Mayer offered to the general public lots and plans for housing. Dr. Joseph Lee Jones, a well-to-do Negro dentist in St. Louis and his wife examined the Mayer brochure, selected a lot and house design, and

★ *Gallagher v. New York Dock Company (Sup. Ct. 1940).*

tendered payment. They were refused because Mayer had a "general policy" of not selling to Negroes.

On behalf of the National Council of Churches, I obtained from the United States Supreme Court leave to intervene and submit a brief *amicus curiae*. The lower courts had dismissed the Jones' complaint. I sought reversal.

In my brief I said:

> *We submit that the decisions below provide an open door for enclaves in our American society of vast quasi-municipalities built on exploitation of racism and discrimination for profit.*

And again:

> *Jim Crowism is alien to American municipalities whether operated directly by the State or operated privately with the assistance of the State.... He [Mayer] and his Missouri corporations and not the United States Constitution will determine the criteria and privileges of eligibility and citizenship in his subdivisions of the State of Missouri.*

On June 17, 1968, the Supreme Court (with one dissent) reversed the lower courts and held (392 U.S. 409*) that the complaint stated a valid case for injunction. The opinion covers forty-five pages; but compresses its essence into the following paragraph (p. 443):

> *Negro citizens North and South, who saw in the Thirteenth Amendment a promise of freedom—freedom to "go and come at pleasure" and to "buy and sell when they please"— would be left with "a mere paper guarantee" if Congress were powerless to assure that a dollar in the hands of a Negro will purchase the same thing as a dollar in the hands of a white man. At the very least, the freedom that Congress is empowered to secure under the Thirteenth Amendment includes the freedom to buy whatever a white man can buy, the right to live wherever a white man can live. If Congress cannot say that being a free man means at least this much, then the Thirteenth Amendment made a promise the Nation cannot keep.*

★ *Jones v. Alfred H. Mayer (1968).*

If the Supreme Court had not found in the Constitution an insecticide to destroy this weed of apartheid which Mayer was nurturing, its bitter fruit would soon have poisoned the nation and annulled the American creed that all men are created equal and endowed by the Creator with equal inalienable rights. The Court has wrested from private prerogative this evil power.

SECTION 21

A Taxpayer's Right to Challenge Public Expenditures as Violative of the First Amendment's Religion Clauses.

IN 1923 THE SUPREME COURT of the United States had seemingly held in *Frothingham v. Mellon* (262 U.S. 447) that, as regards public expenditures, the interest of the taxpayer was so "infinitesimal" that he had no "standing" to challenge in the courts the expenditure's legality. For forty-five years the barrier of that decision remained unbreached.

But in 1968 there came before the Supreme Court the question whether such a barrier could constitutionally exist where the taxpayer charged violation of the Free Exercise and Establishment Clauses in the First Amendment, and thus of his own personal liberty, and not mere illegal use of money.

The three-judge District Court had held (2 to 1) that even in such case *Frothingham* denied the taxpayer a standing.

In the Supreme Court, Professor Norman Dorsen and I filed a brief on behalf of the National Council of the Churches of Christ advocating reversal. The brief's tenor is manifested by the following quotations (pp. 9, 10):

The substance of the Bill of Rights is freedom, not money, and the dominant inducement for this action is the protection of individual and social freedom, which the Constitution requires the national and state governments to respect.

To deny the citizen access to the courts for the protection of the rights so solemnly reserved to him by the Constitution unless he can show major financial damage is, we submit, to degrade the Bill of Rights from a declaration of fundamental liberties to a mere declaration of monetary rights, or to rhetorical abstractions.

Freedom of conscience is justifiable, no less than the freedoms of speech, and press, not because of monetary evaluation but because of its intrinsic value—a value beyond mere money and the pocketbook.

The brief distinguished the *Frothingham* case because in that case no rights of personal liberty under the First Amendment were involved.

On June 10, 1968, the Supreme Court reversed, with one Justice dissenting (392 U.S. 83*). The court's opinion declared (p. 103) that the taxpayer's complaint "alleged that the challenged expenditures violate the Establishment and Free Exercise Clauses of the First Amendment," and hence (p. 106) that "his tax money is being extracted and spent in violation of specific constitutional protections against such abuses of legislative power."

In his concurring opinion (p. 108) Justice Douglas likened the status of the taxpayer on such a constitutional issue to that of "a private attorney general seeking to vindicate the public interest." To quote him further (p. 111):

The Constitution, even with the judicial gloss it has acquired, plainly is not adequate to protect the individual against the growing bureaucracy in the Legislative and Executive Branches. He faces a formidable opponent in government, even when he is endowed with funds and with courage. The individual is almost certain to be plowed under, unless he has a well-organized,

* *Flast v. Cohen.*

active political group to speak for him. The church is one. The press is another. The union is a third. But if a powerful sponsor is lacking, individual liberty withers—in spite of glowing opinions and resounding constitutional phrases.

I would not be niggardly therefore in giving private attorneys general standing to sue.

The decision breathed the faith of the American hymn that God, not the Mint, was the "Author of Liberty."

------◆◆◆◆------

SECTION 22

The Right of Corporations To Equal Protection under the Fourteenth Amendment of the U.S. Constitution.

THE NATIONAL DISTILLERS Products Corporation, a Virginia corporation, had its statutory office and held its annual stockholders' meeting in that State. It was authorized to do business in Ohio, where it maintained a distillery and warehouse, as it did in six other states.

Under an Ohio statute, its Tax Commissioner levied an *ad valorem* tax on all the corporation's accounts receivable derived from sales of goods manufactured by it in Ohio, although not used in the conduct of its business in Ohio but in its general business. Ohio residents and Ohio corporations doing an identical business were exempt from the tax.

The imposition of this tax on the National Distillers Products Corporation was upheld by the Ohio State Supreme Court (150 Ohio St. 229★).

★ *National Distillers Products Corp, NY v. Glander (1948).*

CHARLES H. TUTTLE

by Raymond Perry Rodgers Neilson (1881–1964)

This 1949 portrait was presented by the "Tuttle Boys" as a gift to Charles Tuttle in celebration of his 70th birthday.

On National's appeal in 1949 to the United States Supreme Court, I was retained. I briefed and argued the case on the contention that this scheme of taxation of receivables was arbitrarily discriminatory in favor of residents of Ohio as against non-residents doing an identical business, and hence violated the clause in the Fourteenth Amendment to the United States Constitution which forbade any state to "deny to any person within its jurisdiction the equal protection of the laws." As I said in my brief, the Ohio statute "loads the dice of taxation to the advantage of the Ohio businessman."

But was a corporation a "person" within the meaning of this clause?

By a vote of seven to two, the Supreme Court upheld my contention that a corporation was such a "person." In consequence, the Supreme Court reversed the Ohio Supreme Court and the Ohio Tax Commissioner (337 U.S. 562 [1949]). The minority held that the word "person" meant only a "human," saying (p. 578):

> *The Fourteenth Amendment was framed to protect the Negroes from oppression by the whites, not to protect corporations from oppression by the legislature.*

As a citizen I am glad that this narrow minority review did not prevail.

The Fourteenth Amendment was an act of statesmanship designed to preserve the fabric of our nation against the disruptive consequence, moral and economic, of legislation corrupted by inequality and favoritism in the enactment of law.

"Oppression" is not a word for which there is much countenance in the United States Constitution.

CHAPTER NINE

CONTINUED PUBLIC LIFE AFTER THE 1930 ELECTION

——➤◄●►◄——

SECTION 1

The Board of Higher Education of the City of New York.

M Y INTENSE INVOLVEMENT with public higher education in the City, described earlier★, continued. On November 18, 1930, I attended New York's Board of Higher Education meeting and continued as Chairman of the Board's Executive Committee—an office I held thereafter for many years.

★ Chapter 4, Sections 1–4.

The great expansion of free higher education was already making itself manifest. There were: City College on Washington Heights; City College at 23rd Street and Lexington Avenue; Hunter College at 68th Street and Park Avenue; Hunter College in the Bronx; and a Brooklyn College in process of establishment. A University of the City of New York was already in the discussion stage.

Hereafter★ I shall write a firsthand account of the era when the university dream became a reality, for I continued on the Board until June 1966.

<hr>

SECTION 2

Co-Chairmanship of the Metropolitan Rapid Transit Commission, 1954-1958. A Last Effort at Unified Mass Transportation.

THE METROPOLITAN RAPID TRANSIT COMMISSION came into being on June 14, 1954, as a bi-state agency created by Chapter 801, Laws of 1954, of the State of New York, and Chapter 44, Laws of 1954, of the State of New Jersey.

As stated in Section 5 of the legislation, the Commission was established to "study present and prospective rapid transit needs of the New York–New Jersey Metropolitan Area and develop, recommend and report as soon possible measures for meeting such needs." The Commission had no governmental powers.

The Commission consisted of five members from New York and five from New Jersey, appointed by the respective governors. The New Jersey Co-Chairman was Edward J. O'Mara and I was the New York Co-Chairman.

★ Chapter 13, Section 3.

For the Commission's assistance, $800,000 was provided by the Port of New York Authority to be used solely for the interstate (trans-Hudson) part of the study; $150,000 was provided by each of the two States for the intrastate studies.

The Commission employed an expert staff and retained outstanding consultants of national repute who functioned under the coordinating direction of an eminent Project Director, Arthur W. Page. It reviewed carefully all previous studies. It heard all parties who desired to propose plans, and it received many written memoranda and suggestions from many sources. It conducted public hearings in New York and New Jersey on the proposals recommended by the consultants and the Project Director. All proposals submitted and all views expressed at the public hearings were thoroughly considered in reaching the Commission's findings.

In its report, the Commission stated its conviction that any adequate plan for mass transportation to serve the needs of the New York–New Jersey megalopolis must be centered and revolve around the Trans-Hudson situation. To this end the Commission recommended that in this core region there be, under administration by a metropolitan district, *a loop system* of rail mass-transportation operating in both directions.

The system, running north and south, would contact or cross all existing means of transportation on the New Jersey side, and on the Manhattan side would run through or adjoin the executive and commercial centers from the Battery to 59th Street. It would utilize, as far as could be arranged with the New York City Transit Authority, existing subway facilities and transfer rights; and would be so planned to provide cooperative service for other parts of the City and for Westchester and Long Island, and allow for mutual long-range planning for the future.

The loop would cross the Hudson River at 59th Street, New York City, and would return by way of an enlargement of the tubes of the Hudson and Manhattan Railroad, which was then being operated by a Trustee under the Bankruptcy Act (with continuance problematical without public financial assistance).

The metropolitan district to be established as the base for the general program would be adequately empowered to implement the program in accordance with practical requirements as they might develop. In the first instance, it would be bi-state in character and established by a compact between the States of New York and New Jersey, with the consent of Congress. The compact would provide that Connecticut could join on suitable terms if it so requested. A draft of legislation to carry out the recommendations was annexed to the report. The following paragraphs from the report are worth quoting:

> The Commission is convinced that no small, cheap or piece-meal measures will or can begin to meet either the present urgent emergency or the multiplying necessities for the expansion of this Area in the next three decades, including facilitation of urgently needed means of Civil Defense.

> The crisis and the opportunity call for bold, imaginative, unselfish and adequate thinking, planning and action. They also call for full realization that this vast Metropolitan Area is one economic and social unit, that all its parts are interdependent, and that their welfare and progress depend on and derive from the welfare and progress of the community as a whole. . . .

> It is stark realism to say that the moment for action is now, or, perhaps never. The cost will be large; but the cost of inaction is already far larger and will progressively grow still larger.

> The Commission keenly realizes the dismaying obstacles and complexities, economic, legal and operational, which have accumulated during the decades when repeated studies and proposals continuously failed of action because bi-state cooperation was absent and because the ever-present negative criticisms by private and sectional interests wrought paralysis. Nevertheless, this Commission has faith that, however late the hour, a way forward can yet be opened if the voices which concentrate on public interest will not again be silenced by self-interested voices of negation. . . .

The Commission's Report is designed not to be read and used as an academic treatise but as a guidepost for direction and a tool for action. It is designed not to bring a final solution to a problem that will pass but to bring progress to a problem that will be with us always in ever-changing form.

In this Commission's opinion there is no other effective way for this vast New York–New Jersey Metropolitan Area, the executive center of the nation and the Capital of the World, to face up to its indispensable rapid transit needs in the present and for its future. . . .

The Commission recommends that the question of costs, both capital and annual deficit, be left for future development of the general plan by the new Metropolitan Transit District which can be submitted for approval of the respective Governors and Legislatures of the two states upon the firm basis of complete negotiations which the District should be authorized to undertake.

The report of the Commission was unanimous. It and the accompanying enabling legislation were approved by Governor Averell Harriman of New York, and, with only three dissenting votes, by the New York Legislature. It was also approved by Governor Robert Meyner of

Courtesy of FDR Library

New Jersey and by the New Jersey Senate. But the self-interest and the clamor of local interests and political demagogy in and around Journal Square and Newark, New Jersey, was such that the Report lost in the New Jersey Assembly by a slight margin. As a result, the dream and its realization for unified and unifying transit in the metropolitan area of New York and New Jersey was once again defeated by the sacrifice of the interest of the many to the self interest of a few. The loss was and is vast, and it appears to be permanent.

AVERELL HARRIMAN   The last desperate effort had been made.

SECTION 3

The First Law in the United States against Discrimination in Employment for Race, Creed, Color or National Origin.

IN MARCH 1944, GOVERNOR Thomas E. Dewey recommended to the Legislature the creation of a non-partisan, non-political temporary commission to recommend legislation against discrimination in employment because of race, creed, color or national origin. The next month, the Legislature created such a commission, consisting of twenty-three members (L. 1944, Ch. 692).

The Commission organized in Albany on June 19, 1944. It elected Assemblyman Irving M. Ives as Chairman, Dr. Alvin Johnson as Vice-Chairman, and Senator Louis B. Heller as Secretary. I was designated as Counsel. In accepting the post, I stated that I intended to serve without compensation.

After appropriate notices in the public press, widely attended hearings were held by the whole Commission in Albany, Syracuse, Rochester, Buffalo and New York City, with a final public hearing before a Joint Session of the Legislature. Everyone who wished to speak was heard without curtailment of time. Numerous memoranda were filed.

Notwithstanding the highly controversial and emotional subject matter, the exemplary course of all the hearings was to confirm faith in the democratic process even in wartime.

As Counsel I prepared alternative drafts in the form of possible legislation; and these drafts were the bases of the public discussion at the hearings. As a result, the people of the State of New York themselves actively participated in writing the final legislation which the Commission later approved and recommended to the Legislature.

Two incidents at these hearings are especially worth noting.

At one of the hearings in New York City, an hour was consumed by a florid orator from what I will call "the extreme right." He saw nothing but disaster in the proposed legislation. If it were enacted, "grass would grow in the streets." "Blood would be shed." I could not resist some cross-examination, perhaps not altogether gentle.

When the recess for lunch came, I stepped down from the dais. A young woman in a bright red dress ran up to me, bubbling with joy:

O, Mr. Tuttle, for what you did in those questions to that awful man, our group is most grateful! We want the privilege of making you an honorary member.

Thereupon she eagerly offered me a card. Naturally, one extends a receptive hand; but, as I was doing so, my guardian angel rushed down all in a flutter: "Don't touch it!" Thus warned, I asked the card-offerer: "And what is your group?" With sparkling eyes, she said: "The Communist Party!"

The other incident occurred during the crowded public hearing held in the Assembly Chamber before a Joint Session of the Legislature. The Joint Session had been called at the instance of the opposition, who hoped that the legislators would be overwhelmed by denunciations and gloomy foreboding such as that by the aforementioned orator in New York City. Yes, it seemed, the world could come to an end if there were a square deal for all in employment.

The opposition had not anticipated that, on the contrary, proponents from all over the state would swamp the hearing. In the course of the oratory one leader of the opposition said to me ruefully: "We made an awful mistake in engineering a public hearing before this Joint Session!"

I replied that I was grateful to them for assuring the passage of our Bill.

The Commission had asked me to open to the Joint Session the case for the Bill. The date was February 20, 1945—in between the days then nationally memorializing Abraham Lincoln and George Washington. I still have a copy of that address. I quote its conclusion:

The whole country is watching this battle in New York. It senses that here at last is a serious effort to come to grips with this great paradox in our American way of life—this malignant contradiction which, as this Legislature has itself declared, "menaces the institutions and foundations of a free democratic state."

If this battle fails here, it cannot be undertaken elsewhere. The verdict will be that racial and religious discrimination is too thoroughly established in our economy to be outlawed.

We will then be plunging into the turbulent tensions, derangements and fevers of the post-war period with a cancer in the economic body of the nation. We will be weakening our over-burdened democracy with the moral strains of racial and religious discriminations. We will inoculate millions of our fellow-citizens with the disillusion, cynicism and hopelessness which are fertile fields for alien ideologies and false messiahs at home and abroad. We will find ourselves up against the impossible task of trying to balance the books of social injustice with other than red ink.

Perhaps it is no accident that, under Providence, this great debate occurs in the middle of Brotherhood Week, and while Race Relations Sunday and the anniversary of the Great Emancipator still find the mystic chords of fraternity touched by the better angels of our nature.

Let us have faith in our minorities, and be fair with them. They also hold the title deeds to God's blessing upon America.

Courtesy of Truman Library

A few days later the bill passed both houses with only a few dissenting votes. Governor Dewey signed it into law on March 12, 1945, in the presence of a distinguished company. It is commonly referred to as "the Ives–Quinn Law" because its sponsor in the Assembly was Irving M. Ives, a Republican from Chenango County, and

THOMAS DEWEY

its sponsor in the Senate was Elmer F. Quinn, a Democrat from New York County. The law has been added to from time to time as other areas have been legislatively closed to racial and religious discrimination. It has withstood all attacks upon its constitutionality.

This enactment was pioneering legislation in 1945, but it was soon copied in other states, and has been reflected in Federal legislation.

The Commission accompanied its introduction of the Bill into the Legislature with a report signed by its members and carried into the State's archives as "Legislative Document (1945) No. 6." On the fly-leaf of the report is the following:

IN APPRECIATION

The Commission takes this opportunity to express its profound gratitude to Charles H. Tuttle, Esq., who has served as Counsel to the Commission. When Mr. Tuttle was asked to act as Counsel, he consented to do so upon condition that he personally would perform all services required by Counsel and that he would do so without remuneration. The Commission accepted this offer at its meeting on August 7, 1944, and recorded its deep sense of appreciation for his public-spirited attitude. Mr. Tuttle has served as Counsel since that date. He has attended every meeting of the Commission, including the four upstate hearings and the three hearings held in New York City, and actively participated in the conduct of all such hearings, contributing greatly to their success. He has attended all meetings of the three sub-committees and has advised the Commission from time to time with reference to various matters of research upon which the Commission sought guidance.

The following report owes its clarity and effectiveness largely to his draftsmanship. It would be difficult for the Commission adequately to express what a deep debt it owes Mr. Tuttle for his invaluable services in this significant and far-reaching effort.

We want the citizens of the State of New York to know of the unselfish service which Mr. Tuttle has rendered, and the Commission gladly takes this opportunity of expressing to him and of spreading on the record its deep sense of appreciation.

With this enactment, the great Declaration in the Fourteenth Amendment to the United States Constitution that all persons were entitled to "the equal protection of the laws" had begun to move out from the letter into the spirit of the American creed.

SECTION 4

Codification of the Cooperative Corporations Law of the State. Equality versus Privilege.

IN 1945 THE LEGISLATURE PASSED an Act (Chapter 494) creating a Temporary State Commission to make studies and recommendations designed to improve agricultural conditions within the state.

The Commission had fifteen members. Its duties ran to all farm activities, industrial utilization and marketing of farm produce, forest products, the labor and technological situations of agriculture, and the recommendation of laws and other measures as to production, marketing and consumption practices.

The Commission employed me as its Counsel. I undertook a comprehensive study of the very confused state of the laws governing cooperatives, due mainly to the fact that promoters of new cooperatives almost invariably had sought to obtain from the Legislature special charters with special provisions deemed in aid of their particular operations. There were thirty or more of these special enactments.

The aim was to telescope the sprawling, poorly coordinated and overly detailed provisions of the existing separate laws into a single, simplified, much abbreviated and consolidated statute, expressed in every day language which the members of the cooperatives could themselves easily understand without the aid of lawyers, and unburdened with the need of a book of supplementary departmental regulations from government sources.

To this end I prepared alternative drafts which were utilized by the Commission in its various public hearings around the State, to which were invited all cooperatives and agricultural interests.

Finally the Commission settled on a draft which was submitted to the Legislature and adopted by it *without a dissenting vote*. It is titled "Cooperative Corporations Law" and became effective, with the Governor's approval, on April 11, 1951 (L. 1951, Ch. 712; Chapter 77 of the Consolidated Laws).

The whole codification can readily be read in fifteen minutes. All existing special laws as to particular cooperatives were repealed, so that the new codification would constitute a common operative statute. Since its enactment in 1951, there have been few amendments. No portion of it has been adjudged unconstitutional.

In the Foreword to the Commission's report, its Chairman, Senator Austin W. Erwin, wrote:

> *The Commission is of the opinion that this enactment will meet a long-standing need in the field of cooperative business.*

Section 2 of the Codification contained this brief but comprehensive "Declaration of policy":

> *It is the declared policy of this state, as one means of improving the economic welfare of its people, particularly those who are producers, marketers or consumers of food products, to encourage their effective organization in cooperative associations for the rendering of mutual help and service.*

The essence of the new Code was the substitution of uniformity in cooperation instead of varying prodigality's in special privilege.

SECTION 5

Proposals for Change
and Simplification
of the State Constitution.

IN 1956 THE LEGISLATURE passed an Act (Chapter 814) creating a Temporary State Commission for the purposes cited in this section's title. In addition, the Commission was charged with collecting data and pertinent information to aid the voters at the 1957 general election to decide whether there should be a State Convention to revise the State Constitution.

Governor Averell Harriman appointed me as a member. The Commission consisted of fifteen members, of whom eight were Republicans and seven were Democrats.

The Commission organized promptly; elected Nelson A. Rockefeller chairman and Francis Bergan (later an Associate Judge of the Court of Appeals) as vice chairman; chose counsel; employed an expert staff and established its main headquarters in New York City. The principal committee to which I was assigned was that on home rule for counties, cities, towns and villages.

The State Constitution was an enormous document of nearly 200 pages, with many accretions and amendments since its adoption by the people in 1938. It contained many patches sewed into it over the years by local or special interests seeking to put themselves beyond the vicissitudes of legislative power. It also contained much that was mere legislation and not of constitutional substance, and also much that remained on the beach of Time as flotsam and jetsam from issues long since dead.

Nevertheless, we soon found that nearly every provision was the very ark of some covenant to some group or interest, and in their eyes far too sacrosanct ever to be breathed upon. Wherever we held hearings voices of consternation clamored.

Gradually, however, we made progress because of the masterful leadership of the Chairman in avoiding the paralysis of partisan contention within the Commission itself. When Rockefeller was elected Governor on November 4, 1958, David W. Peck, formerly the Presiding Justice of the Appellate Division, First Department, succeeded him as the Commission's Chairman.

We made and published extended studies of the history of the constitutional development in the State; of the relation between state and federal constitutions; and of the principles which should separate constitution framing from legislation.

The Legislature, however, did not provide the legislation necessary for convening a state convention to revise the Constitution as a whole. As a result, the Commission was thrown back on proposing particular amendments.

The existing Constitution required that any such proposed amendment must first be presented to the legislature. If approved by concurrent resolutions of the Senate and Assembly at two successive Legislatures with a general election intervening, it would then be submitted to the People by way of a referendum at the next general election.

At the general elections in 1962 and 1963, the people of New York adopted a number of such amendments submitted by the Commission and processed by concurrent resolutions of the Senate and Assembly. These amendments greatly simplified and shortened many sections of the Constitution.

Nonetheless, the Commission never reached such major constitutional matters as apportionment, education, and taxation. The last appropriation for it to my knowledge was in 1961 (L. 1961, ch. 193).

Some years later, when a State Constitutional Convention submitted a new Constitution in the form of a total revision and substitution, it was overwhelmingly defeated in the popular referendum.

SECTION 6

Presidency of the National Republican Club.
The 1952 Republican National Convention.

I N 1951 THE TRUMAN ADMINISTRATION was near its close. The
Republican Party began marshalling its troops for the 1952 presidential election.

The National Republican Club, with its headquarters at 54 West
40th Street, New York City, had been founded after the Civil War.
Both in name, membership and influence it was truly national and
Republican. The term of the Club's president was for one year and was
filled by membership election.

I was elected for 1951 and reelected for 1952 and 1953. On taking
office I found that the building was overhung with fire violations
which (I was discreetly told) could continue to be disregarded because
of the Club's political standing. Continued laissez faire was urged. I
replied that I did not propose to be headlined as the Club's president if
a disastrous fire occurred. Accordingly, we raised the initiation fees,
the dues, the room rentals, and the dining room and bar charges,
secured the required $40,000, and cleared off the violations.

Monthly meetings, with notable speakers and open debates on current vital topics, were instituted. We held luncheons and dinners periodically when nationally known Republicans were in town and available. The Club's membership and bank account swelled.

The Event of the Year was the annual Lincoln Day Dinner in the
Waldorf Astoria—a triple dais affair with a baby elephant from the Cir-
cus, an opera singer, and a battery of headline orators.

An unbilled feature of one of these dinners could easily have
been my public suicide! Pride, it has been authoritatively said, goeth

before a fall. When the waiters had cleared the tables, I arose in the full sartorial dignity of the presidential office to open by loading with praise the officers and committeemen who had created this "Mammoth Dinner."

Confident that I needed no notes, I reeled off the names and the eulogies, until I finally came to the last. Suddenly I could not remember the hero's name. Governor Dewey was on my right and a United States Senator on my left, and 1500 elite were in front of me. I played for time by piling up wordy laudation, until continuance reached the brink of the yawning precipice.

The only way out was to stage a heart attack, fall off the dais at the feet of Mrs. Tuttle sitting at the table directly below the podium, and break my neck. Just as I was poising myself for the dive my guardian angel — God bless her — came rushing down to the rescue, and whispered that the first letter was "C". Association flashed! Fortissimo! "Our great and good friend and beloved treasurer, Conrad Pitcher! May his tribe increase!" Deafening applause!

In the taxi on the way home I asked Mrs. Tuttle if she had sensed how close she had come to being a widow. She said that she had never seen me in better form. I kissed her. Lesson for after-dinner speakers:

Don't be too proud to have a few lowly notes!

IN 1952 I WAS ELECTED a delegate to the Republican National Convention which met in Chicago in July to nominate the Party's candidate for President of the United States. In preparation for the Convention, we had strenuous debates at the Club between the Eisenhower and Taft forces. The overwhelming sentiment was for Eisenhower.

The Convention met in weather that matched the superheat of the contest. I was elected teller for the 96 votes of the New York delegation, and was pictured on nationwide television standing up beside the New York banner and calling out "90 votes for Eisenhower and 6 for Taft."

When my third term was expiring, I felt that the responsibility had been carried long enough. I settled for a banquet.

———◆◆◆———

SECTION 7

The Judgeships I Declined—and Why.

S HORTLY AFTER I HAD TAKEN OFFICE as United States Attorney,
President Coolidge offered to appoint me United States District
Judge.

I went into what, to borrow a phrase, might be called "transcen-
dental meditation." As a judge, one would be a sort of cloistered judicial monk, together with a few fellow monks. The daily grind would
be playing critic to other people's dramas, good or bad. Was it an
acceptable career? And above all, as I looked into myself, was I really
qualified?

While I was balancing the scales of judgment, my friend Frank J.
Coleman, Republican leader of the Silk Stocking District, invited me
to lunch with him at the Singer Building. During the second course he
said:

> Charlie, can you let me know whether you are taking that
> judgeship? If you aren't, I am next in line.

I replied:

> Frank, do you remember that in English history there was
> once a man called "Warwick, the King Maker"? I am now
> "Tuttle, the Judge Maker" Get yourself measured for a silk
> robe, and accept my condolence.

Appointed on June 1, 1927, Judge Coleman served with distinction
until his death.

Two other offers came while I was still United States Attorney.
One was from President Hoover in the latter part of my service. The
other was Judge Manton's proposal to recommend me for a seat in his
Court—the United States Court of Appeals. I declined both.

CHARLES H. TUTTLE ON JUDGESHIP OFFERS:

"I never had had ambition for a judgeship, and felt no talent or taste for its obligations and confinements."

Years later, the office held by Judge Philip J. McCook in the Supreme Court, First Judicial District, became vacant. It was early in 1943. Governor Dewey offered me the appointment for the unexpired term and spoke with confidence that I could be assured of a bi-partisan endorsement at the following election, with a reasonable prospect of moving up later to the Appellate Division.

Again, I respectfully declined, and recommended for his consideration David W. Peck, who had been one of my ablest assistants in the United States Attorney's office and had already become outstanding in the profession. David was appointed on July 15, 1943, and later created a most memorable record as Presiding Judge of the Appellate Division.

One hot June day I had a business engagement in the 23rd Street area. At its conclusion, I found I had half an hour to kill before going to a friend's home for dinner. The trees in the Park extended an inviting shade; but all the benches were occupied with habitual practitioners of unemployment. Eventually I found a seat between two of them, and became absorbed in the evening newspaper. After a while I was conscious that two men were passing me on the asphalt path. One was saying to the other:

Isn't it too bad that Charlie Tuttle has sunk so low!

I looked up. The speaker was his Honor, David W. Peck, who had just left the Appellate Division court house across the street. My protest was wasted on their backs.

As one reviews one's life, among the most fascinating speculations is this: *Where would the other road have led, if I had chosen it?*

I did, however, once act as a referee, and in a rather large matter.

Involved was the settlement of the accounts of the United States Trust Company as trustee under the will of Theron R. Butler. The question was the proper disposition of the proceeds of the trustee's sale of 2,100 shares of the stock of the Lake Shore & Michigan Southern Railway Company for $500 a share, thus aggregating $1,050,000.

The trustee had credited the entire sum to capital. The life beneficiaries claimed that income should have been credited with a fair share.

The matter was sent to me as referee. Much testimony was taken. In an extended report I directed the transfer from principal to income of $261,471.00, to be apportioned according to the number of shares sold. I was promptly reversed by the Surrogate who ruled the entire proceeds to be principal (106 Misc. 375★).

But this gall and wormwood became custard pie, when the Appellate Division unanimously reversed the Surrogate and unanimously sustained my decision (190 App. Div. 494★★). Further sweetening was added when the Court of Appeals unanimously affirmed the Appellate Division and "directed the Surrogate to enter a decree confirming the report of the referee" (229 N.Y. 598 [1920]).

Perhaps one reason I never accepted a judgeship was because *Matter of United States Trust Company* left me with a judicial record which could only be worsened and never bettered.

SECTION 8

A Degree of Doctor of Laws from Syracuse University, Chancellor Tolley.

I N A CEREMONY PRESIDED OVER by Chancellor William Pearson Tolley, Syracuse University conferred upon me the degree of Doctor of Laws and the accompanying Orange Hood on June 11, 1952.★★★ The framed parchment hangs on my office wall beside the framed parchment of a like degree subsequently conferred by City College and the State Board of Regents.

Chancellor Tolley was a most gracious host on that mid-June day, escorting Hélène and me on a leisurely tour of the principal academic buildings and of the spreading handsome campuses.

★ *In re Butler's Estate (Sur. Ct. 1919)*

★★ *In re United States Trust Co. of New York.*

★★★ In the investiture citation to Charles Tuttle, Chancellor Tolley described the degree recipient in words prized by the Tuttle family: *"Citizenship at its Best."*

Here was a University that gave physical and spiritual witness to the American faith that the right to search for the Truth is the inalienable endowment of every man and is the essential element whereby human society can maintain itself and progress in freedom, justice and brother-hood. Here was a University dedicated as a center for recruitment against the neo-barbarism of the present times.

While what was outward in structures and grounds was a temple of learning, what was inward was the inborn urge of the Spirit of Man to seek filiation with the Spirit of Truth.

The passage of several millennia has not dimmed in the slightest the truth of Socrates' profound saying that "the life which is unexamined is not worth living." The inculcation of capacity for such examination should be a prime educational objective. Rightly pursued it can give to personal and community living the expanded space of a new dimension.

SECTION 9

Some Unforgettable Recollections of an Unforgettable Man, Fiorello H. La Guardia.

I HAVE ALREADY WRITTEN of my first meeting with Fiorello La Guardia at a Republican Rally in a smoke-filled room two flights up on East 125th Street when in 1916 he was running for Congress and I was making my first political speech.★

I have also written how what happened there led, many years later, to my leaving the Republican City Caucus in 1933 as chairman of its committee to meet with Judge Samuel Seabury to put together a Fusion Ticket with La Guardia for Mayor.★★

Now I will go on from there.

★ See Chapter 5, Section 1, pp. 95-96.
★★ See Chapter 5, Section 1, pp. 96–97.

Part I: THE VOW

FIORELLO LA GUARDIA took office as mayor of New York on January 1, 1934. The then chairman of the Board of Higher Education was Mark Eisner—one of the best chairmen in all my fifty-three years on the Board. His nine-year term was to expire on June 30th of the next year. My colleagues urged me to ask La Guardia's assurance that Mark would be reappointed. They were concerned that, because Mark was a law partner of Tammany Boss George Olvany, La Guardia would not reappoint him.

Soon I was sitting with the Mayor. After some reminiscences, there followed a conversation so remarkable that I have always remembered it nearly verbatim:

Fiorello, in your campaign you pledged yourself to appoint men on ability rather than political affiliation. Mark Eisner has been a chairman of outstanding ability. We of the Board unanimously and earnestly hope that you will reappoint him.

Charlie, don't you know that I am an Italian, and that when an Italian makes a vow he keeps it?

Fiorello, I know about the Italian part but not about the vow.

Charlie, when I was elected Mayor I made a vow that I would not reappoint to the Board of Higher Education or the Board of Education anyone who had been appointed by a Tammany Mayor. You will have to tell Mark that I will keep my vow.

What the h--- are you laughing at?

Fiorello, I am laughing because I have been appointed and reappointed by four Tammany Mayors. To apply that vow to me, you will have to be reelected. Your term as Mayor runs only four years, whereas the balance of my term on the Board runs for five years.

I told this to Mark Eisner, and he resigned at once without waiting till June.

Four years went by. I ran around making speeches for La Guardia's renomination and reelection. My fourth term on the Board of Higher Education would expire on June 30 in the first year of La Guardia's second term. My colleagues on the Board wanted to send a committee to tell him that I was (to use their exaggerated term) "indispensable." I forbade it. I wanted nothing said to him about me by anyone. To myself, I said that that "vow" would be interesting to watch. June 30 came. No word. *The vow!*

At 5:00 p.m. the Mayor's secretary telephoned that the Mayor wished to see me at once. I walked up Nassau Street to City Hall composing a pretty speech. "It's all right, Fiorello, you must not break a vow because of me. Hereafter if you have some nice civic committee which pays no salary I will be happy to serve on it."

Fiorello was alone, writing fiercely. I stood in the doorway. Finally, conscious that someone was gazing at him, he looked up and scowled darkly. "Charlie, hold up your right hand and be sworn before I change my mind!"

Part II: THE WEDDING

IN THE SUMMER OF 1934, my daughter Charlotte, who had inherited my love of the law and had become one of the first women editors of the *Columbia Law Review,* married Howard Westwood, a previous year's *Review* editor, who had served as a law clerk to Justice Harlan F. Stone of the United States Supreme Court. The wedding was to be in St. James Episcopal Church in the Village of Lake George, New York.

Several days before the wedding, I was getting ready to leave my office and head north to "give the bride away." The telephone rang. "This is Fiorello. I wanted you to know that I will attend your daughter's wedding." I asked if he was aware that the distance was 210 miles. He was; but he would drive up with his wife in the morning and back in the afternoon.

> *Make no mistake, Charlie. I am doing this for your daughter, not for you. I have followed her career from the time she was in Vassar. She is a **real** progressive.*

I hurried to Lake George, and got hold of Henry Gabb, the Village mayor. After filling him in about our last-minute surprise guest, I told

Courtesy of Lake George Village

FIORELLO LA GUARDIA *(left)*
AND CHARLES H. TUTTLE
Lake George Wedding, 1934

Mr. Gabb that it would be up to him to do the honors—as one mayor to another. I advised him to turn out the entire Village motorcycle police force *(one man!)* to meet New York City's Mayor at the Village line and escort him in—with a finger kept pressed down hard on the siren. Later, I arranged refreshments for Fiorello and his wife at the venerable Fort William Henry Hotel.

When I walked up the aisle with my daughter on my arm that Saturday, there sat Fiorello La Guardia and his wife, beaming, *in the front pew.* After the ceremony they went to Rockledge, my summer home, mingled graciously with our guests, and then jumped into their car for the 210-mile return trip to the City.

It was a crazy thing for him to do. But that was La Guardia, one hundred percent. When he did a fine thing, nothing could be finer!

Part III: THE TEMPLE

A WORLD'S FAIR was held in Flushing Meadows in 1939-40, with the theme "The America of Tomorrow."

An interfaith group of which I was a member firmly believed that such a worldwide portrayal of the American dream of "Tomorrow" could not be truthful and complete without the inclusion of a portrayal of the American dream of "Religion in the World of Tomorrow."

Accordingly, our group incorporated itself as "The Temple of Religion at the World's Fair," raised a large fund—contributed generously by Catholics, Jews and Protestants—and erected a handsome ecclesiastical edifice, with accompanying landscaping, dedicated to the "Fatherhood of God and the Brotherhood of Man."

This temple was to be available without charge for any religious group wishing to use it for worship or a brotherhood purpose. The public was admitted free. No collection or solicitation of money and no sales were allowed either in the Temple or its grounds.

When the day for the Temple's dedication approached, our group sought out Mayor La Guardia with the request that he issue a citywide proclamation dedicating the day to this Temple of Religion at the World's Fair.

He asked for a draft. When we submitted it, he said it did not have much "ring." The following day's newspapers carried in full a proclamation wholly of his own composition which rivaled in "ring" the best trumpet calls of Old Testament Prophets.

He followed this up by presiding at an overflow luncheon at the Hotel Astor where each table was equally divided among the religious groups. The addresses were made by Alfred E. Smith for the Catholics, Mark Eisner for the Jews, and myself for the Protestants. When La Guardia went "all out," he pushed for the zenith. A citywide fund-raising campaign followed.

After two years the Fair closed. Although nearly all other features finished *in the red,* the Temple of Religion, which charged nothing, sold nothing, and took up no collections, finished *in the black*. With all bills paid, we were left with a net of about $100. Religion without dogma had proved good economics.

"FREEDOM OF WORSHIP"
by Norman Rockwell

The directors voted this munificent surplus to the interfaith group sponsoring the Released Time Program for Religious Education of children in the City's public schools.

If any individual was the ***deus ex machina*** behind this unimaginable miracle, that individual was Fiorello La Guardia.

CHAPTER TEN

SELECTIVE SERVICE CHAIRMAN: WORLD WARS I and II

————◆◆◆————

SECTION 1

Chairman during World War I of Selective Service Board, Local 141.

With all thy faults I love thee still. My Country.

— COWPER, *The Task*

WHEN WE ENTERED WORLD WAR I, I was appointed Chairman of Selective Service Board, Local 141, with offices in the Main Hall of City College, on Morningside Heights. I had two associate members, a government appeal agent and a small staff. Our Board was the first in the City to operate. The Government told us that it looked to us as a showcase to convince the people that the draft law, run through local boards by civilians, should have public confidence and cooperation. Some incidents are unforgettable.

Part I: "MY NAME IS MURPHY"

A BLAZING HOT DAY in July 1917 was dull with the monotony of claims for exemptions. The representatives of the press chided me for not providing patriotic stories for publication, and unblushingly intimated that, if I wanted to see the War won, I should invent a thriller. I hesitated.

In the middle of the evening there entered an old lady with a shawl over her head. She was followed by a youth seemingly just within the draft age. Leaning on a cane, she was panting from walking up the long hill to City College and up two flights of stairs. I seated her. She said she was a widow, and that the lad was her only child and her main support. I was directing her to the exemption desk when she startled me by saying that she did not wish to claim exemption. I told her that it was the policy of the law to grant exemption in such a case as hers. She persisted. She would not claim exemption. I asked why. Then there came into her old eyes a light of a kind one is seldom privileged to see. She said simply: "My name is Murphy. The Murphys never claim exemption."

Reverently I called over the representatives of the press. Next day there were banner headlines: **MURPHYS NEVER CLAIM EXEMPTION.**

Part II: THE IMMORTAL STORY OF "CASEY"

CASEY WAS UNATTACHED. He had been reared in the school of the saloons along Amsterdam Avenue. Nevertheless he had become dimly conscious that his Uncle Sam was in a tough fight and needed him badly. He kept coming, more or less maudlin, to demand that we send him at once. He could not seem to understand that, because his draft number was far down the line, he would have to wait, perhaps for months.

One day came our first call for men, twelve in number. We were told that in honor of the occasion we could call for volunteers regardless of draft numbers. Casey heard and rushed in quite ablaze with enthusiasm, natural and artificial. It took our whole staff to subdue him to the tragic reality that he was the *thirteenth* to volunteer and hence could not go.

At last the great day came when, with a band, flags and our feminine staff gaily appareled, we took our twelve heroes to the Pennsylvania Station. After they were well kissed by the girls, we put them on the train to Camp Upton, Long Island.

Then an appalling apparition appeared. As the train started, Casey stepped out on the back platform and put his fingers to his nose in a gesture which through the ages has not been indicative of much respect. My associates inquired whether we could all be court martialed for sending thirteen men when only twelve were allowed. Bumptiously I said: "Leave it to me."

Next morning, an angry officer telephoned me from Camp Upton to demand that we get Casey out of the Camp, because the Army was not succeeding in doing so. I said: "Hold it, Officer! Do you want to win this war? If you do, keep that thirteenth man, and the War is all over." I hung up.

Some months later, I was doing paperwork in the evening at the Draft Board. I became conscious that someone was looking down at me. I glanced up. *Behold, it was Casey!* He was in full uniform. His back was straight. His eyes were bright. His cheeks were ruddy. Saluting, he said that he had stopped in to thank me. He was leaving soon.

Months later, during the decisive battle of San Mihiel*, we received a telegram from the War Department. Our Casey had been elevated into the Valhalla of American heroes who had given their all. He had indeed fought for his Uncle Sam.

Part III: "YOU THOUGHT I WAS 'YELLOW'"

ONE MORE UNFORGETTABLE STORY. An old man had two sons, one over and the other just below the draft age but within enlistment age. They and their father ran a small store on Amsterdam Avenue. We drafted the older son. The old man and his wife were in tears. I do not know whether we acted within the law's letter, but finally said that, if the younger son enlisted and appeared before us in uniform, we would defer the older. This was done.

---

* During World War I, the San Mihiel salient, held by the Germans from 1914, commanded two important railroads. It was captured by the U.S. Army under General Pershing in the autumn of 1918.

Several months later I was told at my law office that a young man with the name of the older son wanted to see me. I sent word that I did draft business only at the Draft Board. Word came back it was urgent.

In came the older son, in uniform!

> *Mr. Tuttle, I know you thought I was "yellow." I have come to think so too. I could not sleep nights. I kept dreaming of my younger brother dead on the battlefield. I had traded away his life for mine. I know I cannot get him out of the Army, but I can join him. I am on my way.*

He had found his own answer to the age old question: *"Am I my brother's keeper?"* (Genesis 4:9).

SECTION 2

Chairmanship During World War II of the Selective Service Appeal Board.

DURING WORLD WAR II the Selective Service System established an Appeal Board of five members to hear and determine appeals from the many Local Boards in Manhattan. I was designated Chairman.

The Board's work was huge and daily. We received every week one hundred or more appeals by draftees or the Government. Our practice was to write a brief memorandum in every case, so that both the Local Board, the draftee and the Government would know the reasons for our decisions. Many of the records on appeal were voluminous. Nevertheless the exigencies of the War required almost immediate decisions.

There was much human drama in many of the appeals.

Part I: "DON'T PAY ANY ATTENTION"

THE MEMORY of one of them leaves me torn between laughing and crying.

The young man was the only child of extremely wealthy parents. He was in good health, unmarried, and without any dependents. The difficulty was that he was "the apple of his mother's eye" — too precious to be hazarded with the public's youths. She had educated him at home with expensive tutors. The psychiatric experts employed by the parents made affidavits that her mind, to say nothing of her life, would be imperiled by the thought of his being thrown with a crowd of crude recruits and tough sergeants. The Local Board slapped him into 1A. Up came an appeal, with a voluminous record full of medical affidavits and terminologies. In thumbing through them, a slip of paper fell out. On it in the boy's handwriting was this confidential message: "I took this appeal because my mother made me, but please don't pay any attention to it." We didn't!

Part II: THE "MANHATTAN PROJECT"

THEN THERE WAS THE CASE of the "Manhattan Project." The Local Board had put in 1A two students in the Science Department at Columbia. The record had cryptic references to a "Manhattan Project." The term meant nothing to the Local Board. The students had no dependents. Columbia appealed. Could it possibly be that this obscure fancy term had some relation to the War? I called up the Army Colonel who was the Draft System's Administrator for Manhattan.

"Colonel, we have an appeal, with the words 'Manhattan Project.'" Before I could get further, there came back a stream of Army vernacular that, with some editing, amounted to asking whether I wanted to be shot for uttering those words on the telephone. None of us did, so we meekly and discreetly granted deferment because of essential employment.

Later, when the Manhattan Project fell on Hiroshima, we all began boasting that through our Appeal Board we had won the War.

Of course there were indirect and, at times, adroitly managed efforts to influence our decisions.

Part III: A Very Simple Formula

After the War was over and our Appeal Board members had been accorded Selective Service medals and been discharged, a very distinguished citizen who was a close friend and bridge crony, told me that he had a very simple formula for discouraging appeals from 1A classifications by Local Boards. Parents who knew of his friendship with me had come to him and tactfully suggested that, although they would not think of asking him to use his friendship with Mr. Tuttle to urge a reversal and deferment, nevertheless would he please tactfully suggest to Mr. Tuttle that Mr. Tuttle take a special interest in so-and-so's appeal.

My friend said that his formula was to compliment the parents on their patriotic purpose to get their son into the military forces immediately. When they protested that that was the very last thing they wanted, he replied that if he made mention to Mr. Tuttle of so-and-so's appeal, the lad's 1A would be affirmed before sunset. In consternation the parents said that on second thought they would prefer nothing be said.

Thereafter, in his case, I renounced one of the chief enchantments of contract bridge—chiding your partner for his *(in your eyes)* moronic errors.

CHAPTER ELEVEN

RELIGIOUS AND PHILANTHROPIC ORGANIZATIONS AND ACTIVITIES

———⟫◆⟪———

SECTION 1

Released Time for Religious Education of Public School Children.

IN 1925 AN INTERFAITH GROUP of fifteen began meeting in the rectory of St. Patrick's Cathedral amid all the sacred symbols dear to the Catholic heart.

The Catholic group of five was headed by Monsignor Lavelle, the rector of the Cathedral; the Jewish group of five by Dr. David de Sola Pool, the Rabbi of the Portuguese Synagogue; and the Protestant group of five by myself, then President of the Greater New York Federation of Churches.

CHARLES TUTTLE, RELIGIOUS LEADER

Seated above, right: Conferring with leaders of the Protestant
Council of the City of New York; *Below, right:* Meeting with
religious leaders in the rectory of St. Patrick's Cathedral. In
1925, an interfaith group of Protestants, Catholics and Jews
had begun meeting at the Cathedral. These historic meetings
were chaired by Charles Tuttle, who was then also serving as
president of the Greater New York Federation of Churches.

These groups met to discuss and to agree upon methods within the Education Law and the constitutional separation of Church and State whereby religious instruction could be given to public school children — in a manner offsetting the possible implications of a purely secular system of public education that religion was a thing apart from the American way of life and negligible. I had the honor of being elected chairman, with Monsignor Lavelle and Rabbi Pool as vice-chairmen.

These meetings were, I believe, one of the first steps forward in the present worldwide movement known as Ecumenism.

A consensus was reached; and what is known as "the Released Time Program" was born in 1925. On the request of the parent, a child would be excused during school time for up to one hour a week to attend religious instruction at a center designated by the parent and off school grounds. No public funds or property were used to support the Program.

The School Board of White Plains, Westchester County, accepted the Plan and put it into effect, with the tacit assent of the State Commissioner of Education.

Immediately, Joseph Lewis, President of the Free Thinker's Society of America (an atheist group) sued for a peremptory order of mandamus to compel the State Commissioner of Education to direct discontinuance of the Plan. One of the counsel for Lewis was Arthur Garfield Hays, who had shared with Clarence S. Darrow the fame of "the Monkey Trial" in Tennessee. My role was that of counsel for the Greater New York Federation of Churches and the New York State Sunday School Association as *amici curiae*.

The Lewis application was denied unanimously in all the New York courts (127 Misc. 135★; aff'd 219 App. Div. 233; aff'd 245 N.Y. 195; motion for reargument denied, 245 N.Y. 620).

Mr. Lewis charged that this program for Released Time was put forward "at the instigation of an aggregation of ecclesiastical and political medievalists (Rec. on App., p. 61). In a contemporaneous

★ *People ex rel. Lewis v. Graves (Sup. Ct. 1926).*

public statement quoted by *The New York Times* of February 22, 1926,
Mr. Lewis said:

> *Modern civilization rests upon physical science. . . . The*
> *public schools of the great state of New York are under abject*
> *subservience to two sinister forces which are and always will be*
> *inimical to true education and scientific progress—Fundamen-*
> *talism in the Protestant and the Roman Catholic Church, its*
> *logical counterpart.*

Mr. Lewis' brief of 220 pages in the Court of Appeals devoted
many pages of diatribe at me by name. A typical ironic phrasing was:
"Mr. Charles H. Tuttle's unmaterialistic, un-pagan and perfectly
altruistic and humanitarian projects for illegal injection of religious
instruction into the public schools" (pp. 126-7).

The interfaith group that thus came together in the rectory of St.
Patrick's Cathedral in 1925 continues as sponsor for this Released
Time Program, and I continue to have the honor of being its Chairman. After the foregoing court decisions the Program was given statutory backing by the Legislature for use throughout the State. In New
York City the parents of some 100,000 public school children have
annually taken advantage of it.

Judge Ellis J. Staley, in his memorable opinion at Special Term,
declared that the Released Time Program was lawfully based on the
following propositions (p. 140):

> *That the right of the parent to direct the training and nur-*
> *ture of the child is a fundamental right;*
>
> *That the obligations of citizenship require the promotion of*
> *a spirit of patriotic and civic service and the fostering in children*
> *of moral as well as intellectual qualities;*
>
> *That the religious conscience, conviction and accountability*
> *are the least dispensable foundations for good citizenship and*
> *real patriotism;*
>
> *That moral growth and intellectual growth go hand in hand*
> *to make the essential elements of character and good citizenship;*

That the right of the State to enforce school attendance does not mean that the mental and moral development of all children must be limited to a common mold, and that all children must be standardized;

That the regulation does not create a union between church and State, or teach any sectarianism in the schools or invade the religious freedom or conscience of any individual.

Some years later the opposition again attacked, and after losing again in the New York courts (198 Misc. 631⋆; aff'd 278 App. Div. 573; aff'd 303 N.Y. 161), went to the Supreme Court of the United States in a suit entitled *Zorach v. Clauson.*

Counsel for the appellants argued that, under this Released Time Plan, "the weight and influence of the (public) school is put behind a program for religious instruction; the school is a crutch on which the churches are leaning for support in their religious training."

I argued for affirmance in behalf of the Greater New York Coordinating Committee on Released Time of Jews, Protestants and Roman Catholics. Briefs *amici curiae* were submitted in support by the Attorneys General of California, Indiana, Kentucky, Maine, Massachusetts, Oregon, Pennsylvania, and West Virginia.

The issues to quote the Supreme Court's opinion were (343 U.S. 306, 310):

Whether New York by this system has either prohibited the "free exercise" of religion or has made a law "respecting an establishment of religion" within the meaning of the First Amendment.

On April 28, 1952, the Supreme Court upheld the New York Plan by a vote of six to three. Justice William O. Douglas wrote the prevailing opinion. In it he emphasized that the Court adhered to its prior decision in the *McCollum* case on the ground that in that case "the classrooms were used for religious instruction and the force of the public school was used to promote that instruction." On the other hand,

---

⋆ *Zorach v. Clauson (Sup. Ct. 1950).*

he said that, under the New York Plan "the public schools do no more than accommodate their schedules to a program of outside religious instruction." He further said, in speaking for the Court (pp. 313-4):

> *When the state encourages religious instruction or cooperates with religious authorities by adjusting the schedule of public events to sectarian needs, it follows the best of traditions. For it then respects the religious nature of our people and accommodates the public service to their spiritual needs. To hold that it may not would be to find in the Constitution a requirement that the government show callous indifference to religious groups. That would be preferring those who believe in no religion over those who do believe.*

In short, the Church is not a poor relative in the house of the State.

Presently, some three million or more public school children throughout the United States are receiving religious instruction under the aegis of this Program's ecumenical beginning in the rectory of St. Patrick's Cathedral in 1925.

SECTION 2

The Protestant Council of the City of New York. The National Council of Churches. Help from a Catholic.

That they all may be one.
— ST. JOHN 17:21

SEVERAL YEARS AFTER the 1927 decision of the State Court of Appeals upholding the constitutionality of the Released Time Program, I was elected President of the Greater New York Federation of Churches, and have held various offices therein.

An immediate task was to enlarge the constituency of the Federation so as to include other Protestant agencies in the City. To this end and after much negotiation, the Protestant Council of the City of New York was incorporated in October 1943, as a New York membership corporation. In 1955 I received the Council's DISTINGUISHED SERVICE AWARD "for untiring labor for Christian Education of Children and Youth."

In 1950 the Federal Council of Churches of Christ in America and various other large Protestant national organizations agreed upon a plan of union under the name of the National Council of the Churches of Christ in the United States of America. I was asked to prepare and arrange for a charter.

The leaders in this movement agreed with me that such a national organization deserved a national charter, such as those of the Boy Scouts and the Girl Scouts. A committee of three, of which I was one, then visited President Harry Truman on June 24, 1950. The President told us that he would advocate such a charter, directing us to convey his advocacy to the Vice President and the Speaker of the House. Appointments were accordingly made, but the next day North Korea invaded South Korea, and both the President and Congress became preoccupied with the international crisis.

I therefore drew a charter for the new National Council under the Membership Corporations Law of the State of New York. The draft was unanimously adopted at the December 1950 organization meeting in Cleveland, Ohio, and was signed by representatives of all the constituent communions.

Courtesy of Harry S. Truman Library / NARA

HARRY S. TRUMAN in the Oval Office

Before carrying the draft to Cleveland, I had taken the precaution to have its legality also approved in writing by the office of the New York Secretary of State, where after such approval the law required the executed certificates to be filed.

On returning to New York, I sent a messenger to Albany to file the executed certificate. He telephoned me in great consternation that an assistant in the office of the Secretary of State now claimed that a clause as to power to receive gifts was deemed illegal and that filing was positively refused. I protested, in vain, that the draft's legality had already been approved in writing.

In great concern I then telephoned directly to the Secretary of State himself, the Honorable Thomas J. Curran, who had been one of my principal assistants while I was United States Attorney and who was an ardent Roman Catholic. I emphasized the devastating embarrassment to me and some forty million Protestants consequent upon this belated withdrawal by his office of written approval. His reply was: "Chief, it would never do for one Roman Catholic to hold up *forty million Protestants*. I will personally file their certificate at once." Ecumenism smiled happily on the legitimizing of that Charter.

The certificate was a brief statement of the purpose and powers of the National Council of Churches as "an inclusive cooperative agency of Christian Churches in the United States of America" organized "to bring churches into further united service for Christ and the world," and "to promote the application of the law of Christ in every relation of life." A Constitution and General bylaws followed. From then until the present I have served as the National Council's "general counsel." Some events in my service as such are narrated separately.

—————◄◆►—————

SECTION 3

Presidency of Brotherhood-in-Action. A Presiding Justice and His Vision.

ONE DAY IN 1960 the Honorable George Beldock, Presiding Justice of the Appellate Division, Second Department, inquired by telephone when he could see me at my office. He over-ruled my protest that I would come to his Chambers.

When he arrived, he outlined "a vision" which he had had for years and in the attainment of which he was asking my participation. I will tell the "vision" in his own words when as "Founder" he later laid the "vision's" cornerstone at the northwest corner of 40th Street and Seventh Avenue, Manhattan, on September 12, 1962:

> *Brotherhood-in-Action is the culmination of a vision that took shape in the minds of a few men as long ago as 1945.*
>
> *World War II had just ended in a cataclysm of destruction. Once again, man's inhumanity to man had brought death and ruin to millions all over the world. New forces had been unleashed that presented mankind with the necessity for developing means of communication for better understanding between all men. Although the fighting had at last ended, the ideal of Brotherhood among men seemed as far from realization as ever.*
>
> *This was the background against which a small group of idealistic businessmen and civic leaders in midtown New York began to seek ways in which men could be persuaded to turn away from conflict to cooperation and improve human relations. Out of their efforts grew the idea of Brotherhood-in-Action as a program fostering that ideal.*
>
> *Brotherhood-in-Action represents the carefully thought out views not only of its founders but also of those who were later attracted by the vision that had inspired them and joined with them in helping to make it come true.*

During his visit, Judge Beldock told me that the "Vision" would be incorporated. He asked me to share in it as president.

Hence, when the cornerstone was laid in the presence of New York's Governor Nelson Rockefeller, Senator Jacob Javits and Mayor Robert Wagner, I had the privilege of following Judge Beldock's address and saying:

Nowhere on our planet is there a pedestal loftier than this World-City from which to radiate the eternal light of Brotherhood.

Here within the compass of a few miles are the greatest concentrations of all things human, the ethnic center of mankind, the fullest intermingling of all cultures and beliefs, the economic center of the commerce of the oceans, the council of chambers of international finance.

Here also in this microcosm of humanity there will now be the Home and the Witness of Brotherhood-in-Action, a Center of Hospitality beside these crossroads of the world, to which all men of goodwill, singly or in association, may repair and find encouragement to rekindle the flame of their dedication to the tearing down of the walls dividing men from men.

Those who come as strangers from far parts will find within this edifice the symbols of that harmony and beauty which wordlessly supply a communication of fraternity among all men.

Its great purpose is to provide well-planned facilities and a center which all who are so inclined may find helpful for their objectives.

On that cornerstone there has since been reared a huge six-story building in which there is daily fulfillment of the unique purpose of Brotherhood-in-Action to encourage and assist the multiplicity of programs represented by the various organizations, local and national, which share and work in the commitment by men and women of all faiths to the one supreme ideal which all faiths share in common—the faith that all men are brothers.

The distinctive and unique goal of Brotherhood-in-Action is to help all such other agencies to achieve their own goals in their own ways, and to do so in the hope that thereby the goals of each will be better attained by common cooperation. To these ends the building provides gratuitously a theatre-auditorium, a library, seminar and conference rooms, radio and television studios, and offices. As had been well said, the building combines the monumental with the functional.

On May 16, 1966, the building was dedicated symbolically at a huge dinner at the Hotel Americana attended by more than 1,400 persons. Governor Rockefeller made the dedicatory address. Francis Cardinal Spellman was the special guest of honor.

At the dinner I was presented a bronze plaque with the words:

BROTHERHOOD-IN-ACTION
HUMAN RELATIONS AWARD

to

HON. CHARLES H. TUTTLE
FORMER UNITED STATES ATTORNEY
GENERAL COUNSEL TO THE NATIONAL
COUNCIL OF CHURCHES OF CHRIST
FOR HIS LIFETIME OF DEDICATION
TO THE ADVANCEMENT OF
BROTHERHOOD AMONG ALL MEN

The full text of my address in response was published in the Congressional Record of May 25, 1966, pp. A 2814-15.

The Board of Governors of Brotherhood-in-Action is a large and uniquely distinguished roll call of our city's foremost citizens representing all faiths and ethnic groups. In their own persons as well as in their deeds they symbolize the common bond of fraternity which was Judge Beldock's "vision" of long ago.

> *Grant us brotherhood,*
> *not only for this day but for all our years —*
> *a brotherhood not of words but of acts and deeds.*

> – from a prayer by President
> Franklin D. Roosevelt
> *Flag Day, June 14, 1942*

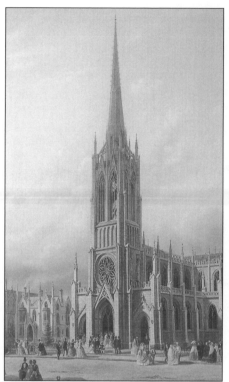

Detail of 1858 painting by Ferdinand Richardt; courtesy of Grace Church Archives

SECTION 4

Grace Episcopal Church: A National Shrine

S HORTLY AFTER MY WIFE
HÉLÈNE and I had moved
from Convent Avenue to University Place in 1939, Dr. Louis
W. Pitt, the rector of Grace
Church and an eminent clergyman of the Episcopal Diocese,
invited us to join his parish.

Grace Church is quite
understandably an official
national shrine. Its pure Gothic
architecture, its cathedral-like
design and romantic beauty, and
its prominent identification

GRACE CHURCH
Broadway and Fourth Avenue
New York City

with and contributions to New York City's history for a century and a
half, have caused the federal government to enroll it among the price-
less legacies of art, beauty and faith from our nation's past.

When at night I see the illumined spire of Grace Church towering
over the length of lower Broadway and making its gleaming contribution to the radiance of the Light of the World, I feel the awe of its
voiceless message to the humanity hurrying by: "Remember, 'Man
does not live by bread alone.'"

From its clergy Grace Church has continuously given strong leadership to the spiritual life of our City—three bishops including Bishop
Henry Codman Potter of New York, and the distinguished theologians
and civic leaders, William Reed Huntington, Charles Lewis Slattery,
Walter Russell Bowie, and Louis Wetherbee Pitt.

The present [1970] rector, the Rev. Benjamin Minifie, wears on his shoulders the same mantle of consecrated ministry worn by this unique succession of predecessors.

From the first, Grace Church has not been merely another parish church, living (or barely living) unto itself. The day for such a sectarianized church has passed. The walls of a church dedicated to service in the present world may contain the sanctuary and assemblages for worship, but the road which leads from the front door must be the road to Jericho—the road beside which a "neighbor" lies waiting succor. Pope John XXIII called for throwing "open the windows" for a clearer view of that road; and now Grace Church is proposing to set out with enlargement of heart and means on that selfsame road, locally known as Broadway on its west and Fourth Avenue on its east. The road is long and it can lead afar.

The social involvement of Grace Church has been manifested for 75 years by Grace Church School, which presently is a co-educational, integrated, eight-grade elementary school with a kindergarten.

But now the Church's social involvement is in process of being greatly expanded by present plans for enlargement and modernization of its physical facilities on Fourth Avenue. These plans will preserve the consistent row of landmarks on Fourth Avenue that make such a visible contribution to the community. There will be remodeling for additional classrooms, living facilities for the staff and a large community auditorium.

The vision, the planning, the energy and the faith for all this expansion and for the raising of the large required funds have chiefly been supplied by the Rector and by the Honorable Whitney North Seymour who for many years has been Junior Warden in the Church, but in the Nation has been president of the American Bar Association and a member of many government commissions by appointment of the President and the Mayor.

At a vestry meeting last September, Mr. Seymour, with the aid of the architect and a projection camera, portrayed on a screen these extensive expansions and their value to the Church and all beyond. He then moved their approval in principle, and astonished me with including a resolution that the all-purpose community-church-school

Rendering by Elliot Schulnick; courtesy of Grace Church

CHARLES H. TUTTLE HALL★
As shown in 1969 Grace brochure

auditorium be named the "Charles H. Tuttle Hall." I passionately protested. Such honors were only for those who had left this life and I did not intend to be hustled out of it. I had no title deed to any such memorial. Mr. Seymour was the one who had breathed life into those dry bones on Fourth Avenue and should be the one laurelled.

My protests went unheeded. Soon there was a brochure portraying the whole monumental development, and with this preface by the Mayor of the City:

> The plans of Grace Church and its friends for Fourth Avenue are very exciting, since both the Church and the Church School have played a great role in the New York community. Preserving the beautiful Renwick buildings on Fourth Avenue (which share the landmark quality of the Church), making them come alive again, especially adding a Church-School-Community auditorium honoring Charles H. Tuttle, will insure continuation of that role in the challenging city of tomorrow. Charles Tuttle has been a leader in many good causes, and I am delighted that he is to be thus honored in connection with his ninetieth birthday.

> THE HON. JOHN V. LINDSAY
> *Mayor of New York*

Hereafter, if I live long enough and pass in erected state what is now pictured in this brochure, I shall pause to wonder — to wonder "Why?" Can it be that friendship has depths which no plumb line of reason can fathom?

★ *Editor's Note:* In the twenty-first century, "Tuttle Hall" continues as a multi-purpose facility at Grace Church, serving as an auditorium, theater, gym, reception hall and gathering center for the Church and surrounding community.

SECTION 5

My First Diocesan Convention. Can Conscience Exempt from the Law of the Land?

I N MAY 1968, under pressure from the rector of Grace Church, I found myself at the Cathedral of St. John the Divine as a lay delegate to the Diocesan Convention. I assumed that, dutifully and as a "first," I would go along with the prefabricated agenda and be seen and not heard.

But a stumbling block lay in wait. The sixteenth of the printed proposed resolutions advocated an amendment of the Selective Service Law in such wise as to exempt from the draft those who, while not conscientiously opposed to war "in general," nevertheless "discriminate between wars on grounds of moral justification."

The underlying principle of the resolution was that citizenship entitled individual exemption from a law personally deemed morally unjustified and contrary to his private conscience.

In accordance therewith, the resolution advocated the above alternative to the four requirements combined in the existing Selective Service Law as conditioning conscientious exemption, namely:

1. *Conscientious objection to war "in any form";*
2. *"Religious training and belief," creating a sense of duty imposed outside and above oneself;*
3. *Exclusion of any "essentially political, sociological, or philosophical views";*
4. *Exclusion of "a merely personal and moral code."*

Accordingly, when the proposed resolution was reached, I opened the debate by speaking against it in substance as follows:

> Doubtless the resolution reflected the Vietnam War, but neither the resolution nor its underlying principle was or could be limited. Both would introduce into the nature and obligations of American citizenship a preferential and disintegrating personal selectivity as between laws.
>
> Particularly in a population of multifold national origins, creeds and ethnic diversities, such a doctrine of personal selectivity could and would quickly germinate seeds of disunity, personal privilege and disaster, present and future. Already it was being used by hostile powers to stimulate desertions from our armed forces at home and abroad, to disrupt the morale and effectiveness of our men in uniform, and to create among them a sense of injustice which on the brink of combat could be destructive to their unit, their comrades, and our country.
>
> Moreover, if law and order were to be subjected to such a preferential doctrine of personal privilege and exemption, where would its erosion stop or be stopped? Is an individual to be allowed to declare himself exempt from the payment of taxes because some of the tax fund will support purposes which he personally regards as morally unjustified and contrary to his personal conscience? Where will be the line between personal choice and legal obligation? Is a personal moral code to be substitutable for the law of the land?
>
> Furthermore, as the current events showed, this doctrine easily led to efforts by men, themselves secure from the draft because of age, to urge younger men in the name of conscience to resist the draft law and to burn or throw away their draft cards.

At the conclusion of my address there was a standing ovation. But there followed a number of clergymen who sought to picture how deeply distressed in conscience were some young men over the Vietnam war and who felt that therefore they should be left to enjoy *their* private lives in the security which Congress was requiring other young men to protect at the hazard of *their* private lives.

After an hour's discussion, a "vote by orders" was called for, with the consequence that concurrence of the clerical and lay orders was necessary to adoption. The clerical order voted three to two for the resolution. The lay order voted five to one against it. Thus the resolution was defeated.

The interesting question lingers: To what extent and under what conditions is the lay judgment in matters political influenced, if at all, by the clerical judgment?

On the personal side, I now cannot be accused by St. Peter or any other appraiser of having gone through life without having attended at least one Diocesan Convention. I am not sure that St. Peter would want me to go through another.

SECTION 6

Separation of Church and State. Argument before Congress Opposing the So-Called "Becker Amendment"

IN 1962-63 THE UNITED STATES SUPREME COURT twice held uncompromisingly that the First and Fourteenth Amendments to the Constitution of the United States forbade any inculcation or exercise of religion in any public school or other tax-supported building. *Engel v. Vitale,* 370 U.S. 421 (1962); *Abington School District v. Schempp,* 374 U.S. 203 (1963).

These decisions caused great consternation in certain religious circles. Loud was the outcry that the Supreme Court had sided "against God" and was promoting a wholly secular nation.

A powerful movement arose to overrule the Court by the so-called "Becker Amendment" to the Constitution. It read:

SECTION 1. *Nothing in this Constitution shall be deemed to prohibit the offering, reading from, or listening to, prayers or Biblical Scriptures, if participation therein is on a voluntary basis, in any governmental or public school, institution, or place.*

SECTION 2. *Nothing in this Constitution shall be deemed to prohibit making reference to belief in, reliance upon, or invoking the aid of God or a Supreme Being in any governmental or public document, proceeding, activity, ceremony, school, institution, or place, or upon any coinage, currency, or obligation of the United States.*

The House Judiciary Committee held public hearings. As a private citizen and also as the General Counsel of the National Council of Churches, I spoke at length before the Committee in strong opposition to the proposed Amendment. I was questioned at length by the Committee's members.

Thereafter a summary of my address was printed in the Congressional Record (House, p. 11453) of May 20, 1964, and my full address was later printed in the Congressional Record Appendix of June 24, 1964 (p. A3470). Selected paragraphs from the summary read:

It [the Becker Amendment] ties religion, personal liberty, and individual freedom of conscience to National, State, and local ballot boxes. The potentials lurking in its political words throw into reverse the whole theory of our Constitution that the minority and the individual have certain inalienable rights which cannot be abridged by Government or by the majority of the moment....

By its very terms it makes of itself and its subject matter a separate, independent and exclusive constitution....What were prohibitions are replaced by permissions....

There is no escaping the facts that a public school represents an audience assembled by government by compulsion of law; that the program and procedure therein are governmental activities by law; that such activities are paid for by public funds raised by public, general taxation from persons of all beliefs and no beliefs; and that in our pluralistic society any government formulation of a religious exercise in the public schools must entail in the last analysis the overriding by way of the ballot box of the religious beliefs or disbeliefs of dissenting minorities and individuals.

Furthermore, and equally fundamental to personal liberty, is the right and high duty of parents to nurture and direct the destiny of their children. Our children are not the property of the State; and nothing could be more fatal to the substance of liberty than acceptance of any general power of the State to standardize them in matters of religion. . . .

True religion has been authoritatively said to be "the perfect law of liberty." What has true religion to fear from being true to itself?

Thereafter sentiment for the Becker Amendment steadily receded in Congress and throughout the country, and finally vanished.

I close by quoting the following from an address in the House of Representatives on June 2, 1964, by the Honorable John V. Lindsay*.

Courtesy of NYC

MR. LINDSAY: *Mr. Speaker, Mr. Charles H. Tuttle, Counsel to the National Council of Churches of Christ, and one of New York's most distinguished lawyers, testified before and submitted to the Committee on the Judiciary a most perceptive analysis of House Joint Resolution 693 relating to prayer and Bible reading in the public schools and religious references in public affairs. Mr. Tuttle has done a service to the Congress in his thoughtful presentation.* (Congressional Record Appendix, p. A2945)

I cannot understand the belief that God is served by fanning fires of contention about Him among our people. If peace and brotherhood are not what real religion is all about, what is?

---

* Congressman **John Lindsay** *(pictured above)* served as a U.S. Representative for New York's 17th District from 1959 until 1965. He then became Mayor of New York City, serving in that role from 1966 to 1973.

Above: ON TOP O' THE WORLD, 1970
Below: HALCYON, LAKE GEORGE

Photo by Alice H. Schmidt, 2001

CHAPTER TWELVE

LAKE GEORGE. "TOP O' THE WORLD." THE ADIRONDACKS.

Editor's Introduction

THE AUTHOR OF THESE memoirs wrote extensively about his beloved Lake George: its geologic history; its military significance in the mid-eighteenth century; the establishment of the family summer home in the mid-nineteenth century; the development of his mountain resort in the mid-twentieth century; his many activities to protect the Lake's clarity and beauty; the family participation in their village church, St. James; and his connections with many people and projects in the area.

To reflect the author's lifetime Lake George involvement somewhat more fully than is shown in the five sections he provided for this chapter in his autobiography, the editor has included four additional sections drawn from his other published writings. The first is Section One of this chapter which is his second half of "The Family Story" (1896-1956), appearing in the booklet entitled *One Hundred Years on Lake George, 1856-1956*. The booklet was written alternately by him and his wife, inspired by the hundredth anniversary of the Tuttle family's summer residence on the Lake. It was dedicated "to the two generations which have preceded us" and commended "to the many who are succeeding us."

The pen and ink drawings framing the booklet's pages and illustrating its text were by his son-in-law, David D. Lloyd (1911-1962).

The other three additional sections— 7, 8, and 9—are taken from the author's 1970 book, *A Supplement to My Family Memorabilia of April 21, 1969*. Those sections are brief letters to his children rejoicing in tributes to him in appreciation of his various areas of service to the Lake George community.

— THE EDITOR

SECTION 1

An Excerpt from "One Hundred Years on Lake George":
The Family Story, 1896–1956

(reprinted on the following two pages)

THE FAMILY STORY
(The second fifty years)

by Charles Tuttle

Upon my grandfather's death in 1896, I was seventeen, and a freshman in Columbia College, New York City.

It was impossible for me to come to the Lake George property, except occasionally. Travelling as economically as possibly, I made infrequent trips by nightboat to Albany and thence to Lake George by trolley car. I continued as caretaker Mr. Miles Latham, my grandfather's superintendent for the property; and I endeavored to rent Rockledge and Wayside. The rentals were very small, and woefully insufficient to carry the property. Nevertheless, I could not bring myself to sell it.

In 1899 I graduated from Columbia College and in 1902 from Columbia Law School. I became a law clerk in the large law firm of Davies, Stone & Auerbach, and early in 1906 became a junior partner.

On the death of Mr. Miles Latham about 1905, I engaged as superintendent Mr. Charles H. Bly, who has been with us as a beloved friend and co-worker ever since.

On June 1, 1907, Miss Hélène Wheeler, of Oswego, N. Y., and I were married in St. Luke's Church, Convent Avenue and 141st Street, New York City,—a church built under the rectorship of my grandfather.

We came on our honeymoon to Rockledge, travelling by nightboat to Albany and by trolley car to Lake George. A cold rain fell all the first day at Rockledge.

Thereafter for ten years we spent our summers in Wayside, and rented Rockledge to a series of tenants, among whom were the Ambassador from Siam, Dr. William Breyfogle, and Sidney and Louise Homer. During this Wayside period, our four children were born in New York City. Then we moved to Rockledge.

During the ensuing Rockledge period I held the office of United States Attorney for the Southern District of New York from April 1927 to September 1930, in which latter month I was nominated by the Republican Party for Governor of the State. In the election next November I was defeated.

Also during this Rockledge period two other important events occurred.

The first was in 1934 when I purchased back into the Tuttle family "Bonnie Nook," then called "Halcyon." My grandfather had built it and later sold it to Mrs. Maria J. Kempe Cooke. Successor owners were Mr. Fredrick T. Gates and Mr. Eugene W. Small. After Mr. Small's death I purchased it and Tea Island from his family.

Thereafter we rented Halcyon to various tenants until 1945, when our family began its own summer occupancy thereof.

A second important event during the Rockledge period occurred in 1926 when I purchased the first tract of land now part of "Top O' The World" on French Mountain. The story of that purchase will be told by Hélène Tuttle.

SECTION 2

The Story of "Top O' The World." "The Lone Pine" and "The Sentinel Mountain."

O N THE EAST SIDE OF LAKE GEORGE and directly across from our family's summer home is French Mountain — by far the most historic mountain in the United States. It looms as a frowning sentinel at the gateway from the Albany plain into the serried battlements of the towering Adirondacks.

Long before the white man came, the Iroquois from the south and the Algonquins from the north fought at this gateway for the possession of the hunting grounds which it guarded. With the white man came the battles for empire over the New World. For the French in the north this martial mountain blocked conquest of the Hudson to the sea. For the English and Colonials in the south it blocked conquest of Canada. Armies stormed against it from both directions. In the War of the Revolution, battles again surged around it on land and water; and in the War of 1812 the English from Canada overran it briefly. Its name and its story linger from those ancient days when Montcalm posted on it the banner and cannon of France in his successful siege of Fort William Henry since immortalized in James Fenimore Cooper's *The Last of the Mohicans.*

In the summer of 1926 someone told Mrs. Tuttle and me that there was a wonderful view from a high shelf on the mountain's northern shoulder, and that on the shelf there was a huge weather-beaten solitary tree, "a Lone Pine" which had already become old in the days of Montcalm. So up we went, hand in hand over a wood road and through the buttercups and daisies of an abandoned farm. We viewed and spooned for a while under the Lone Pine, and then walked reverently in the adjoining forest primeval where the long huge branches seemed to extend a benediction over our heads.

LAKE GEORGE *from* **TOP O' THE WORLD**

For us it was a new world—and irresistible. I bought the site of the Lone Pine, and as time passed, more acres, 1500 in all. We called it "Top O' The World." Mrs. Tuttle began to have visions for it. Several old abandoned farm houses were glorified. Clearings were made, and paths pushed upward to and along the crest. Yielding to memories of the meadow brook and its finny denizens at Oak Ridge, New Jersey, I built a stone dam across the mountain brook to create a small pond. Thinking it to be a grand idea, I stocked the pond with trout—until discovering that I was in fact stocking, unthanked, some of the larders of the countryside.

During several summers Mrs. Tuttle and I lived in one of the old houses which she had modernized. In the middle of one of those summers, while both of us were in the City for a few days, she excitedly telephoned me at the office that she had discovered "a wonderful prefabricated house" at Wanamakers; I must, she insisted, come up at once to buy and then erect it on one of the Top O' The World outlooks over the Lake. There it has stood for fifteen years, known as "Horizon Cottage" and annually rented by a family who had fallen in love with it.

In the early 1960s, Mrs. Tuttle and I turned over Top O' The World for further development and management to our son who carries forward my father's name, H. Croswell Tuttle. Under his direction it became the site of a great summer resort — Lodge, Club House, motels, cottages, swimming pool, golf course, tennis court, horseback riding, boating, and more.

I am very thankful to have had a son who enjoyed managing it. With great delight, I've been able to spend most of my own summer at "Halcyon" on the west shore of the Lake and look across at this fabulous mountain. If it had a tongue, the story the mountain could tell would begin in the opening pages of the Geological History of the World. As from its crest the Dawn pursues the shadows of the Night, I pause in wonder why God did not end creation with such majesty. Did He move on to make Man in order to have someone to sense its glory?

SECTION 3

Presidency of the Lake George Association. The Bishop and the Bass.

IN 1885 THE LAKE GEORGE ASSOCIATION was founded by public-spirited residents of the Lake George area who believed that the Lake was one of the most beautiful in the world, and that it and its waters, mountains, and historical sites must be preserved as an inviolable heritage and inspiration for the people of our state and nation.

In 1927 and again in the following two years, I was elected president of the Association and ever since have been its counsel. During my presidency the Association continued to pursue vigorous measures to prevent the corporation owning the dam and paper mill at Ticonderoga from using the Lake as a mill pond; to preserve the forest from commercialism, fire and disease; to protect the unique purity of the waters; to improve the safety of navigation; to regulate fishing and game hunting; and to preserve in public trust the many historical sites. To these ends laws were sought from the legislature and regulations from state departments. A sanitation inspection service was maintained.

As I look back on those three years as president of the Lake George Association, I recall one amusing incident. Bishop Ernest Stires, the Episcopal Bishop of the Diocese of Long Island, was a summer resident of Lake George. In the fall, winter and spring he was a dedicated and ardent fisher of men; but in the summer he was an equally dedicated and ardent fisher of smallmouth bass. He was often out on the lake, it was said, before breakfast, before lunch, and before dinner, with the aid of a fast motorboat and a helper to work the engine, the anchor and the bait.

At an annual meeting of the Association one August, I was presiding and the good Bishop was sitting in the front row opposite me. Debate was lively as to how to have more smallmouth bass in the Lake. I surrendered the chair, and said that one sure way to do it was to petition the legislature to enact a law to forbid "any bishop" to fish for bass in Lake George. I pointed out that there was nothing "personal" in my motion, for I said "*any* bishop." The motion was uproariously adopted. Even Bishop Stires voted for it.

Photo by Richard Dean

THE "ISLAND–STUDDED NARROWS" OF LAKE GEORGE

SECTION 4

A Secretary of War at Lake George in the Nude.

URING WORLD WAR II Henry L. Stimson, Secretary of War,
came to Lake George for a moment of revival in its mountain
air. I had long known him at the Bar and as a former United States
Attorney.

What more exhilarating change from crash programs of war than a
program of "search and destroy" marshaled against some virile and wily
smallmouth bass?

So the Secretary of War and I went down in my motorboat to the wild
and island-studded Narrows of the Lake, under the frowning escarpment
of Black Mountain. I knew a very secret spot among the rocks in thirty
feet of water where the bass lurked in anticipation of unwary minnows.
The high wind would keep the boat yawing widely on the pivot of the
anchor rope, which was supplemented by the loosely hung "trip rope" for
use if the heavy anchor became jammed among the rocks.

As Admiral of the Fleet (one boat) I assigned the Secretary of War
to the plebe's task of watching that the loose trip rope did not entan-
gle itself with the propeller. After half an hour, with the last bass in the
basket, the time came to return for lunch. All of a sudden I saw the
Secretary of War standing up and removing his clothes. He said he was
court-martialing and sentencing himself to dive under the boat and
disentangle the needed trip rope from the propeller!

The Admiral countered by starting to take off his own clothes. This
led to an argument between the Army and the Navy, terminated by
tossing a coin. The Army lost. Later its Secretary of War reappeared
from under the boat holding up triumphantly the loose trip rope. We
both redressed before leaving the privacy of the wilderness. What an
opportunity the photographers of the mass media had missed!

My own mental souvenir is that, without a stitch on, neither the
Army nor the Navy displays much martial pomp.

SECTION 5

The Case of the Lake George Water Levels. Lake or Mill Pond?

LAKE GEORGE is undoubtedly one of the most beautiful lakes in the world. Its long valley sheltered between ancient mountains, its crystal-clear waters, and its jewelry of some 200 islands guarded with the battlements of steeply rising cliffs, perpetuate the wonderment of the story of creation.

The Lake's natural grandeur has also been the theatre for centuries-old human drama. History textbooks carry the name of Father Isaac Jogues (the discoverer), General Montcalm and Ethan Allen adorning with romance and legend the Lake's northern end; the names of Generals William Johnson, Lord Geoffrey Amherst and General Philip R. Schuyler adorning the southern end; and in between, that unforgettable aforementioned American classic, *The Last of the Mohicans*.

The geology of Lake George underlies what I am now about to tell. At the Northern end there is the 400-foot long formation known as the Natural Dam, over which in their natural state the waters of the Lake flowed out and fell in a series of waterfalls into Lake Champlain with a total drop of 220 feet in a distance of three-and-a-half miles.

The commercial development of water power finally led to the erection on the Natural Dam of a huge masonry dam with gates, sluice-ways and flashboards. Thereby Lake George was turned into a mill pond. Water from the melting snows would be stored in the Spring, thus overflowing the docks, islands and shore lines, and conversely, leaving them by Fall far above water level.

The Lake George Association (LGA) thus became involved in continuous conflict with the power interests. It succeeded in enlisting the State as an ally; and in 1947 there began the historic suit for a declaratory judgment, *People of the State of New York v. System Properties, Inc.* The LGA became an intervenor with myself as the Association's attorney.

The trial was held in Elizabethtown, Essex County, before Judge Andrew W. Ryan, who rendered a judgment upholding the contention of the Association and directing System Properties to operate the dam so as to maintain the level of the Lake between a maximum of 4.0 feet and a minimum of 2.5 feet on the Rogers Rock Gauge — a government mechanism for measuring the water level. The court appointed the State Superintendent of Public Works as its agent to enforce its decision (189 Misc. 991).

On appeal, this judgment was reversed by the Appellate Division, Third Department, on the ground that, although it afforded "an equitable solution of what had long been a troublesome problem," nevertheless it was beyond judicial power, since only "the State had the power to regulate the water level of Lake George," and such power must be exercised by the Legislature (281 App. Div. 433).

This ruling was affirmed by the State Court of Appeals (2 N.Y. 2d 330); but that Court significantly said (p. 345):

> *The trial court's plan was probably a fair and practicable one and the invalidation thereof by the Appellate Division leaves a vacuum as to control, but expediency cannot transfer legislative power to the courts. . . . But the State's own rights being sovereign in character remain unimpaired and there is no reason to suppose that the Legislature will neglect to exercise them as its collective judgment dictates.*

The Legislature immediately accepted this suggestion by the Court of Appeals and enacted into statute law the maximum and minimum levels on the Rogers Rock Gauge embodied in Judge Ryan's judgment. (Laws 1957; Chapter 1035.)

This legislation has been continuously effective. Thereby the water levels of Lake George have been stabilized ever since, thus perpetually assuring the safety of navigation, the rights of riparian owners, and the full enjoyment of the Lake by the public. *Lake, not Mill Pond!*

Courtesy of NARA

SECTION 6

The Case for the Protection of the Adirondack Forest Preserve and the Constitution's "Forever Wild" Clause.

IN 1949 THE BOARD of the Black River Regulating District (a state incorporated agency) determined to construct and operate a dam on the south branch of the Moose River near Panther Mountain in Herkimer County for the purpose of regulating the Moose and Black Rivers which ultimately joined and flowed into Lake Ontario at Watertown.

The project required the taking and flooding of 1500 acres of the State Forest Preserve and 3500 acres of the land of the Adirondack League Club in the very heart of the Adirondack wilderness.

I was retained by the Club to prevent these takings, and to do so by court or legislative action.

The issue at hand centered in the provision and policy of the State Constitution which guaranteed that:

> the lands of the state now owned or hereafter acquired, consti-
> tuting the forest preserve as now fixed by law, shall be forever
> kept as wild forest land. They shall not be leased, sold or
> exchanged, or be taken by any corporation, public or private.

In the Fall of 1949 the Appellate Division, Fourth Department, unanimously upheld the project★ (275 App. Div. 618) on the ground that, in its opinion, "there is a reasonable doubt" as to whether the Constitution prevented a limited use of the Forest Preserve "to regulate the flow of streams."

★ *Adirondack League Club v. Board of Black River Regulating District.*

We appealed to the Court of Appeals which, in 1950, reversed the Appellate Division's order and dismissed the whole proceeding "upon the ground that the issues are moot" (301 N.Y. 219).

The Court of Appeals opinion based itself on the fact that on April 20, 1950, and after the Appellate Division's decision, there took effect an Act of the Legislature (L. 1950, ch. 803) which overruled the plan of the Board of the Black River Regulating District for this dam and reservoir.

The Board argued in the Court of Appeals that this Act of Legislature was unconstitutional; but the Court of Appeals refused so to determine.

The result of these efforts in the court and the Legislature has been that the policy of the State in preserving as "forever wild" large tracts of the Adirondacks and the Catskills was firmly and broadly established and, with a few small instances voted by the people as special amendments to the Constitution, has remained so to this day.

Every man should make and keep appointment with the wilderness, for there he has a special business with the earth and sky, with the potency of silence, and with his own soul.

SECTION 7

Once More Commissioned for Lake George

February 10, 1970

To my dear Children:

The mail has just brought me from the Governor, with the approval of the State Senate, my appointment for a second nine-year term as a member of the Lake George Park Commission.

Many public offices have come my way but none has seemed more like the touch of the sword of knighthood upon my shoulder. I have been in love with Lake George. From my youth up I have been her liegeman in realm of Natural Beauty. Hence the weight of my present years is lightened by the thought of being continued as one of the Palace Guard for this Queen of Lakes.

The Lake George Park holds within its embrace as an inviolable treasure the thirty-two miles of water and the land for a mile back from its shore lines. The Commission is the agency of the State for the protection and enhancement of the Lake's beauty, water purity, navigation, policing, recreation areas, and safety against the desecrations of commercialism.

But the Park and its area are much more than a dwelling place of beauty. Here on display to all who will see is the story of creation, the earth's billions of years, the coming of life and ultimately of Man, and the birth of our Nation. On the sides of the mountains there are the sandbanks of primeval oceans. In the rocks there are the fossil records of the beginnings of life. The mountains are scarred with the assaults of the Ice Ages. The artifacts of the Esquimaux tell the story of human millennia before the arrival of the Indians out of the West. Recorded history marks its commencement and progress with far-scattered monuments and the fashioning of civilization as the White Man arrived with his ways of good and evil. Here, in immensity, is a University of Learning, founded in the Dawn Age and with admission open to all with the will to study, profit and enjoy.

The gates of this Enchanted Region were opened to me by a benign Providence in 1879, and within them there have been the great joys of my life—early playmates, my incomparable bride, my children, grandchildren and great grandchildren. On a hillside overlooking the Lake there sleeps in dedicated ground the one who shared with me the honor and the joy of founding our noble family. Above her stands as an eternal guard the majesty of Prospect Mountain.

Hence, you will understand why in my old age [of 90 years] I have been happy at receiving this renewed commission in Lake George's Honor Guard. When and if I see the Lake again she and I will hail each other with a smile and in comradeship as we have done throughout all the years of our love. Doubtless she will parade the procession of her changing moods—the calm of her meditation in the serene sunlight, the dance of her moonbeam children at play upon her midnight waters, or the charge of her white-plumed knights of the wind riding her waves in assault against the battlements of the shore.

— FATHER

SECTION 8

L.G.A. Citation and a Letter from the Governor

September 9, 1970

To my dear Children:

On September 4, 1970, at the Top O' The World Club House, there was held the largest and most constructive annual meeting of the Lake George Association in its history.

In the course of the meeting there was presented to me by President Lysle W. Morton and Executive Secretary Cyrus H. Woodbury a large and very handsome tablet bearing the following inscription:

To

CHARLES H. TUTTLE, *Esq.*
from
THE LAKE GEORGE ASSOCIATION

PRESENTED IN APPRECIATION *of a* LIFE DEVOTED TO EFFORTS ON
BEHALF OF LAKE GEORGE *and with* PERSONAL AFFECTION OF
THE LAKE GEORGE ASSOCIATION

The Association establishes this date the

CHARLES H. TUTTLE CITATION
September 4, 1970★

In connection with the event there came to me from Governor Nelson A. Rockefeller the following letter *(see next page):*

★ *Editor's Note:* Although Charles Tuttle died only four months after receiving this cherished honor from the Lake George Association, his legacy with the LGA continues into the twenty-first century. The Charles H. Tuttle Citation is awarded periodically to an Association member whose achievements have significantly benefited Lake George. *(See Appendix D, page 364.)*

Courtesy of NARA

STATE OF NEW YORK
Executive Chamber
Albany 12224

September 2, 1970

Dear Charlie:

I am delighted that your many years of service to the commu-nity are being recognized by the Lake George Association with the presentation of a commemorative plaque at the dinner in your honor.

Your record of unselfish, sustained effort on behalf of the residents of the area is well known far beyond the environs of Lake George. I know your many other friends feel as I do—that this accolade from your neighbors is indeed well merited.

Congratulations to you and best wishes to everyone in atten-dance at the dinner.

Sincerely,

NELSON

One of the rewards of living to an age as venerable as mine is that there is additional time within which expressions such as the above have a chance to catch up with you.

Love to you all.

— FATHER

My Collection of Titles "Emeritus."
St. James Church.

July 22, 1970

RESIGNATION AS SENIOR WARDEN OF
ST. JAMES EPISCOPAL CHURCH, LAKE GEORGE

To all my Children:

Another long chapter in my life has just come to a close—a happy close.

On Wednesday, July 22, I again hosted the annual summer parish dinner of St. James held at Top O' The World. The attendance was far larger than ever. The cuisine outdid itself. There was full observance of the biblical injunction to *"make a joyful noise unto the Lord."*

During the meeting I confirmed my previously announced purpose to resign as Senior Warden. There were many reasons—not the least my many years. The future of St. James must be founded on its community. Room must be made for the younger men to move up. Furthermore, since my home and my law practice were in New York City, I could only attend about two vestry meetings in the year.

Accordingly, I determinedly stepped out as Senior Warden and was thereupon invited to step back in as "Senior Warden *Emeritus.*"

My collection of titles "Emeritus" continues to grow luxuriantly under the fertilization of ninety years.

Member "Emeritus" of the Board of Higher Education of the City of New York—after fifty-three years of service.

Chairman "Emeritus" of the Interfaith Committee for Released Time for Religious Education—after forty-six years of service.

Vestryman "Emeritus" of Grace Episcopal Church, New York City—after more years of service than I can recall.

Member "Emeritus" (the technical title is "Counsel") of my law firm Breed, Abbott & Morgan—after thirty-six years of service.

Other "Emeriti" are, I believe, waiting for me just around Time's next corner.

The title "Emeritus" is a sort if honorary epitaph carved for you on a sort of trial tombstone erected by associates and friends along the roadway of one's life as a sort of preliminary obituary before you have given them the sad occasion to attend your funeral proper.

St. James has always been, and while I live always will be, very close to me. Founded by my grandfather in 1855, it still contains a pew gra-

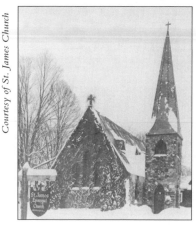

Courtesy of St. James Church

ciously but informally associated with the Tuttle family. I believe I have been in that pew on at least several occasions every year including babyhood.

My daughter Charlotte was married in St. James, with Mayor Fiorello La Guardia as one of her distinguished attending friends. My daughter Jasmine was also married in St. James, and her first-born was baptized in St. James. My marvelous wife, after her long years of devotion to St. James, was carried through its door into eternal life.

ST. JAMES CHURCH, *Lake George*

For many years I have stood in its pulpit in the Sunday nearest July 4th to make what was kindly called an inspirational address. On Sundays in the summer, after the morning service, I have often had the privilege of joining with the congregation for "a coffee break" under "the Maple Tree" in the Church Close. Some of the trees around the borders of the Close were planted by my wife and me in the early days of our marriage.

The name "St. James" occurred to my grandfather as he was rowing down to attend the organizing meeting in the old Village Court House. The stars above him shone like angelic beings. They seemed to have voices reciting from on high the seventeenth verse of the first chapter of the Epistle of St. James:

> *Every good gift and every perfect gift is from above,*
> *and cometh down from the Father of lights, with whom*
> *is no variableness, neither shadow of turning.*

— FATHER

CHAPTER THIRTEEN

FACING UP TO OLD AGE

SECTION 1

Kindly Accolades in the Sunset.

S O MUCH WAS continuously going on in life that only slowly did I
recognize that I had long passed the scriptural utmost allotment of
four score years. The fields of Time still stood full of ripening events,
and harvesting was both fun and life.

But early in 1966 necessity surprised me with a summons for
major surgery and a stay of several months in a hospital. There followed medical warnings and much family concern. The strange word
"retire" cropped up from somewhere. I was sure it was of such recent
coinage that it could not as yet have found lodgment in the dictionary,
or perhaps the word was the invention of younger men seeking to
empty the next higher rung on the ladder.

Yet, on second thought, perhaps one would find the zest of battle even keener by laying aside a little armor. Did Job have this vision of the old war-horse?:

> *He saith among the trumpets, Ha, ha!*
> *And he smelleth the battle afar off,*
> *the thunder of the captains, and the shouting.*
>
>   – JOB 39:25

In any event, old age was something to rejoice in, particularly if one stopped long enough to consider the alternative.

I began to get the kind of accolades which usually are given in the sunset of life. The balancing of Life's account was beginning.

Hence I was by no means prepared to fulfill the last line of the familiar couplet that:

> *Old soldiers never die;*
> *They only fade away!*

On the contrary, if the time was coming to leave the hotly burning hearth which had warmed so many years, it seemed better to take with me not the ashes but embers still afire.

Happiness will be continuing to love what you loved when you and all were young.

A CITY HONORS HER ILLUSTRIOUS CITIZEN

New York's Mayor Robert Wagner *(left)* honored Charles Tuttle in 1964 with the City's "Illustrious Citizen of New York" bronze medal *(pictured on next two pages)*. Praising him for "services to our fellow citizens for more than half a century," the Mayor described Charles Tuttle as "a model for a democratic society."

SECTION 2

The Mayor of New York City Cites An "Illustrious Citizen."

IN A CEREMONY AT CITY HALL, Mayor Robert F. Wagner presented to me the Bronze Medal of the City of New York, bearing the following inscription:

PRESENTED TO

CHARLES H. TUTTLE, LL.D.

ILLUSTRIOUS CITIZEN

OF NEW YORK

— May 7, 1964 —

In making the presentation the Mayor said:

*The City of New York is deeply and wholeheartedly com-
mitted to the education of its young people—and specifically to
the ideal of a free education of every child, from kindergarten
through college.*

*You have served the youth of the City of New York through
your dedication to the continuing development and expansion of
excellence in education, now represented in the ten colleges of
The City University of New York.*

*Your staunch devotion to free tuition in institutions of
higher education in the City is based upon your knowledge of
the results of such education, and
the civic loss which would be
suffered if free tuition was
no more.*

*You have been a
pioneer in inter-group
relations—when you
served as legal coun-
sel to the New York
Temporary Commis-
sion Against Discrimi-
nation—and when you
served as Chairman of the
Greater New York Commit-
tee on Released Time of Jews,
Protestants and Roman Catholics.*

*Your conscientious, whole-hearted participation in civic
affairs establishes a model for a democratic society.*

*It is with pleasure and pride that I present this bronze
Medal of the City of New York to you, Dr. Charles H. Tuttle,
illustrious citizen of our City, in recognition of your services to
our fellow citizens for more than half a century.*

— ROBERT F. WAGNER, *Mayor*

In accepting the medal, I said to the Mayor:

> If there is any luster to it, it comes to me because of you. You've done more than any other man to fashion this 10-star crown on the brow of this great city.... The best hope I have for higher education is that you remain Mayor for a long time to come.

Attending the ceremony were my wife, the Chairman and members of the Board of Higher Education and officials of the City University.

Concerning the presentation of this medal, the Honorable John V. Lindsay (then a member of Congress and later the mayor of New York City), made the following recorded statements in the House of Representatives on June 23, 1964 (Congressional Record, Appendix, p. A2915):

> MR. LINDSAY: *Mr. Speaker, I would like to call this body's attention to one of New York City's most distinguished citizens, Mr. Charles H. Tuttle, member of the board of higher education, who recently was honored for his 50 years of public service. Late last month Dr. Tuttle was presented with a bronze medal by Mayor Wagner for a half-century of invaluable service to the people of New York.*
>
> *Of Dr. Tuttle's many contributions, he must be particularly remembered for his dedication to the education of young people and to the concept of free education for every child—from kindergarten through college. During his 50 years of service, Dr. Tuttle has been instrumental in the impressive and dramatic growth of the City University of New York. When school doors open this Fall, the system will include four senior colleges and six community colleges with a total enrollment of more than 250,000 students. Dr. Tuttle has made an impact on New York education which will be lasting. As Dr. Gustave Rosenberg, chairman of the Board Of Higher Education, described him:*
>
> **He has never failed us. He has truly been a servant of the people.**

---◆◈◆---

SECTION 3

Retirement after Fifty-Three Years as a
Member of the Board of Higher Education.

M Y SIXTH TERM as a member of the Board of Higher Education of the City of New York was ending on June 30, 1966. Many urged me to stand for another term, but I said that I was afraid lest "the man upstairs" would think me irreverently presumptuous if in my eighty-seventh year I took on another nine-year term.

To avoid such a hazard I fired off the following letter, dated May 23, 1966, to Dr. Alan Pifer, Chairman of the Mayor's Screening Committee:

> *Dear Dr. Pifer:*
>
> *My current term as a member of the Board of Higher Education of the City of New York expires on June 30 next—two months after my 87th birthday.*
>
> *I was first appointed by Mayor Gaynor in 1913, and have been reappointed for successive terms by Mayors Hylan, Walker, La Guardia, O'Dwyer and Wagner.*
>
> *The time has come to stop. I ask, therefore, that, in making your selections for recommendation to Mayor Lindsay, you do not consider me.*
>
> *The term of my colleague, Hon. Louis Quero-Chiesa, also expires on June 30 next. I have no information as to his wishes, but I feel it a privilege to tell you that he has proven himself a very valuable member of the Board—constructive, faithful and held in high esteem by all his fellow Members. I warmly commend him to you.*

When you make your report to Mayor Lindsay, please include this letter or the substance of it.

With best wises to you and your Committee in this important task, I am

Yours respectfully,

CHARLES H. TUTTLE

I mailed this letter at noon of its date and then read it to the Board of Higher Education at the conclusion of its regular meeting that evening.

I received from Mayor Lindsay the following reply dated May 27, 1966:

Dear Mr. Tuttle:

I understand that you have decided to withdraw your name from consideration for reappointment to the Board of Higher Education.

I want to thank you personally for your many years of dedicated service to the interests of higher education in New York City. For more than half a century the Board of Higher Education and its predecessor, the Board of Trustees of City College, have benefited from your insight, experience and energetic participation. If in the future years, the City University of New York can profit from the guidance and dedication of men such as yourself, I am confident that our higher educational system will continue to be among the best in the world.

With best personal regards,

Sincerely,

JOHN V. LINDSAY
MAYOR

Governor Nelson Rockefeller, in the course of a public statement, said:

Charlie Tuttle is one of the most outstanding citizens of New York. His keen legal mind has been of great assistance to me as Governor throughout the years I have served in this capacity.

Dr. Buell G. Gallagher, President of City College, with whom I had worked for many years as Chairman of the Board of Higher Education's Committee on City College, wrote me the following letter dated May 26, 1966:

Dear Charles:

I was stunned by the final moments of the Board meeting Monday night and you will remember that in our conversation on the way to University Place, I did not attempt to express myself.

Even today, I have great difficulty in finding words which might suggest the depth of my feelings. I suspect that it will have to remain that way simply because there are no words which can fully express the appreciation and affection which cry for expression at this time.

One of the few things that we can do will be done. I don't want any arguments from you about it. On the night of June 15 in the Lewisohn Stadium we will drape the Lavender Hood on your shoulders. I started the machinery rolling on this one early Tuesday morning and now I have the informal assurance of the Regents that it will be permitted. I share this with you in confidence and we shall privately keep the matter as a surprise rather than to publicize it in advance.

June and I have greatly enjoyed the "Dedication Dinner" documents and I know that Hélène must also be very proud of her Charlie.

Yours ever,

BUELL G. GALLAGHER

PRESIDENT

In a letter dated June 23, 1966, United States Senator Robert F. Kennedy wrote me:

Your great contribution to the educational well-being of the youth of New York City during your fifty-three years of service on the Board is widely acknowledged by leaders in higher education in the city. You have long been one of the Board's most active and influential members, and have been in the forefront of many important causes, including the preservation of the City University's free-tuition system and the protection of the University's autonomy.

Courtesy of NARA

In addition, as president of Brotherhood-in-Action Inc., you have contributed significantly to the betterment of the inter-racial and inter-religious relations. I want to take this opportunity to congratulate you on both the City College honorary Doctor of Laws degree and the "Brotherhood-in-Action" award recently conferred upon you, and to offer you my very best wishes on the occasion of your retirement from the Board of Higher Education.

With kindest regards,

Sincerely,

ROBERT F. KENNEDY

Editor's Postscript: On May 25, 1966, *The New York Times* featured a lengthy story about Charles Tuttle's retirement from New York City's Board of Higher Education. The article quoted Board Chairman Gustave G. Rosenberg's profound reaction:

This man has been the heart and soul of this board. I cannot imagine what it will be like without him.

The *Times* article described Charles Tuttle as "one of the most active members of the Board," noting admiringly of Mr. Tuttle: "despite his age, his voice is firm and resonant, and his 5-foot-11-inch frame is still erect and trim." The 1966 *Times* account also reported that the departure of the eighty-seven-year-old Charles Tuttle from the Board of Higher Education was expected to spark demands that the City impose a mandatory retirement age. "However," explained the *Times,* "as long as Mr. Tuttle remained, his presence was regarded as an effective deterrent to any attempt to impose an age limit."

SECTION 4

A Degree of Doctor of Laws from the College of the City of New York and the State Board of Regents.

O N JUNE 15, 1966, there was conferred upon me by the College of the City of New York, with the authorization of the State Board of Regents, the degree of Doctor of Laws and the lavender hood. In presenting me to President Buell G. Gallagher, Associate Dean Samuel Middlebrook said at the commencement exercises held in the Lewisohn Stadium:

> With this ceremony tonight we celebrate one of the most extraordinary careers in the guardianship of free public higher education in New York. Appointed by Mayor Gaynor in 1913 to the nine-member Board of Trustees of the College of the City of New York, this good and faithful man has served during the administrations of nine mayors of the city and five of the seven presidents of the College. He took part in the fusion of the Boards of Trustees of City and Hunter into the present Board of Higher Education in 1926 and the subsequent creation of the senior colleges in all boroughs, and the City University.
>
> During these 53 years—almost half its lifetime—his concern for **City College** has been paramount; since 1932 he has been chairman of the City College committee of the present Board. No member of the staff today outranks him in length of service. Under our present retirement rules none ever can exceed his record. In classical terms, we can say that he began as our Mentor; he developed into our Odysseus, strong in wisdom and counsel; he remained to become our Master; tonight he is our Laureate and in a moment he will be our Valedictorian **summa cum laude.**

*Mr. President, I have the privilege of presenting to you the Honorable Charles Henry Tuttle, upon whom I ask you to confer **honoris causa,** the degree of Doctor of Laws.*

President Gallagher then came forward with the lavender hood and said:

Courtesy of CCNY

The honorary degrees of the City College are jealously guarded. Only a dozen times in 119 years have we made such an award, and only once before to a non-alumnus. But tonight's award is as inevitable as it is merited.

All that we could have done earlier to signal our respect and affection for Doctor Tuttle has been done. He has received the

DR. BUELL GALLAGHER

40-year plaque marking four decades of service. The Alumni Association has conferred upon him its Alumni Service Award (given only to three non-alumni in the history of the college), its Townsend Harris Medal, and its John H. Finley Award. This last was given not only for his service to free public higher education but also for writing the New York State statute of 1945 outlawing discrimination in employment for reasons of race, creed or national origin—a model for similar legislation throughout the nation. Tonight we legitimize the previous actions of the Alumni Association by making him formally and officially what he has been for so long—a sturdy son of City College.

*Charles Henry Tuttle, by virtue of the authority vested in me, I confer upon you the degree of Doctor of Laws, **honoris causa,** in token whereof I give you the diploma of the College and cause you to be invested with the hood of lavender.*

Next day I received from President Gallagher the following personal letter:

Dear Charles:

I shall always be glad that your career with The City College ended on a note of triumph.

Two Annual Dinners of Breed, Abbott & Morgan

Charles Tuttle *(top, second from left)* in 1936; and *(oval and lower, middle row, sixth from left)* in 1967, the year of his retirement from the firm.

There are few, if any, in American life who, as they look back over a lifetime of activity in behalf of higher education, can have the genuine feelings of satisfaction to which you are entitled.

We are proud of you and hold you in warm affection.

Ever,

BUELL G. GALLAGHER
PRESIDENT

With friends like these no man could feel that his life has been a loss.

———◆———

SECTION 5

Retirement from Full Partnership in Breed, Abbott & Morgan

SHORTLY AFTER MY EIGHTY-EIGHTH BIRTHDAY on April 21, 1967, I conferred with senior partners in the firm and stated that the time had come for me—in the interest of the firm, my family, and myself—to recognize my age and to lay aside the obligations of a partner. A cordial understanding resulted in my becoming as of June 1, 1967 "counsel" to the firm in which I had been a partner for 37 years—over half of my professional life.

My warm friend and comrade, William L. Hanaway, thereupon became "Senior Partner." On May 10, 1967, he wrote the following most cherished letter:

TO: CHARLES H. TUTTLE

This is a great occasion in your life and it must not go by without full recognition. I know of no one who deserves more than you to live a life of ease. After a most distinguished and successful career at the bar of the State and of the United States

*which has extended beyond a half century, during which time
you have represented thousands of clients with honor and distinction, you are now graciously and gently putting aside these
arduous burdens. You are a great credit to your profession and
to this firm. I am sure that every one of us hopes in his own
mind that when his time comes to make this change, it will be
done the same way and with same universal acclaim for a job
well done.*

*We admire your mind as well as your courage and your con-
stitution. As I wrote you on the occasion of your 88th birthday,
I hope that Father Time will be good to you, that you will live
a long time, and that you will be able to enjoy the companion-
ship of other cultured minds. This is the hope of all your partners and associates.*

*We have all been privileged to have been your friend and
partner for all of these years. As we face the future we do it
with courage for we will be able to look to you for guidance and
inspiration.*

> *For the Firm,*
> WILLIAM L. HANAWAY
> *SENIOR PARTNER*

May 10, 1967

I cannot better tell the story of this momentous change in my life
than by quoting from my family letter of May 19, 1967:

To all my dear Children:

*My two long hospitalizations for surgeries by no means
minor, and the stark fact that I am less than two years short of
ninety, have compelled me to think in depth about the
inescapable realities and obligations which in consequences I face.*

*Every day the obituary pages record the constant passing of
far younger prominent and active men, and every day many such
men are stepping aside either voluntarily or because they have
reached the age fixed by public or private law for compulsory
retirement—judges, clergymen, educators, corporation executives,*

military officers, etc. That compulsory age limit usually ranges from 65 to 72, although in the retention of mental powers there can occasionally be unusual exceptions as in the case of Oliver Wendell Holmes, who remained active on the United States Supreme Court until over ninety — there being for that Court no compulsory age limit.

But human experience and the overall need for maintaining efficiency of organization require the imposition of a common and non-discriminatory limit, which usually is 70 or under, depending on the nature of the occupation....

In the next two-year partnership agreement, beginning June 1, 1967, and on the firm's letterhead, I will be referred to as "of Counsel" to the firm. I will retain all fringe benefits which I now have as partner; will retain my present room; will receive periodically a very agreeable lump-sum allowance in each of the two years, together with my share of the undistributed balance of this year's profits and the return of my capital in the capital account of the firm, and at the firm's expense I will be furnished with a secretary, stenographic and telephone service and insurances as at present, and with continued membership in the Wall Street Luncheon Club.

Hence, to the extent of my health I will continue in the full practice of my beloved profession, tempered with such leisure as I may choose and find agreeable — a leisure which I will find the happier the smaller I can keep it. My present and future clients will be carried by me in association with one or more of my present partners but as formal clients of Breed, Abbott & Morgan, and they will be billed by and for the firm.

All this, of course, is the opening of a new chapter in my already lengthy book of life; but there would be no sense, happiness or moral contentment in attempting to ignore or struggle against its inevitability or its present timeliness. Postponement has already been much longer than all known precedents. The firm's professional image would not be advantaged by common talk that it had as its senior partner one who was nearly a nonagenarian. In sum, I owe it to the firm, my family and myself to attempt no further delay. Naturally, having long known that this must come some day, I have not overlooked making prudent provision to meet it.

Hence this letter to you all because I wish you all to know about it before its publicizing. Mother already knows and approves. I urge you to be as happy about it as I am. We are still on course.

With lots of love,

Affectionately,

FATHER

POSTLUDE

———◆◆◆———

SECTION 1

My Wife.
A Last Look Back.

QUIETLY my wife Hélène left me on Saturday, October 5, 1968. Her long illness had gradually closed and shuttered one window after another through which she had looked so joyously at the world and the people around her. At last she left and went where Light would be again.

Hélène, like myself, loved her world. She happily wrote and published much about it, including *Memorial Gift Book: Lake George and Vicinity* (1929), *One Hundred Years on Lake George* (1956), *Houses in the Sun* (1958), and her final book, *On Our Way Rejoicing* (1964). As Emeline Page, editor of *The Villager,* wisely observed in her introduction to Hélène's last book: "Unless countless grandmothers— and grandfathers—across the nation record what they remember, a rich part of American life will be lost."

On Our Way Rejoicing contains very much about "Charlie," but that is understandable, because Hélène and Charlie loved each other very much.

At the beginning of the summer of 1968, I had taken Hélène to our beloved "Halcyon" on Lake George in an ambulance. As the summer drew to a close, I brought her back in an ambulance to a room at Flower Hospital in New York City on September 6.

The day before we left Halcyon, an event happened which was so extraordinary that I described it in a September 17 letter to our children entitled, "A Last Look Back from the Opening Gate of Heaven":

> After I had brought mother by ambulance to Halcyon on June 21, 1968, she continued her slow withdrawal from us. Her consciousness of what was about her faded. Immobility increased. Recognition lessened. Words became rare and indistinct, as if spoken from far away.
>
> Could I break through to the world of love that had been in her soul and which we had always shared together through the long years?
>
> My various efforts had all failed. But finally, as I sat beside her one evening shortly before I was to take her from Halcyon in the ambulance wherein I had brought her, I tried

bending near her lips and narrating softly to her the ineffable story of our first kiss.

In 1905 I was escorting her home from a dance. As we walked her white dress floated beside me in the moonlight. She was as ethereal as an angel. Slowly I extended my hand in a gesture of parting. There was a look of longing and awe in my eyes. Suddenly we were in each other's arms, and our lips clung together in their first kiss. Then she disengaged herself gently, moved through the front door, and closed it slowly and silently behind her.

Nothing had been said. But, as I stumbled blindly down the steps, I knew that I had become an engaged man and that my imperative business was to go for a diamond ring.

As I softly narrated to her this story of a supreme event in our lives some sixty-three years ago, I could see that she was returning. Her eyes opened and were filled with the old lovelight. A smile glorified her wan face. Slowly she withdrew from underneath the covers her left hand and held up the diamond ring toward my lips to be kissed. But only for a moment. Then she left again. Once more the door closed softly and silently behind her.

But I had been part of an immortal moment—the moment of a look back from the opening gate of heaven.

The funeral service was at the Grace Church, Tenth Street and Broadway, on October 7th. All the many whom Hélène had loved, and also the many whose acquaintance with her had seemingly been slight, came to reverence her as her body lay under a pall beneath the soaring Gothic arches and amid the beautiful flowers at the head of the aisle.

In the course of the service I arose, and, standing beside her, I told of the foregoing transcendent event of her return for a moment's kiss by me on her upheld engagement ring.

To me and to the others who had seen it, that event was conclusive proof of the truth of the Christian Hope.

The service closed with the singing by all present of a hymn, the opening line of which entitled her last book— "On Our Way Rejoicing." As we sang in farewell, the words glowed for me as they never had before. She was beside me.

As Hélène was carried down the aisle to begin her last journey to Lake George, there was the sound of triumph in the accompanying reverberation of the last two lines of that great Hymn:

> *On our way rejoicing*
> *Now and evermore!*

She was then taken by hearse to St. James Church in Lake George Village which she had attended with me every summer since marriage. After the sublime words of Burial service in the Book of Common Prayer and the Committal service at the grave, I confided her to the hospitality of Eternity on a hillside sloping toward the lake and under the wardship of Prospect Mountain.

I slowly turned away. Henceforth I was to live alone. My children and their families were far from New York City. The old apartment at One University Place would have but me, the ever faithful Hattie, and the portraits on the wall. But No! It would still be peopled with the companionable memories of sixty-three years—above all, the memory of that final look back!

Besides, there is still so much to do; and so much joy in going on with the doing of it. There are still friends all around—friends with whom association vibrates with Life.

CHARLES AND HÉLÈNE TUTTLE IN 1957

Celebrating 50 years of marriage *(above);* relaxing at
Halcyon with son, Croswell, and his wife, Doris *(below).*

THE TUTTLE FAMILY AT LAKE GEORGE, 1957
Celebrating the *50th Wedding Anniversary Summer* of
Charles and Hélène Tuttle *(seated, center)* at Halcyon

Back row, left to right: Robert S. Bryant, Robert B. Bryant, Jasmine T. Bryant, Doris E. Tuttle, H. Croswell Tuttle, Evelyn T. Horne, Charles F. Horne, Jr., Charlotte T. Lloyd, David D. Lloyd, Andrew M. Lloyd.

Seated beside Grandparents: Rebecca D. Bryant, Charles H. Tuttle II.

Sitting in front: Louisa T. Lloyd, Elizabeth A. Bryant, Julianne H. Tuttle.

INSETS, left: Frederick B. Warder, Jr. and Anne H. Warder; *right:* Flora E. Horne and Charles F. Horne III.

SECTION 2

Our Children.

T HE OLD TESTAMENT CLOSES with this final verse:

> *And he shall turn the heart of the fathers to the*
> *children, and the heart of the children to their fathers,*
> *lest I come and smite the earth with a curse. (MALACHI 4:6)*

It seems evident that the disintegration of family life and its sanctity and discipline are as rot gradually eating through the fairest apple as a "curse." Where the weed of meaninglessness takes root in the home, responsibility and dedication have no environment for flowering. The absence of a common warm heart invites an infection which can spread its poison into the whole community. And the presence of that common heart fosters a loving environment that can shine in the darkness.

Our children have been our great blessing because their hearts and our hearts have been truly turned toward each other. The resultant bond of love has widened to encircle all as our family has grown, now numbering more than two dozen. I could write several volumes about them all, but (in far finer literature than I could hope to imitate) Hélène has already enshrined them in her book *On Our Way Rejoicing,* published in 1964 and dedicated "To My Family, Past, Present and Future."

As I noted earlier in these Memoirs, children are truly "the best answers in the world." Now, as I draw this book to a close, permit me to offer my "best answers"—the four great blessings of Hélène and myself: Evelyn Cressman Tuttle, Charlotte Merrill Tuttle, Henry Croswell Tuttle, and Hélène Jasmine Tuttle. From these four have sprung other great blessings, including the Bryant, Horne, Lloyd, Walkup, Warder and Tuttle families—all blooms on the Tree of Time standing on the bank of the River of Eternity. And, no matter who pens the diary, the script of love is clearly legible, in any language.

SECTION 3

A Song Without Words.

GOD HAS CREATED an exciting Universe, intending that His children should lead exciting lives.

To this end He provided a stage as wide as Infinity. For lighting effects He hung innumerable suns, moons and stars. For scenery He designed endless forms of beauty, from the tiny wild flower hiding shyly in the forest to the towering mountains shoring up the sky. To insure the excitement He added Man.

For those who enter upon His stage with a wish to play adventurously, He has provided for the role parts, scripts and opportunities of endless variety and endings.

But now I am ninety, my story must close—at least for the present.

If there is enough in it to suggest a kindly future epitaph, let it be: *"He was in love with his world."*

Externally there have been failures and successes; much that should have been done but was not; and much that should not have been but was. But I like to think that internally there has been a song at the core. I hope that when at last I move off the stage and disappear into the wings, I may be carrying that song with me.

The song has not been of my own composition. Nor is it in words. It has come as music out of the love in the hearts of those with whom I have been privileged to live. Perhaps also some of it is orchestration by the guardian angel of whom I have written so much.

As I lay down my pen, I do so with gratitude to all without whom there would have been no song at all.

Charles H. Tuttle

CHARLES H. TUTTLE
1879–1971

Chronology

CHARLES H. TUTTLE *(1879-1971)*

1879 Charles Henry Tuttle is born in New York City on April 21 to Henry Croswell Tuttle and Penelope Cook Tuttle.

1882 Charles's father, an 1868 graduate of Columbia Law School, dies of tuberculosis in New York.

1883 His mother takes "Charlie," as he is called by family and friends, to live on a farm in New Jersey to improve their health.

1888 Charlie and his mother commence life at 218 West 46th Street, New York City, the home of his grandfather, the Rev. Isaac H. Tuttle, D.D., rector of St. Luke's Episcopal Church in Greenwich Village, later re-established at Convent Avenue and 141st Street. The Reverend Dr. Tuttle had been one of the first summer settlers at Lake George, New York in the mid–nineteenth century.

1895 Charlie graduates from Trinity Episcopal School in New York City.

1896 The Reverend Doctor Tuttle dies, leaving to his grandson his Lake George property, but little in monetary assets.

1899 Charlie graduates from Columbia College, Columbia University, with honors, and enters Columbia Law School.

1902 Charlie passes the New York Bar Examination, graduates from Columbia Law School, and becomes a law clerk in the New York City law firm of Davies, Stone & Auerbach.

1906 Davies, Stone & Auerbach makes Charlie a partner. He practices law in that firm for another twenty-one years.

1907 On June 1st Charles H. Tuttle and Hélène L. Wheeler are married in St. Luke's Episcopal Church and honeymoon at his Lake George summer home.

1913 Tuttle becomes a member of the Board of Higher Education of the City of New York, a membership which continues for fifty-three years.

1917   Charles Tuttle begins service as Chairman of Local 141 of the
        World War I Selective Service Board.

1925   He becomes President of the Greater New York Federation of
        Churches and chairs the interfaith group which creates the
        Released Time Program, allowing a one-hour a week release,
        on parental request, of public school children for religious
        instruction away from their school.

1927   On April 7th, Tuttle becomes the United States Attorney
        for the Southern District of New York by appointment of
        President Calvin Coolidge.

1927   In this year, and again in 1928 and 1929, Tuttle is elected Presi-
        dent of the Lake George Association, and in 1930 becomes
        its lifelong counsel.

1930   On September 25th, having resigned as U.S. Attorney, Tuttle is
        nominated at the Republican State Convention in Albany as the
        Republican candidate for Governor of New York. He conducts
        a state-wide campaign against Governor Franklin D. Roosevelt.

1930   On November 4th, Tuttle is defeated.

1930   On November 5th, his former staff of the United States Attor-
        ney's Office forms the lifelong "Tuttle Boys Association."
        They will gather to celebrate the "Chief's" birthdays through
        his 91st.

1930   On November 7th, Tuttle accepts an invitation to become a
        partner in the large Wall Street law firm of Breed, Abbott &
        Morgan, in which he will practice throughout the balance of
        his life.

1933   As chairman of the Republican City Caucus committee, Tuttle
        joins with Judge Samuel Seabury to form a Fusion ticket with
        Fiorello La Guardia as the nominee for Mayor of New York
        City, and promotes the successful candidacy.

1942   During World War II Tuttle serves as Chairman of the Selective
        Service Appeals Board.

1944-5 As counsel to the New York State Commission on Anti-Dis-
        crimination, Tuttle drafts and sees enacted the first State statute
        in the United States prohibiting discrimination in employment
        on the basis of race, creed, color, or national origin.

1945   Archbishop Athenagoras, later the Patriarch of Jerusalem, awards Charles H. Tuttle "The Grand Cross of the Order of the Holy Sepulchre."

1947   As counsel to the Lake George Association, Tuttle intervenes in State litigation to establish a fixed range of water levels on Lake George.

1950   Tuttle prepares and obtains filing under New York State law of a charter creating the National Council of Churches.

1952   As counsel to the Greater New York Coordinating Committee for Released Time, Tuttle successfully defends that program in the United States Supreme Court.

1952   Syracuse University confers upon Tuttle the honorary degree of Doctor of Laws, citing him for "citizenship at its best."

1955   Tuttle receives from the Protestant Council of the City of New York its Distinguished Service Award for "untiring labor for Christian education of children and youth."

1956   Tuttle is appointed to the temporary State Commission to study proposed changes in the New York State Constitution.

1962   Tuttle begins presidency of recently formed Brotherhood-in-Action.

1964   Mayor Robert F. Wagner presents Tuttle with the Bronze Medal of the City of New York as "Illustrious Citizen of New York."

1966   Tuttle retires after six terms from the Board of Higher Education and receives the thanks of the City from Mayor John V. Lindsay.

1966   City College confers upon Tuttle the honorary degree of Doctor of Law.

1967   Tuttle resigns as a partner in Breed, Abbott & Morgan and becomes "of counsel" to the firm.

1969   Historic Grace Episcopal Church, Broadway at 10th Street, attended by Charles and Hélène Tuttle for thirty years, names its proposed enlarged auditorium "Charles H. Tuttle Hall."

1970   The Lake George Association honors "Mr. Lake George" with a newly established award, the "Charles H. Tuttle Citation."

1971   On January 21st, Charles H. Tuttle dies in New York City, at the age of 91.

ACKNOWLEDGEMENTS

PART I:

The Genesis of this Book

I HAVE WRITTEN IN THE FOREWORD about our father, Charles H. Tuttle, creating his fascinating autobiography in his lofty Manhattan office during the two years before his death in January 1971. This 2002 publication of his work is our heartfelt thanks to him for that enormous outlay of time, energy, and perseverance expended for us—his children and grandchildren—and for all interested in the law, politics, and causes of his day. It is also a testament to our belief that the stories of his life and times are as compelling today as when he recorded them.

Father wrote his work in longhand on yellow pads. We owe great thanks and praise to his longtime, devoted, capable secretary, Augusta Musterer, who typed his writing into a 500-page book and then made a copy for each of his four children.

When we four children received this gift in 1970, we were still fully engrossed in our work, enterprises, and family responsibilities, playing "their own exciting parts," as Father envisioned for us in his Preface. Later, as his and our descendants multiplied, we needed copies of Father's autobiography for them. My niece, Elizabeth (Lisa) Bryant Escudero, a machine copy expert, reproduced thirty copies, bound them with covers depicting the "Oxcart to Jet" in Father's title to his book, and, in 1989, mailed them to family members as Christmas gifts. Reproduction was a difficult job as the original copies were made on thermal paper which would not take repeated machine copying; so Lisa first had to make a master copy from which to work. Thank you, Lisa, for this first dissemination of Father's work.

The impetus toward publication of the autobiography came as a by-product of the courageous decision by my sister, Jasmine T. Bryant, our Halcyon manager, to clear out and clean the spacious attic of Halcyon, our inherited summer family home on Lake George. This attic was the repository of generations of family papers, books, memorabilia, and discarded furniture. It was July 1996, and a bevy of younger Bryants and their friends went to work carrying boxes and other objects to a protected screened porch. When my husband, Homer Walkup, his daughter, Pamela (Pam), and I arrived in latter July, there were twenty-two boxes of books and papers to be sorted out and appropriately handled. I examined the boxes of Father's papers. These proved to be largely the yellow copies of his fairly routine response correspondence as United States Attorney for the Southern District of New York, 1927–1930, and documents and speeches from his candidacy for Governor in latter 1930. After giving them a rough semblance of order, I was delighted to find that the New York State Historical Library would be glad to accept donation of them and did so. I express our thanks to the State Library.

The ready interest of the State Library in just the three years we had available of Father's papers awakened us to the significant interest there might be in the ninety-year-long record of his life. For the next two years the family's attention was focused on other important matters, but in August 1999, I was authorized to prepare the public chapters of his autobiography for donation to the State Historical Library.

However, in attempting to complete this project, I found that extracting some chapters would require extensive re-editing. I also discovered that if the chapters were to be prepared in publishable form, they would need to be placed on a computer disk. At the August 2000 family meeting, my daughter, Louisa Lloyd Hurley, was commissioned to type the autobiography, minus a few personal chapters edited out by me, for access on a computer disk. This she did, and had the 99,000 words on disk and on 304 printed pages by July 2001.

Our fumbling about with the question as to how best to make Father's story available to the public came to a happy solution in August 2001. My most hoped for publisher was the College Avenue Press in Clinton Corners, N.Y., operated by Joseph J. (Trip) Sinnott, III, a long-time family friend who had known Father. I had read four books, beautifully produced by College Avenue Press, and found them to be excellent in appearance, format, and style. Trip had the opportunity in July to examine Father's original autobiography and the computerized pages typed by Louisa. He prepared a publication proposal for the family. We thank you, Trip Sinnott, for coming forward at just the right time, and for your imaginative suggestions and contagious enthusiasm.

The Tuttle family assembled at Halcyon that August the 11th, to discuss and decide on the publication proposal. The assembly included: my brother, H. Croswell Tuttle, his son, Charles H. Tuttle, II, and daughter Julianne T. Currie, from their homes across the Lake; our Halcyon family, my sister Jasmine, her son, Robert S. Bryant and daughter Rebecca B. Lamont (Lisa B. Escudero was unable to attend); Anne Horne Warder, daughter of my deceased sister, Evelyn, and Anne's son, Frederick B. Warder, III; my daughter, Louisa, and myself. We accepted Trip's proposal with much satisfaction and expectation. We are finding now how much reason we have to thank each other, Trip, and good fortune for this book launching. We rejoiced that a publication in 2002 of Father's work would be a centenary edition, honoring his emergence as a newly-minted attorney in 1902.

Two further decisions were made at that August meeting. I was entrusted with the responsibility of being editor, an undertaking I have enjoyed, and been greatly assisted in fulfilling, by the experience, encouragement, and initiative of the publisher, Trip Sinnott. The second decision was to request Fred Warder to become copyright owner in trust for the Tuttle family. As a partner in a New York City law firm and a younger member of the family, he was most suited for this assignment. Fred agreed, and later in the year drafted the Charles H. Tuttle Literary Trust Agreement, which was executed by all appropriate grantors by January 2002. Thank you, Fred, for becoming Trustee, for the trust agreement, and for later providing the complete citations of the twenty-six New York cases Father discussed.

PART II:

Contributors to the 2002 Publication Process

NOW I TURN to the welcome acknowledgement of the family members and many other persons who have contributed their time and effort, pictures, and supplementary information to this publication.

First and foremost, I must fondly thank my own husband, Homer Walkup, for not only giving advice and support in this undertaking but also for providing the computer facilities and expertise essential for rapid, often daily, communication with Trip Sinnott, Louisa, and others by e-mail and fax; also, he has been unfailingly willing to type up my old-fashioned longhand. Very important was his educated proficiency in using the incredible resources of Westlaw and Lexis-Nexis to find the substance and complete citations for Father's case stories, at first only the federal cases but later State cases as well (in addition to New York case material developed by Fred Warder). On his own initiative Homer explored indices in the Library of Congress for pertinent data, as his informative Appendix article testifies. And in his photography days, he took an exceptional mountaintop picture of Father, reproduced in this book.

Next in assistance has been my daughter, Louisa, whom I have already thanked for computerizing, by July 2001, father's preliminarily edited manuscript. Earlier this year she added to the disk some of father's omitted personal story which the publisher and I deemed to provide insight and understanding into his life and person. Then, as the first text emerged, Louisa prepared the lengthy initial Index of Persons. Thank you again, Louisa, three times over.

The first version of the printed text was much enhanced by the reading and commentary given it by Pamela F. Bryant, daughter-in-law of my sister, Jasmine. Pam had offered in August 2001 to give the book a review for contemporary readability. Her perceptive suggestions were largely incorporated.

I especially commend and thank my brother, Croswell, for his persistent reminder of the foremost attention and devotion Father had given to Lake George throughout his life. This emphasis resulted in the addition to the book of a few of Father's previously published reflections on his Lake George activities, as well as the prominence of Lake George in the title and cover of this book.

Much enrichment of the book came about from the day-long search in the Lake George area conducted last March by my sister, Jasmine Bryant, niece, Julie Currie, and Trip Sinnott, for relevant Lake George material. They visited the Lake George Association for archival information and an update on the "Charles H. Tuttle Citation" *(see page 364);* Dean Photography in Glens Falls, assisted by Wendy Dean Chitty, in the pursuit of pertinent pictures; and then a final search at Halcyon, looking through closets, dressers, boxes, and scrapbooks for additional pictures and clippings. The Halcyon search received the timely assistance of family friend, Mike Rich, who found some outstanding political cartoons in scrapbooks. Much aid in this overall effort was also provided by Don Whitefield, who has devotedly taken care of Halcyon for many years.

Julie, the family archivist, further enhanced the book by providing early pictures of Father and Mother in Oswego, New York, treasures saved by Julie's mother, Doris Tuttle. Two much-needed pictures were provided by my niece, Anne Warder, one of her mother (my sister, Evelyn) for the gubernatorial candidate's family picture, and one of herself and her husband, Frederick B. Warder, Jr., for the 50th wedding anniversary Tuttle family picture of 1957.

The wealth of pictures and other graphic art which brings so much life to this book is due to the initiative and enterprise of Trip Sinnott. In addition to enlisting the family in providing pictures, he tirelessly researched into Father's world, obtaining pictures of the mayors, governors, and presidents in Father's life, and other leaders and colleagues he had worked with,as well as the City College of New York, four of the churches he had attended or represented, and other important places.

To accomplish this, our publisher contacted the following people who responded with interest and grace. He and I, for myself as editor and for all the family, herewith thank each by name or entity:

Karen Anson, archivist in the Franklin D. Roosevelt Library, for her ongoing enthusiastic guidance in helping Trip locate archival photographs in the collection of the FDR Library, and for kindly steering him toward other treasures obtained for the book through the vast collection offered by NARA (National Archives and Records Administration);

The Still Pictures Branch in Maryland of the National Archives and Records Administration, which was the source of presidential photographs and related pictures;

The Office of the Mayor of New York City for the pictures of seven mayors;

Charles DeCicco, Director of Public Relations of the City College of New York/CUNY, for the pictures of the college and of its former president, Dr. Buell Gallagher;

Margaret (Peggy) Edwards, Lake George Historian, for pictures of Lake George and Mayor La Guardia's visit, and for information about former Lake George mayor, Henry J. Gabb;

Mona Seeger, office manager of the Lake George Association, for her assistance in amplifying and updating information on the LGA and Father's longstanding involvement with the Association;

Lynn Hoke, archivist, and Linda Hall, receptionist, of Grace Church, New York City, for their help in providing pictures of the Church, the Fourth Street façade, and updated information on Tuttle Hall;

The Rev. Julie McPartlin, rector of St. James Church, Lake George, for the lovely picture of the church;

The Rev. Canon Harry E. Kraus, Senior Curate of St. Thomas Church (NYC), and his assistant, Linda Crosier, for their enthusiastic assistance in offering information and photographs related to the Scott Memorial statues on the Fifth Avenue facade;

The Rev. John Gill for his successful effort in tracking down and carefully reproducing old photographs of Patriarch Athenagoras from his personal archives;

Thomas Rockwell for his gracious consent to our use of two classic paintings by his father, Norman Rockwell.

Dr. Madelon Delany Stent for her gracious cooperation in lending pictures of her father, Hubert T. Delany;

Max Andrews for his permission to use the 1929 drawing of Charles Tuttle, which first appeared in *The New Yorker* and was created by Max's late uncle, Abe Birnbaum;

Eric Glass, a Maine artist, for his skilled work in rendering several 21st Century sketches, depicting a lawyer as Charles H. Tuttle might have appeared a half century earlier;

Bob and Nancy Quinlan for their generous offer of time and talent in aerial photography of New York City, and for the use of the photographic gems of Highway Aerial Photography appearing in this book;

Barry and Leigh Knickerbocker for their gracious help with digital photographic processing and related computer work;

Kathleen Corby of Corby Design for consultation and creative input on the cover design of the book from its earliest renderings.

IN ADDITION TO all the foregoing assistance with the procurement and use of the many graphic reproductions, office assistance was given to the publisher by Irene Decker, Trip's invaluable part-time assistant. We join him in thanking her for her many hours of computer work, formatting, draft binding, photocopying, shipping, and general office support.

Special thanks also go to Jeff Tremper of UPS for literally "going the extra mile," and to Marilyn Grieco, Kathy O'Connor and Becky Hicks of the Clinton Corners Post Office for literally "going the extra minute" to ensure timely deliveries between publisher and editor.

Throughout this production I have heard from Trip of the ongoing review and helpful commentary given to him by his friends and neighbors, the Angell family, including a lawyer's review of *LIFE STORIES* by Thomas Angell. Janet, Nathaniel and Hannah Angell offered timely assistance with proofing of the Index. Many thanks to all the members of this supportive family.

Finally, we give our specially fond gratitude to our friend of many decades, Sally Marsh Sinnott Guernsey, for her early and continuing support, insight, and encouragement of this unique project at College Avenue Press.

———◆———

IN FURTHER CELEBRATION of Charles Tuttle's life and legacy, we present a special five-part Appendix in this Commemorative Edition of his memoirs. Released exactly one hundred years after Charles Tuttle began his illustrious legal career in the "dog hole" of a New York law firm, LIFE STORIES includes these additional illuminating glimpses of his life, beginning with a treasured handwritten letter.

———◆———

Appendix A
A WRITER'S FIRST LETTER

Dear Grandpa,
Mamma told me that you had a birthday this month.
I want to tell you that I think of you very often and love you very dearly.
I wish you were here to see the good time I have with my sled.
It was my wish to send you the first letter I have written.
Your loving grandson
Charles Henry Tuttle

"FIRST LETTER I HAVE WRITTEN," *1885*

Penned by five-and-a-half-year old Charles Tuttle, this loving correspondence was mailed to "Grandpa" Isaac Tuttle on February 25, 1885. It is the first of many letters sent to family and friends from the gifted writer during nearly a century of letter-writing.

Appendix B
THE TUTTLE BOYS: "Truly Remarkable"

"AND WHO ARE these 'Tuttle Boys'? asked Charles Tuttle rhetorically in his memoirs. "They are," he answered, "all truly remarkable men with outstanding lives and careers in their own right."

Exactly fifty years ago, the Tuttle Boys gathered for a special dinner to celebrate the fiftieth anniversary of the Chief's admission to the bar, the twenty-fifth anniversary of his appointment as U.S. Attorney, and more than two decades of annual gatherings as the Tuttle Boys. The April 21, 1952 gathering included a musical "satirony" *(see page 178)* and the following staff list, described as "Assistant U.S. Attorneys under Mr. Tuttle during his term of office as U.S. Attorney, 1927–1930"— including the Tuttle Boys and their office colleagues.

Seymour D. Altmark	Isaac Gutman	John M. Ryan
Richard L. Baltimore	Harry G. Herman	George B Schoonmaker
Earle N. Bishopp	Ben Herzberg	Walter H. Schulman
John M. Blake	Clare P. Johnson	Arthur H. Schwartz
Leonard Bronner, Jr.	W. Houston Kenyon, Jr.	Crenna Sellers
Reuben T. Carlson	Thomas E. Kerwin	Maxwell Shapiro
Frank P. Catinella	Emanuel G Klied	Joseph F. Sharp
Frank Chambers	Ernest Lappano	Edward S. Silver
Porter R. Chandler	George S. Leisure	Kenneth F. Simpson
Maurice Cohen	J. Edward Lumbard, Jr.	Leon E. Spencer
Samuel C. Coleman	Robert E. Manley	Irving Spieler
Thomas T. Cooke	Andrew W. McLean	Herman T. Stichman
Thomas J. Crawford	Vito Marcantonio	Alvin McK. Sylvester
Thomas J. Curran	Nathan R. Margold	Charles L. Sylvester
Hubert T. Delany	Jacob Meirowitz	James H. Terry
Mario G. DiPirro	Henry D. Mildeberger	Owen S. M. Tierney
Ellamarye Failor	George J. Mintzer	Thomas J. Todarelli
Charles H. Finkelstein	Abbot L. Moffat	Bernard Tompkins
Frank W. Ford	James Oliver Murdock	Mary R. Towle
Edward Feldman	Carl E. Newton	Lowell Wadmond
John J. Fogarty	Israel B. Oseas	Robert B. Watts
Herman Forster	Rocco A. Parella	John A. Wilson
Ulysses S. Grant	David W. Peck	
Henry Gerson	C. Frank Reavis, Jr	

The Tuttle Boys: A Lyrical View of
Charles Tuttle and the 1930 Election

HE RAN THROUGH THE STATE
WITH THE GREATEST OF EASE

(MUSIC: *"Man on the Flying Trapeze"*)

He ran through the state with the greatest of ease,
He thought he would win in a walk and a breeze,
He spoke to the workers and farmers as well,
And sought Charlie Tuttle to sell.
Then he urged they discard prohibition,
Oh with this he should never have dealt,
For the upstaters made their decision,
And clamored for Frank Roosevelt, OH-O-O!
They drank wet upstate but they all voted dry,
Just why this should be, Charlie never knew why,
They wanted their wine and beer under their belt,
But they voted for Frank Roosevelt.

Then back to the farm with the greatest of ease,
Poor Charlie repaired to his birds and his bees,
Convinced that if voters he could not arouse,
He'd better just stick to his cows.
His friends gave him great consolation,
And they told him how sorry they felt,
But in spite of their cordial relation,
They had voted for Frank Roosevelt, OH-H-H!
And tho' history tells us that he failed to win,
They've got to admit that he lost with a grin,
And what was important he kept his good health,
Tho' he ran against Frank Roosevelt.

Photo by Evening Journal Staff Photographer.

Among those who will watch the election returns tonight with more than ordinary interest is this little family group—composed of Charles H. Tuttle, Republican candidate for Governor, and his wife and daughters. Left to right they are Charlotte M. Tuttle, Mrs. Tuttle, Mr. Tuttle and Hélène Jasmine. The picture was taken in their home at 339 Convent Ave., on Washington Heights.

Appendix C

THE 1930 ELECTION RESULTS: WATCHING for SIGNALS in the SKY

EDITOR'S NOTE: Before the era of television, instant on–line news, exit polls, and computer projections, voters were offered a 1930s version of "up-to-the-minute" election results in the Tuttle–Roosevelt governor's match–up. *The New York Times* explained to its readers on election day their unique method for signalling the ongoing results as the returns came in for the New York gubernatorial race of 1930.

Election Results Will Be Shown By Times Bulletins and Signals

THE NEW YORK TIMES will signal the results of the New York Governorship election by flashlight signals, both from The Times Building in Times Square and from the tower of the Empire State Building, by means of a General Electric air beacon. The Times will also report this and other results of the election on its electric bulletin board which encircles The Times Building and will display elections bulletins at several places in the city.

New York Gubernatorial Election

ROOSEVELT IN LEAD—Searchlight swinging to north up and down.

ROOSEVELT ELECTED—Searchlight to north, steady horizontal shaft.

TUTTLE IN LEAD—Searchlight swinging to south up and down.

TUTTLE ELECTED—Searchlight to south, steady horizontal shaft.

— Originally published in *The New York Times*
November 4, 1930

Appendix D

THE CHARLES H. TUTTLE CITATION
of the LAKE GEORGE ASSOCIATION

Lake George Association

Originally established in 1970 by the Lake George Association to honor the man they called "Mr. Lake George," the **Charles H. Tuttle Citation** has since been awarded to more than a dozen honorees over the past three decades. Each recipient has demonstrated outstanding achievement in fostering the LGA's mission since 1885 to "protect, conserve, and improve the beauty and quality of Lake George" — a mission embraced by Charles Tuttle throughout his life as an ardent and loyal guardian of the Queen of American Lakes.

YEAR	RECIPIENT
1970	Cyrus H. Woodbury
1971	Lysle W. Morton
1972	Arthur S. Knight
1973	David F. Davis
1977	Victor C. Glider
1978	Henry R. Merrill
1979	C. Guy Suits
1979	Stephen T. Birdsall
1980	Alton C. Warner
1983	Frank Leonbruno
1984	David M. Darrin Family
1985	James D. Corbett
1987	John K. Ryder
1989	Carl D. Simmonds
1994	Tupper C. Limbert

Appendix E

"PATENT ATTORNEY" TUTTLE: NAB vs. ASCAP

by Homer A. Walkup★

I FIRST ENCOUNTERED the name Charles H. Tuttle in reading Wellman's classic, *The Art of Cross-Examination* as a young upstart lawyer in the coal fields of West Virginia. It was more than a quarter century before I met him face-to-face and heard from his own lips the account of his skillful cross-examination recounted in Wellman's book, a story also found in these memoirs *(see page 67)*.

My meeting Charles Tuttle was one of the joys and benefits of marrying, in 1967, his daughter, Charlotte, the editor of *LIFE STORIES*. We met as neighbors after both being widowed, and found that we shared interests as lawyers—she as an Assistant General Counsel of the U. S. Treasury Department; I as a lawyer in the Office of the Judge Advocate General of the Navy.

I enjoyed periodic association with Mr. Tuttle in New York City and in Lake George during the four-year period preceding his death in January 1971. I came to know him as a gracious, caring, and impressive man, as well as a raconteur par excellence.

When he was writing the account of his life within the two years before his death, he spoke of his memoirs during our infrequent meetings, but without detailed discussion of the issues of law, public policy, and morality underlying his advocacy. I did not recognize the true greatness of this man as a lawyer until reading some of the cases in which

---

★*A.B., West Virginia University, 1935; LL.B., WVU College of Law, 1938; LL.M., Georgetown Law School, 1947; U.S. Naval Reserve, active duty as a lawyer, 1942-1973; retired Captain, Judge Advocate General's Corps, 1973; member, West Virginia State Bar.*

he participated. This happened while assisting Charlotte in preparing a Table of Cases for this Commemorative Edition of his memoirs.

For the first time I was struck with the realization that one would be a far better lawyer after having had an opportunity to consider Mr. Tuttle's work in the actual framework of the philosophical propositions involved in his courtroom experience.

In the course of researching a related matter in the 1920's *New York Times Index,* I encountered references to a "Mr. Tuttle" and a "Patent Attorney Tuttle" having represented the National Association of Broadcasters during 1924–1926. This led to the discovery of an area of Mr. Tuttle's expertise not recounted in his autobiography, but one clearly worth emphatic mention.

My search yielded a rare copy of a 462-page Report of Joint Hearings before the Committees on Patents, 69th Congress, 1st Session, on S. 2328 and H.R. 10353, Bills to Amend the Copyright Act, April 5, 6, 7, 8, and 9, 1926. The bills were termed the Dill and Vestal Bills, and my father-in-law, then a senior partner in the firm of Davies, Auerbach, and Cornell (previously Davies, Stone & Auerbach), had represented the National Association of Broadcasters in a vigorous effort over a two-year period to obtain Congressional action upon an intricate series of copyright problems of national concern.

A few words of "background" to refresh, revive, or create understanding of the issues concerned: By 1905, when Mr. Tuttle was three years out of law school, slaving in the "dog hole" of Davies, Stone & Auerbach, three technologies affecting authors and composers were apparent. They were the typewriter; the automatic piano on which music could be reproduced by using perforated rolls; and the motion picture which, although not itself then containing sound, could be accompanied by either human musicians or an automatic roll-playing piano. The piano roll was improved upon by printing words on the side to permit persons near and facing the piano to sing the words with the music, thus giving the lyricist a piece of the action.

House and Senate Patent Committees, the jurisdiction of which included copyrights, labored from 1905 to 1909 to meet the emerging technology. Interests to be served and conflicts to be resolved included those of composers, authors, publishers, manufacturers, wholesale and retail outlets, the press, the clergy, and, above all, individuals, whose patronage was required to keep the wheels turning.

The resultant 1909 Act provided in essence that one holding a copyright might bring an action in court against another who, without permission of the copyright owner, performed for profit the copyrighted work. The holder of the copyright could recover such damages as he might be able to prove, or, in the absence of proven actual damages, such damages as the court might deem just.

But read on: With respect to certain specified types of copyrighted works, schedules of allowable damages for infringement were prescribed. The fourth class specified was "a dramatic or dramatico-musical or a choral or orchestral composition," for infringement of which damages were limited to $100 for the first and $50 for every subsequent infringing performance or, in the case of *other* musical compositions, $10 for every infringing performance. Clearly, an individual composer who copyrighted his melody or song could not economically undertake investigation to ascertain infringing performances and litigation to recover damages for them—when the maximum recovery was limited to $10 per performance.

Victor Herbert, a composer whose works are still sometimes played, in 1914 was incensed by hearing performed his song, *Sweethearts,* and realizing that he was not able, as a practical matter, to enforce payment of compensation to him for the performance. He interested other composers and publishers, and they united to form the American Society of Composers, Authors, and Publishers (ASCAP). Upon joining ASCAP, a composer assigned to the organization for a five-year period the right to receive damages or pursue other remedies for infringement of his copyright. This empowered ASCAP to sue to enjoin continuing infringement, thus impeding cash flow to food and entertainment industries. Restauranteurs and early moving picture producers found it wise to pay ASCAP an annual license fee for use of music to which ASCAP held assigned infringement enforcement rights.

In the early 1920's, a new industry—radio—one never contemplated by the 1905-1909 lawmakers, came upon the scene. To get the feet of a twenty-first century reader firmly planted on the earth, note these facts: Warren G. Harding, in the White House from March 1921

until his death in 1923, was (a) the first American President to own a
personal radio set; (b) the first American President to broadcast an
address by radio; and (c) the first American President to travel in an
automobile to his inauguration. The 1924 national convention of the
Democratic Party *("Alabama casts 24 votes for Underwood")* was the
first nationally broadcast political event.

Mr. Tuttle pointed out in the spring 1926 hearings that at a recent
conference between ASCAP and broadcasters representatives, it had
been mutually recognized that 90% of radio broadcasts consisted of
musical selections, and that at least 90% of available music was controlled by ASCAP as assignee of composers' enforcement rights.

Senator C. C. Dill of Washington State, Chairman of the Senate
Patents Committee, had some constituent smaller broadcasting stations
in the Northwest that were concerned that inadequacy of the 1909
Copyright Act placed their livelihood at the mercy of ASCAP. Representative Albert H. Vestal of Indiana, House Majority Whip, was Chairman of the House Patents Committee. Both had witnessed unsuccessful attempts in 1924 to obtain legislation exempting broadcasters from
copyright infringement penalties. The case for exemption was that benefits to composers in having their works broadcast outweighed any
amount they would receive individually out of license fees paid by
broadcasters to ASCAP.

The strategy in 1926 was to concede that broadcasting had emerged
in two years as a profitable economic venture, and should properly pay
some compensation to composers of works broadcast. The amount of
such compensation and the formulae for determining it were, however,
matters to be worked out by the legislative process: Hearing advocates
for all interests concerned and, variously, resolving, compromising, and
settling conflicts involved. Mr. Tuttle came to Washington from New
York and testified before the joint committees on Tuesday, April 6, and
on Friday, April 9. He was certainly *a* principal, and perhaps *the* principal witness, rehearsing needs and interests of broadcasters, and
demonstrating throughout his complete mastery and understanding of
the matters involved.

Mr. Tuttle showed that ASCAP, as a privately operated alternative
to regulation by statute, was in violation of the 1890 Sherman Anti-
Trust Act. He placed on the record the Articles of Association of

ASCAP, revealing that it was governed by a board of twenty-four persons having absolute and permanent control of its own membership and tenure. Three persons employed by the board operated ASCAP without board direction or oversight. He cited precedents establishing that the Society was a combination in restraint of trade and a monopolistic enterprise. His quest was one of principle—to obtain public legislative regulation of compensation of composers for broadcasts of their copyrighted creations. It is apparent from his testimony that his genius would have remained available to legislators and committee staffs as long as they continued in pursuit of that end.

The obstacle to the Tuttle endeavor was Representative Sol Bloom, Democrat, of New York, a member of the House Patents Committee and a former music publisher. Representative Bloom was openly challenging and antagonistic, and asserted a basic position that the 1909 Copyright Act should stand as immutable as the laws of the Medes and the Persians. Mr. Tuttle's dialogue with and bearing toward Representative Bloom during the public hearings, could serve as models for another lawyer placed in a similar setting.

Mr. Tuttle's acceptance, in early 1927, of an appointment as United States Attorney for the Southern District of New York, foreclosed further personal representation by him of the National Association of Broadcasters.

No change in the 1909 Act was to take place until 1976—five years after Mr. Tuttle's death at age 91. The Anti-Trust Act violations pointed out by Mr. Tuttle became nationally apparent in 1939, when ASCAP's blocking of copyrighted music broadcasts relegated broadcasting stations to hymns and folk music. The Department of Justice instituted anti-trust actions and obtained consent decrees from ASCAP, enabling the closing of prosecutions. New technology confronted the judiciary with problems toward whose solution no legislative help was available. How much better had the principle of Congressional regulation by statutory law, espoused by Mr. Tuttle in 1924-26, triumphed over political expediency!

Table of Cases

Listed alphabetically

CASE/CITATION   PAGE

Abington School District v. Schempp   301
374 US 203, 10 L.Ed. 2d 844, 83 S.Ct 1560 (1963) *aff'd.* 201 F.Supp. 815

Adirondack League Club v. Board of Black River Reg. Dist   316
275 A.D. 618 (1949), 301 N.Y. 219, 93 NE 2d 647 (1950) L. 1950, ch. 803

Alexander Theater Ticket Office v. United States   135
23 F2d. 44 (CA 2nd 1927)

**American Brake Shoe & Foundry Co. v.
Interborough Rapid Transit Co.**   212
4 F. Supp. 68, D.C. NY 1933) (Manton, C.J.)

American League Baseball Club of New York v. Johnson   55
109 Misc. 138, 179 N.Y.S. 498 (Sup. Ct. 1919) *aff'd.* 190 A.D. 932,
179 N.Y.S. 898 (App. Div. 1st Dept. 1920)

Ballard v. United States   218
329 US 187, 91 L.Ed. 181, 67 S.Ct. 261 (1944)

Blair v. City of Chicago (Originated as Govin v. City of Chicago)   45
201 U.S.400, 50 L.Ed. 801 26 S. Ct. 427 (1906) 132 F. 848, (CC Ill., 1904)

***In re* Butler's Estate**   273
106 Misc. 375, 174 N.Y.S. 880 (Sur. Ct. 1919)
(rev'd sub nom.) In re United States Trust Co. of New York
190 A.D. 494, 180 N.Y.S. 12 (Ap p. Div. 1st Dept.) *aff'd.*
229 N.Y. 598, 129 N.E. 923 (1920)

Cadman Memorial Congregational Society of Brooklyn v. Kenyon 222
197 Misc. 124, 95 N.Y.S. 2d 133 (Sup. Ct. 1950)
rev'd 279 A.D. 1015, 111 N.Y.S. 2d 808, (App. Div. 2d Dept. 1952),
judgment aff'd. 306 N. Y. 151 116 N.E.2d 481 (1953)

Catapodis v. Onassis 201
2 Misc. 2d 234, 151 N.Y.S. 2d 39 (Sup. Ct. 1956)

College of the City of New York v. Hylan 90
120 Misc. 314, 199 N.Y.S. 634 (Sup. Ct.), *aff'd.* 205 AD 372,
199 N.Y.S. 804 (App. Div. 1st Dept.), *aff'd.* 236 N.Y. 594,
142 N. E. 297 (1923)

Continental Securities Co. v. Belmont 50
168 A.D. 483, 154 N.Y.S. 54 (App. Div. 2nd Dept. 1915)
Aff'd. 222 N.Y. 673, 119 N.E. 1036 (1918)

Contogeorge v. Spyrou 230
7 F.R.D. 223 (US Dist Ct, SD NY 1946)

Engel v. Vitale 301
370 US 421, 8 L.Ed. 2d 601, 82 S.Ct. 1261 (1962) *rvsd,*
18 Misc. 2d 659, 191 N.Y.S. 2d 453, *aff'd.* 11 AD2d 340,
206 N.Y.S. 2d 183, *aff'd.* 10 N.Y.S. 2d 174, 218 N.Y.S. 2d 659,
176 N.E. 2d 579

Fendler v. Morosco, Motion for reargument denied 59
217 App. Div. 791, 253 N.Y. 281, 171 N.E. 56 (1930)
254 N.Y. 563, 173 N.E. 867 (1930)

Fink v. Cole 211
277 A. D. 861, 98 N.Y.S. 2d 207 (App. Div. 1st Dept 1950)
Rev'd. 302 N.Y. 216, 97 N.E. 2d 873 (1951)

Fisher v. Fisher 57
250 N.Y. 313, 164 N.E. 460 (1929)

Flast v. Cohen 251
392 US 83, 20 L.Ed. 2d 947, 88 S.Ct. 1942 (1968)
Notation of National Council of Churches *amicus* brief
20 L.Ed. 2d 1668

Foerster v. Ridder   226
    275 A.D. 665, 87 N.Y.S.2d 419 (App.Div. 1st Dept. 1949)

Frothingham v. Mellon   250
    262 US 447, 67 L Ed 1078, 43 S.Ct. 597 (1923)

Gallagher v. New York Dock Company   248
    19 N.Y.S. 2d 789 (Sup. Ct. 1940), aff'd. 263 A.D.878,
    32 N.Y.S.2d 348 (App. Div. 2d Dept. 1942), 288 NY 737

Hostetter v. Idlewild Bon Voyage Liquor Corp.   246
    377 US 324, 12 L.Ed.2d 350, 84 S.Ct.1293 (1964)

Idlewild Bon Voyage Liquor Corp. v. Rohan   245
    188 F. Supp. 434 (Dist. Ct. NY, 1960)
    289 F.2d 426 (CA 2d, 1961)

Idlewild Bon Voyage Liquor Corp. v. Hostetter   246
    212 F. Supp. 376 (SD NY 1962)
petition for certiorari
    368 US 812, 7L.Ed. 2d 794, 82 S.Ct. 1294 (1961)

Idlewild Bon Voyage Liquor Corp. v. Epstein and
    Hon. Alexander Bicks et al., Dist Ct. Judges   246
    370 US 713, 81 L.Ed.2d 794, 82 S.Ct. 1294 (1962)

Hotel Woodward Co. v. Ford Motor Co.   62
    258 F. 322 (CA 2nd 1919)
Pet. for certiorari denied
    256 US 698, 65 L.Ed. 1177, 41 S.Ct. 537 (1921)

Hotel Woodward Co. v. Ford Motor Co.   64
    271 F. 625 (CA 2nd 1921)
Pet. for certiorari denied
    259 US 588, 66 L.Ed. 1078, 42 S.Ct. 590 (1922)

Johnson v. Manhattan Ry. Co.   213
    1 F. Supp. 809 (DC NY, 1932) 61 F.2d 934 (CA 2d, 1932, L. Hand, C.J.)
    289 US 479, 77 L.Ed. 1331, 53 S.Ct. 721, (1933) aff'd. 61 F.2d 934

Jones v. Alfred H. Mayer Co. 249

392 US 409, 20 L.Ed. 2d 1189, 88 S.Ct. 2186 (1968)

Notation National Council Churches *amicus* brief

20 L.Ed. 2d 1764

Kay v. Board of Higher Education City of N.Y. 85

173 Misc. 943, 18 N.Y.S. 2d 821 (Sup. Ct.), *aff'd.*

259 A.D. 879, 20 N.Y.S .2d 1016 (App.Div. 1st Dept. 1940)

Kedroff v. St. Nicholas Cathedral of the
Russian Orthodox Church in North America 237

344 U.S. 94, 97 L.Ed. 120, 73 S.Ct. 143 (1952)

302 N.Y. 1, 96 NE 2d 56, *remittitur* amended 302 N.Y. 689,

98 NE 2d 485, *rev'd.* 276 App. Div. 309, 94 N.Y.S. 2d 453,

which *aff'd.* 192 Misc. 327, 77 N.Y.S. 2d 333 (1948)

Kreshik et al., Petitioner v. St. Nicholas Cathedral of the
Russian Orthodox Church of North America 237

7 N.Y. 2d 191, 196 N.Y.S. 2d 655, 164 NE 2d 687

Reversed per curiam

363 US 190, 4 L.Ed.2d 1140, 80 S.Ct. 1037 (1960)

Lordi v. Epstein 247

389 US 29, 19 L.Ed. 29, 88 S.Ct. 106 (1967)

McCann v. New York Stock Exchange 204

107 F.2d 903 (CA 2d., L. Hand, Cir.J. Nov. 13, 1939)

Petition for certiorari denied

309 U.S. 684, 84 L.Ed. 1027, 60 S.Ct. 807, Apr. 8, 1940

Petition for rehearing denied

310 U.S. 656, 84 L.Ed. 1420, 60 S.Ct.974, May 6, 1940

McCormick v. McCarton 25

86 N.Y.S. 1140, *aff'd.* 95 A.D. 426, 88 N.Y.S. 722 (App. Div. 1st Dept 1904)

Miller v. United States 121

24 F 2d 353 (CA 2nd 1928)

Petition for certiorari denied

284 US 661, 78 L.Ed. 745, 48 S.Ct. 421 (1928)

Mount v. Daniel S. Tuttle 32
  99 A.D. 433, 91 N.Y.S. 195 (App. Div. 1st Dept. 1904)
  aff'd 183 N.Y. 358, 76 N.E. 873 (1906)

Muller v. Thomas W. Evans Museum and Institute Society 74
  113 A.D. 92, 99 N.Y.S. 93 (App. Div. 1st Dept. 1906)

National Distillers Products Corp., NY v. Glander 254
  337 US 562, 93 L.Ed. 1544, 69 S.Ct. 129 (1949)
  Rev'd 150 Oho St.229. 80 NE 2d 963 (1948) 252

Occidental Petroleum Corporation v. Chandler 240
  303 F2d 55 (CA 10 (Oklahoma) 1962)
  Chandler v. Occid, Pet. Corp. Petition denied 240
  372 US 915, 9 L.Ed. 2d 722, 83 S. Ct. 718 (1963)
  Petition for rehearing denied
  373 US 906, 10 L.Ed. 2d 201, 83 S.Ct. 1288 (1963)

O'Connell v. United States 124
  40 F.2d 201 (CA 2nd 1930)
  Petition for certiorari granted (May 26, 1930)
  281 US 716, 74 L. Ed. 1136, 30 S. Ct. 462
  Petition for certiorari dismissed, pursuant stipulation of counsel (June 12, 1930)
  296 US 667, 75 L.Ed. 1472, 51 S.Ct. 658

People ex rel. Collins v. McLaughlin 51
  23 N.Y.Crim. R. 92, 128 AD 599, (App. Div. 1st Dept. 1908)

People ex rel. Lewis v. Graves 287
  127 Misc. 135, 215 N.Y.S. 632 (Sup. Ct. 1926)
  aff'd. 219 A.D. 233, 219 N.Y.S. 189 (App.Div. 3d Dept.),
  aff'd. 245 N.Y. 195, 156 N.E. 663 (1927)

People v. Marcus 209
  235 A.D. 397, 257 N.Y.S. 424 (App.Div. 1st Dept. 1932)
  aff'd. in part; *rev'd.* in part 261 N.Y. 268, 185 N.E. 97 (1933)

People ex rel. Sturgis v. Fallon 51
  4 App. Div. 76 (1896); *aff'd.* 152 N.Y. 1 (1897)
  46 N.E. 302

People v. System Properties, Inc.   315

      189 Misc. 991, 76 N.Y.S. 2d 758 (Sup.Ct.1947), *rev'd.*

      281 A.D. 433, 120 N.Y.S. 2d 269 (App. Div. 3d Dept. 1953),

      judgment modified 2 N.Y.2d 330, 141 NE 2d 429, 160 N.Y.S. 2d 859 (1957)

Romanian Orthodox Missionary Episcopate of America v. Trutza   238

      120 F. Supp. 183 (US DC, D Ohio 1952), 205 F.2d 107 (CA 6, 1953).

      Cert. denied, 346 US 1915, 98 L.Ed. 410, 74 S.Ct. 274 (1953)

Rose v. Rose   228

      282 A.D. 682, 122 N.Y.S. 2d 819. (App. Div. 1st Dept 1953)

Russian Orthodox Greek Catholic St. Peter
and St. Paul's Church of Lorain v. Burdikoff   238

      117 Ohio Sup. 1, 189 N.E.2d 451 (Ohio App. 9 Dist. 1962)

      App. Dism. 174 Ohio St. 140, 186 N.E;2d 847 (1962)

   Cert. denied sub nom. Burdikoff v. Church,

      374 U.S. 808, 10 L.Ed.2d 1033, 83 S.Ct. 1694 (1963)

      Reh. den. 375 U.S. 870, ll L.Ed.2d 100, 84 S.Ct. 29 (1963)

in re Scott's Estate   215

      19 Misc.2d 18, 189 N.Y.S. 2d 87 (Sur. Ct., 1959)

      aff'd. 10 A.D.2d 556, 196 N.Y.S. 2d 597 (App. Div.1 st Dept.)

      judgment rev'd 8 N.Y.2d 419, 171 N.E.2d 326, 208 N.Y.S. 2d 984 (1960)

Small v. Housman   71

      220 N.Y.504, 116 N.E. 359 (1917)

United States v. Dachis   130

      36 F 2d 601 (SD NY 1929)

United States v. Hutcheson, et al.   243

      312 US 219, 85 L.Ed. 788, 61 S.Ct. 463 (1941), *aff'ng.*

      32 F. Supp. 600 (USDC D Mo. 1940)

United States v. Manton   214

      107 F 2d 834 (CA 2d, 1939)

   Petitions for certiorari denied   214

      309 US 664, 84 L.Ed. 1012, 60 S.Ct. 590 (1940)

United States v. Vause   118
    53 F.2d 346 (CA 2nd 1931)
  Petition for certiorari denied
    284 U.S. 661, 76 L.Ed. 560, 52 S. Ct; 37 (1931)

In re **Wallace & Tiernan Co.**   219
    76 F. Supp. 215 (US DC, Dist. RI, 1948)

Youngstown Sheet & Tube Co. v. Sawyer   196
    343 US 579, 96 L. Ed., 1153, 72 S.Ct. 863 (1952)
  Sawyer v. United States Steel Co.   195
    197 F 2d 582 (US Ct. App. DC, 1952)
  Youngstown S & T Co. v. Sawyer
    103 F. Supp. 562 (US Dist. Ct., DC, Apr. 1952)
  Youngstown S & T Co. v. Sawyer
    103 F. Supp. 978 (US Dist. Ct., DC, Apr. 1952)

Zorach v. Clauson   289
    198 Misc. 631, 99 N.Y.S. 2d 339 (Sup. Ct. 1950)
    aff'd. 278 A.D. 573, 102 N.Y.S. 2d 27 (App. Div. 2d Dept)
    aff'd. 303 N.Y. 161, 100 NE 2d 463 (1951)
    aff'd. 343 U.S. 306, 96 L.Ed. 954, 72 S.Ct. 679 (1952).

INDEX
of Persons and Places

(For an extensive list of **topics**, see
the Table of Contents, pp. vii–xiv.)

Page numbers listed in italics refer to illustrations.

Adel, Justice 223
Aedita, Countess 56
Albany, NY 35, 101, 123, 124, 150, 260, 292, 307
Adirondack Mountains 11, 39, 309, 316, *316*
Adirondack Forest Preserve 316
Allen, Ethan 314
Amherst, General Lord Geoffrey 314
Andrews, Max 356
Angell, Hannah 357
Angell, Janet 357
Angell, Nathaniel 357
Angell, Thomas 357
Anson, Karen 355
Armstrong, Sir Henry G. 108
Arnold, Professor Thurman xx, 243, 244
Athenagoras, Archbishop/Patriarch xx, 229, 230, *230*, 233, 235, 356
Atwell, Judge William H. 135
Auchincloss, Louis 193
Auerbach, Joseph S. 49–51, 77

Baird, Mary S. 186
Baker, Charles 34
Baldridge, Holmes 196
Baldwin, Richard 179

Baldwin, Stephen C. 55, 56, 63–65, 80, 81
Balfour, Lord Alfred 1
Barnard College 39
Baruch, Bernard 210, 211
Battice, Earl 143
Battle, George Gordon 57
Beecher, Henry Ward 19
Beecher, Julia 14
Beecher (Tuttle), Sarah Parmelee 4, 7, *17*
Beldock, Hon. George 292, 293
Bellush, Professor Bernard 159, 160, 163, 164
Belmont, August 49, 50, 77
Bergan, Francis 266
Berger, Samuel A. 126, 129–132
Bertini, Judge 162, 163
Birnbaum, Abe 142, 356
Bishopp, Earl N. 177
Black Mountain 313
Bly, Charles H. 307
Bohan, Judge Owen W. 187
Bondy, Judge William 230, 231
Bonnie Nook, Lake George 308
Bowie, Walter Russell 296
Bowles, Assemblyman 95
Breed, William C. 168, 169

Breyfogle, Dr. William 308

Britton, Nan 105

Bronner, Leonard 179

Brooklyn College 82, 256

Brooklyn, NY 80, 82, 118, 162, 166, 220, 222, 248, 256

Brophy, Thomas P. 130

Brotherhood-in-Action, NYC 292–295, 331

Brownell, Bishop Thomas 4

Bryant, Elizabeth A. (granddaughter) *344*, 351-352, 353

Bryant, Jasmine T.
   See Tuttle, Hélène Jasmine

Bryant, Judge Frederick H. 202, 205, 206

Bryant, Mrs. Frederick 205, 206

Bryant, Pamela 354

Bryant, Rebecca D. (granddaughter) *344,* 353

Bryant, Dr. Robert B. (son-in-law) 205–206, *344*

Bryant, Robert S. (grandson) *344,* 353

Buckner, Emory xx, 58, 88, 99–102, 121, 127, 208

Buffalo, NY 169, 260

Burdikoff, Rev. George 238

Burr, Aaron 37

Butler, Theron R. 272

Cadman, Rev. S. Parkes 220–224

Cantin, Eugene 139

Cardozo, Judge Benjamin N. 61, 62, 70

Carpenter, John W. 15

Carroll, Dr. Robert P. 148

Casey (Army volunteer) 280–281

Catapodis, Spyridon 200–202

Cathedral of St. John the Divine 299

Catinella, Frank 179

Cavanaugh, John G. 53, 54

Chandler, Porter R. 177

Chanler, Hon. William C. 87

Chase Manhattan Plaza, NYC xix, 37

Chitty, Wendy Dean 355

Churchill, Justice Thomas W. 83

City College of New York 40, 81–85, 88, 90, *92,* 100, 159, 256, 273, 280, 329-333

City University of New York 256, 326, 327

Coleman, Frank J. 197, 270

Coleman, Samuel C. 103, 177

Columbia College xx, 18-20, 39, 307

Columbia Law School xx, 6, 18, 21, 29, 307

Columbia University 94, 159, 225

Conboy, Martin 112

Convent Avenue, NYC 4, 9, 34, 39, 40, *78,* 296

Conway, Judge 224

Cook (Tuttle), Penelope Turner 6, 7, *30*

Cooke, Mrs. Maria J. Kempe 308

Coolidge, President Calvin 100, *100,* 270

Cooper, James Fenimore 308

Corby, Kathleen 357

Corcoran, Edward 114, 115

Cornell, Edward 76, 77

Corson, Farmer 12, 13

Corson, Harry 13

Corson, Mrs. 13

Corson, Whitfield 13

Coster, Frank Donald 193

Cotter, Garret W. 134

Crain, Thomas C.T. 131, 160

Crater, Judge Joseph F. 120, 121, 162, 163

Crawford, Thomas J. 179

Croker, Richard 94

Crosier, Linda 356

Croswell, Mrs. Mary 14

Curran, Thomas J. 130, 179, 292

Curran, Alderman Henry H. 80, 81

Currie, Julie
   See Tuttle, Julianne

Curry, John F. 120

Dachis, Jacob 130, 131

Dachis, Louis 130, 131

Darrow, Clarence S. 45, 46, 287

Daugherty, Harry M. 121, 122

Davies, Julian 6, 30–34, 41, 44, 45, 74, 75, 77

Davis, John W. 64, 65, 196

Davis, Senator James J. 197–199

DeCicco, Charles 356

Decker, Irene 357

Delany, Elizabeth 181

Delany, Hubert T. 127, 129, 177, 178, 180, 181, *181,* 225, 356

Delany, Sarah 181

Desmond, Judge 224

Devery, Chief of Police 94

Dewey, Governor Thomas E. 187, 188, 260, 262, *262,* 269, 272

DiPirro, Marco G. 179

Donovan, Colonel William J. 169

Doolittle, Isaac 4

Doolittle, Julia 4

Doolittle, Thankful Bellamy 4

Dorsen, Professor Norman 250

Douglas, Justice William O. 251, 289

Dowling, Victor J. 212

Dye, Judge 224

East River xix

Eaton, Stuart 112, 114, 116, 117

Edwards, Margaret 356

Egbert, Professor 18

Eisenhower, Dwight David 226

Eisenstein, Joe 130, 131

Eisner, Mark 275, 278

Elizabethtown, NY 315

Emmons, H.H. 65

Erwin, Senator Austin W. 265

Escudero, Lisa
   See Bryant, Elizabeth A.

Evans, Dr. Thomas W. 73–74

Ewald, Magistrate George F. 160, 161

Fall, Albert 123

Federal Building, NYC 104, *107,* 110, 111, 137, 138, 143, 168, 174, *203,* 219

Felix, Harold A. 177

Fendler, Grace A. 59, 60

Fink, Jules 210, 211

Fisher, Bud 56–58

Fletcher, Senator 108

Flint, Charles R. 77

Foerster, Friedrich Wilhelm 225, 226

Ford, Frank W. 179

French Mountain xxi, 309, *386*

Frischauer, Willi 202

Froessell, Judge 224

Fuld, Judge Stanley 224

Fuller, Justice Melville 46

Gabb, Mayor Henry 276, 277, 356

Gallagher, Dr. Buell G. 330, 332, 333, *333,* 335, 356

Gallagher, Mr. (stockholder) 248

Gates, Frederick T. 308

Gaynor, Mayor William J. 80, *80,* 81, 332

Gerson, Henry 179

Gill, Rev. John 356

Glass, Eric 356

Goddard, Judge Henry W. (Harry) 128, 130, 131, 140

Gold, Justice Samuel M. 200, 201

Gordon, Judge James G. 41–44

Grace Episcopal Church, NYC 296-298, *296, 298,* 299, 321

Grant, Louis J. 26

Grant, Rev. Percy Stickney 77

Greenberg (defendant in *Dachis* case) 129-132

Greenwich Village 4, 40

Grieco, Marilyn 357

Guernsey, Sally Marsh Sinnott 357

Guider, Joseph A. 82

Guthrie, William D. 71

Gutman, Isaac 179

Halcyon, Lake George 11, *304,* 307–308, 311, 340, *343, 344,* 352, 353, *386*

Hall, Linda 356

Hallinan, Justice 248

Hamilton, Alexander 37

Hamilton Terrace, NYC 36, *36,* 37, 40

Hanaway, William 335, 336

Hand, Judge Augustus N. 63, 101

Hand, Judge Learned 124, 204

Hanson, Charles W. 242

Harbord, Major General James G. 150, 151

Harding, President Warren G. 105, 121, 123, 232, 235

Harper, William D. 139

Harriman, Governor Averell 259, *259,* 266

Hartigan, Judge 219

Hartley, Commodore 56, 57

Hays, Arthur Garfield xx, 227, 287

Healy, Martin J. 160

Helfand, Marcus 111, 112, 114, 116

Hellenic Cathedral, New York City 233

Heller, Senator Louis B. 260

Herman, Harry G. 177, 180

Hicks, Becky 357

Hilles, Charles D. 99

Hipsings 133-134

Hoagland, Miss 14

Hodge, J. Aspinwall 49

Hoke, Lynn 356

Homer, Sidney and Louise 308

Hoover, President Herbert 146, 147, *147,* 156, 159, 163, 169

Horne, Charles F., Jr. (son-in-law) *344*

Horne, Charles F., III (grandson) xxii, *344*

Horne, Evelyn T.
    See Tuttle, Evelyn Cressman

Horne, Flora E. (granddaughter-in-law) *344*

Hotchkiss, Charles E. 32

Hudson, NY 4

Hudson River xix, 39, 44, 257, 309

Hudson St., NYC 4, 15, 34

Hughes, Charles Evans 98, 117
Hughes, William J. 65
Hunter College 82, *170,* 256
Huntington, William Reed 296
Hurley, Louisa
   See Lloyd, Louisa
Hutcheson, William L. 242–244
Hylan, Mayor John J. 90, *90,* 328

Ives, Irving M. 260, 262

Javits, Senator Jacob 293
Jessup, Captain E.P. 108
Johnson, Bryon B. (Ban) 54–56
Johnson, Dr. Alvin 260
Johnson, General William 314
Johnson, John G. 45, 46
Johnston, Alva 142
Johnstone, Robert S. 122
Jonas, Ralph 72, 82, 83
Jones, Dr. Joseph Lee 248, 249
Jogues, Father Isaac 314

Kaplan, Abraham 126, 129, 130,
   131
Kay, Jean 85, 86
Keener, Dr. 23
Kennedy, Senator Robert F. 330,
   331, *331*
Kerwin, Thomas 179
King, Martin Luther, Jr. 181, *181*
King, Roswell H. 31–33
Kirchway, Dean 25
Klein, William 61, 62
Knickerbocker, Barry 357
Knickerbocker, Leigh 357
Knox, Judge 111, 121, 138
Koenig, Sam 141, 150

Kraus, Rev. Canon Harry E. 356
Kresel, Isidor J. 206–209

La Guardia, Fiorello xxi, 85, 93, *95,*
   95–97, 274–278, *277,* 322, 328
Lake George xxi, 1, 4, 10-11, *10,*
   17, *17,* 35, 39, 89, 143, 205, 212,
   304, 305–322, *306-308, 310,*
   339-342, *343, 344,* 365, *386*
Lake Ontario 39, 316
Lamont, Rebecca
   See Bryant, Rebecca
Latham, Miles 35, 307
Lavelle, Monsignor 285, 287
Leary, James 53
Lehman, Herbert 163
Leidersdorff, Sam 173
Leisure, George S. 103, 176
Lerner (defendant in *Dachis* case)
   129-131
Lester, Mrs. William C 39
Leviathan (ocean liner) 56–58
Levine, Judge Max S. 131
Lewis, Joseph 287, 288
Lewis, Judge 224
Lindsay, Hon. John V. 298, 303,
   303, 327, 329
Lippmann, Walter 160
Lloyd, Andrew M. (grandson) *344*
Lloyd, Charlotte
   See Tuttle, Charlotte Merrill
Lloyd, David D. (son-in-law) 306,
   344
Lloyd, Louisa T. (granddaughter)
   344, 352, 353, 354
Low, Mayor Seth 18, 93, 94, *94*
Lucking, Alfred 65
Lumbard, Edward J. 177
Lydig, Mrs. Philip 77

MacCrate, Justice 223

Malone, NY 155

Manhattan *xviii,* xix, 63, 82, 101, 109, 126, 220, 257, 282, 293

Manley, Robert E. 156

Manning, Bishop 77, 85

Manton, Judge Martin T. 123, 124, 212–214, 270

Marcus, Bernard K. 206–209

Marcus, Seymour 125

Margiotti, Charles J. 197–199

Marshall, Louis 135

Marx, Karl 236

Mayer, Alfred H. 248–250

Mays, Carl 54, 55

McCann, Gene 202–206

McCarton (Police Benevolent president) 25

McConkey, Captain Henry 108

McCook, Judge Philip J. 272

McCormick (police sergeant) 25–26

McGeehan, Judge John E. 86–89

McKane, John Y. 94

McKee, Eila Haggin 186

McPartlin, Rev. Julie 356

Medalie, George Z. 179, 197

Medina, Harold 207–209

Merton (German agent) 122

Meyner, Governor Robert 259

Middlebrook, Dean Samuel 332

Miller, Thomas W. 121–123

Minifie, Rev. Benjamin 297

Mintzer, George J. 103, 106, 113, 116, 176, 180

Molloy, Henry 34

Montcalm, General 309, 314

Morosco, Oliver 59, 60

Morris, Dr. 217

Morrison, John H. 37

Morrison, Mrs. John H. 37, 38

Morton, Lysle W. 319

Moscahlades, Socrates 127, 128

Moses, Robert 80, 169

Muhlenbergh, Rev. 4

Murphy, Hon. Thomas P. 126

Murphy, Mrs. (widow) 280

Murray, Thomas E. 212

Musterer, Augusta 351

Nathan, Justice Edgar 173

Neilson, Raymond P. R. 175, 253

Newark, NJ 259

Newberger, Justice Joseph E. 71

New Haven 3, 4, 6

New York City
   (See specific topics regarding New York City in TABLE OF CONTENTS, *pp. vii–xiv; see also* LIST OF ILLUSTRATIONS, *pp. xv–xvii.)*

Newton, Carl E. 127, 129, 179

Nicoll, DeLancey 51, 52, 65

Nizer, Louis xx, 226–228

Nolan, Justice 223

Oak Ridge, NJ 12, 14, 16, 25, 310

O'Brien, Judge Morgan J. 33

O'Connell, Daniel P. 123, 124

O'Connor, Kathy 357

O'Dwyer, Mayor (William) 328

Olvany, George 83, 84, 275

O'Mara, Edward J. 256

Onassis, Aristotle Socrates xx, 200–202

O'Neill, Francis A. 106

O'Neill, Thomas A. 137, 138

Onliongs 133-134
Oswego 37, 307

Page, Arthur W. 257
Page, Emeline 339
Palmer, Archibald 114
Parella, Rocco A. 177
Peck, David W. 122, 177, 267, 272
Pecora, Justice 225
Perkins, Alfred P. 139
Perlman, Nathan D. 225
Philadelphia 41-44, 74, 87, 116
Pifer, Dr. Alan 328
Pine, Judge David A. 194, 195, 196
Pinner, Max 113, 115, 117
Pitcher, Conrad 269
Pitt, Dr. Louis Wetherbee 296
Platzek, Judge 67, 70
Pool, Rabbi David de Sola 285, 287
Potter, Bishop Henry Codman 296
Poughkeepsie, NY 164
Proskauer, Joseph M. 120
Prospect Mountain 35, 318, 342
Providence, RI 218, 219

Quero–Chiesa, Hon. Louis 328
Quinlan, Bob 357
Quinlan, Nancy 357
Quinn, Senator Elmer F. 263

Raphael, Benjamin R. 180
Rich, Mike 355
Richardson, Mr. (trial counsel) 204
Ridder, Joseph 225
Ridder, Victor 225, 226
Rittenband, Lawrence J. 179
Rochester, NY 260

Rockefeller, Nelson A. 266, 267,
    293, 295, 319, 320, *320,* 329
Rockledge, Lake George 17, *17,* 35,
    277, 307-308
Rockwell, Norman 217
Rockwell, Thomas 356
Roosevelt, Eleanor 163, *165, 170,*
    170–172
Roosevelt, Franklin D.
    as N.Y. governor xxi, 120, 151,
        152, 159, 160, 162–163, *165,*
        167, *170,* 170–173, *173*
    as U.S. president 232, 235, 243,
        295
Roosevelt, Sara 170
Roosevelt, Theodore 41, 48
Root, Elihu 41
Rose, Billy xx, 227–229
Rose, Eleanor Holm 227, 228
Rosenberg, Dr. Gustave 327
Ruppert, Jacob 54
Russell, Lord Bertrand 84–89
Ryan, General 96
Ryan, Judge Andrew W. 315

St. James Church, Lake George, NY
    4, 276, 305, 318, 321-322, *322*
St. Luke's Church, New York City
    4, 5, 6, 8, *9,* 34, 39, 307
St. Luke's Hospital, New York City
    216, 217
St. Nicholas Cathedral, New York
    City 236
St. Patrick's Cathedral 285-288, *287*
St. Thomas Church, New York City
    214-217, *214, 217*
Sand, Samuel S. 186
Saratoga, NY 52
Sargent, Charles S. 139

Schmidt, Justice 223

Schuyler, General Philip R. 314

Schwartz, Arthur H. 177

Scott, George S. 214–217

Seabury, Judge Samuel 93, 96, 97, 120, 122, 274

Seeger, Mona 356

Seymour, Marcus 125

Seymour, Hon. Whitney North 297, 298

Shapiro, Maxwell 179

Sheldon, George R. 186

Shepard, Edward M. 93, 94

Shubert Brothers 61

Siam 308

Silver, Edward S. 103, 106, 116, 176, 180

Singer, Herbert 206–209

Singer, Saul 206–209

Sinnott, Joseph J., III (Trip) 353, 354, 355, 357

Slattery, Charles Lewis 296

Small, Eugene W. 308

Small, Ida 70, 71

Smith, Alfred E. 97, 98, 228, 278

Smith, Jess 122

Spellman, Francis Cardinal 295

Staley, Judge Ellis J. 288

Stalin, Josef 236–238, *237*

Stanchfield, John B. 51, 52

Steinbrink, Judge Meier 166, 167, 222, 223

Steinhardt, David 111–113, 116, 117

Stent, Dr. Madelon Delany 356

Stephens, Olin J. 139

Steuer, Max xx, 207, 208, 226

Stichman, Herman T. 179

Stimson, Henry L. 313

Stires, Bishop Ernest 312

Stone, Justice Harlan F. 276

Stroock, Moses J. 83–84

Sunderland, Edwin S. 184, 190

Swan, Judge 124

Sylvester, Alvin McK. 179

Syracuse, NY 162, 260

Syracuse University 148, 273

Taft, William Howard 64

Thatcher, Judge Thomas D. 116, 117

Thaw, Harry K. 110

Thomas, Norman 164

Tilden, Governor Samuel 144

Timm, Caroline 119

Timotheos, Patriarch of Jerusalem 234

Todarelli, Thomas J. 177, 180

Tolley, Chancellor William Pearson 273

Tompkins, Bernard 179

Tongs 133-134

Top O' The World xxi, 308–311, *304, 310,* 319

Tremaine, Morris S. 163

Tremper, Jeff 357

Trinity College, CT 4, 5

Trinity Episcopal School 15

Truman, President Harry S. 193, 232, 235, *235,* 291, *291*

Tully, Richard 59–60

Tuttle, Bethuel 3

Tuttle Boys 102, 104, 168, 174–181, *178,* 360

Tuttle, Charles H., II (grandson) *344, 353*

Tuttle, Charles H. *seriatim*
(See specific topics for Charles Tuttle in TABLE OF CONTENTS, pp. vii–xiv; see also LIST OF ILLUSTRATIONS, pp. xv–xvii.)
Tuttle, Charlotte Merrill (daughter) xxii, 23, *78*, 164, 276, 322, *344*, 345, 351–355, *362*
Tuttle, Daniel S. 32
Tuttle, Doris E. (daughter-in-law) *343, 344,* 355
Tuttle, Elizabeth 3
Tuttle, Evelyn Cressman (daughter) xxii, *78, 344,* 345, 355
Tuttle Hall, Grace Church, NYC 298, *298*
Tuttle, Hélène Jasmine (daughter) xxii, *78,* 205–206, 322, *344,* 345, 352, 353, 355, *362*
Tuttle, Hélène Louise (Wheeler) 37–40, *38,* 40, *40, 78,* 136, *165,* 167, 168, *170,* 170–172, 175, 205, 233, 235, 239, *239,* 269, 296, 307, 308, 309–311, 339, 340, *340,* 342, *343, 344, 362*
Tuttle, H. Croswell (son) xxii, *78,* 311, *343, 344,* 345, 353, 354-355
Tuttle, Henry Croswell (father) 6–8, 7, 10, 11, *11,* 12, 15, 16-17, 18, 21, 30, 44, 75, 311
Tuttle, Rev. Isaac (grandfather) 3–6, 7, 8, 10, 14, 15, 16–17, *17,* 34, 35, 40, 322, 359
Tuttle, Julianne H. (granddaughter) *344,* 353, 355
Tuttle, Penelope (Cook) (mother) 6–9, 7, 11, 12–13, 14, 15, 29–30, *30,* 34–38, 40, 44, 75, 100

Tuttle, Sarah Parmelee (Beecher) (grandmother) 4, 7, *17*
Tuttle, William 3

University Place, NYC xix, 40, 330, 342
Untermyer, Samuel 2, 166

Van Kleeck, Miss Ellen 15
Van Voorhis, Judge 216, 217, 226
Vare, Boss (William) 164
Vassar College 164
Vause, Judge W. Bernard 118–121
Venner, Clarence H. 48–50
Vestris (ocean liner) 106–109

Wadmond, Lowell 177, 180
Wagner, Mayor Robert F. 293, 324–326, *324*
Wagner, Judge Robert 54
Walker, Mayor Jimmy 83, 84, *84,* 96, 160–162, 328
Walkup, Charlotte *See* Tuttle, Charlotte Merrill
Walkup, Homer A. (son-in-law) 352, 354, 365-366
Walkup, Pamela 352
Wanamaker, John 41, 42
Warder, Anne H. (granddaughter) xxii, *344,* 353, 355
Warder, Frederick B., Jr. (grandson-in-law) *344,* 355
Warder, Frederick B., III (great-grandson) xxii, 353, 354
Washington, DC 104, 122, 194, 200
Wason, William J. 247, 248
Watts, Robert B. 103
Wayside, Lake George 10, *10,* 11, 36, 307

Weaver, Mayor John 41, 42, 44

Wellman, Francis L 67, 69, 70

Wenzel, Justice 223

Westwood, Howard 276

Wheeler, Hélène
　　See Tuttle, Hélène Louise

White, Chief Justice 64

White, Sanford 110

Whitefield, Don 355

White Plains 50

Whitman, Governor Charles S. 96, 97

Whitney, George 190, 191

Whitney, Mrs. George 190

Whitney, Mrs. Richard (Gertrude) 188

Whitney, Richard xx, 184–193

Wilson, E. Bright 114, 116, 117

Winslow, Judge Francis A. 111–117, 117, 120, 212

Wood, Loren 24, 34

Woodbury, Cyrus H. 319

Woodward, Colin 95

Woollcott, Alexander 61

Woolsey, Judge 213

Worcester, Judge Frances J. 25, 26

Zabriskie, George 71

Photo by Richard K. Dean

TUTTLE FAMILY AND FRIENDS BOATING ON LAKE GEORGE
Halcyon shoreline is in view, with French Mountain in the background.